우표로 보는 태권도 발자취

The Evolution of Taekwondo as Seen Through Postage Stamps

저자 : 김영선   Young Sun Kim

68개국 145종의 태권도 테마 우표 해설서 1.0
A Compilation of 145 Taekwondo-Themed
Stamps from 68 Countries. Ver.1.0

이 책은 국민체육진흥공단의 기금 및 태권도진흥재단 협찬으로 기획됨.
This book is published with the support from the
Korea Sports Promotion Foundation and the Taekwondo Promotion Foundation.

ANG-A

☞ 이 서적 발간을 위해 도와주신 분들

· 태권도진흥재단 이대순 이사장님과 서필환 팀장님
· 미국 캘리포니아 무도연구가인 최의정씨, 진정한 벗인 캐나다 태권도인 론 드주웬카씨,
  제자인 마이클 리와 존 케메론 군이 영문 번역과 교정을 도와주었습니다.
· 우표 종주국인 영국의 태권도인이자 우취인인 마이크 히스씨
· 이준구 대사범님, 이강희 대사범님, 이규석 교수님, 한상진 교수님
· 태권도문화연구소 이경명 소장님
· 한국우취연합 김장환 회장님
· 연세목우회 신명순 회장님
· 이란태권도협회 기술위원장 및 수원 남창태권도장 관장 강신철님
· 전문우취인으로서 한국우편사업지원단에 근무하시는 김용진님과 이석연님
· 태권도 서적 전문출판사 상아기획의 문상필 사장님
· 연세국제태권도장 사범진 김태엽, 박민재, 김봉현, 황성준님

☞ Contributors to this book :

· Mr. Dai Soon Lee, Chairman of the Taekwondo Promotion Foundation
· Mr. Pil-Hwan Seo, Director of Business Development for the Taekwondo Promotion Foundation
· Mr. Alexander E.J. Choi (Headmaster of Choi's Martial Art's in the U.S.A.)
· My best friend, Canadian Taekwondoist Mr. Ron Dziwenka (PH.D, Arizona University),
· Yonsei International Students, Michael Lee & John Cameron Korean English translation.
· Mr. Mike Heath, Taekwondo Blackbelt and Philatelist of Great Britain.
· Grandmasters Jhoon Rhee & Kang Rhee, Professor Kyu-Seok Lee, Master Shin-Chul Kang
· Mr. Kyong Myong Lee, Chairman of the Institute of Taekwondo Culture
· Mr. Chang Hwan Kim, President, Philatelic Federation of Korea
· Professor Myung-Soon Shin, President of the Yonsei Professors Philatelic Club
· Master Shin-Chul Kang, Chairman of Technical Committee, Iran Taekwondo Association
· Mr. Yong-Jin Kim & Mr. Seok Yeon Lee, KOVIX for philatelic advice
· Mr. Sang Phil Moon, President and Owner of the Sang-A Publishing Company
· Instructors at Yonsei International Taekwondo Academy Master Tae-Yeop Kim,
  Master Min Jae Park, Mr. Bong Hyun Kim and Mr. Sung Jun Hwang supported my efforts.

E.J. Alexander Choi

Ron Dziwenka

Michael Lee

John Cameron

– 태권도의 가치   The Values of Taekwondo –

어린이들의 심신 성장 발육에 도움을 주는 체육 활동
For the Growth and Development in Children

자기방어 호신술
For Self-Defense

올림픽 경기에서 국위 선양과 명예 획득
The Glory of The Olympic Sport

스트레스 해소와 건강한 몸매 관리 운동
For Stress Relief and Fitness

자신감 등 정신력 배양
Confidence and Discipline

명사(名士)들의 건전한 취미
A Sound Hobby for Celebrities

영화, TV 액션 능력
Action for Movies & TV

추천사 이 대 순 (태권도진흥재단 이사장)

세계 태권도 우표를 소재로 한 단행본 '우표로 보는 태권도 발자취' 의 발간을 진심으로 축하드립니다. 이 저서는 세계 각국 정부에서 발행한 태권도 우표를 수집하여 저자의 많은 노력과 정성으로 태권도가 세계적인 무도 스포츠로 발전되어가는 전 과정을 한눈에 바라볼 수 있도록 집대성한 아주 특별한 서적입니다

어떻게 이 많은 태권도 우표들이 발행되었는지! 그 수량이 무려 68개국 145종으로써 우표 하나하나에 대한 도안과 발행 경위, 역사적 배경 등에 대하여 저자의 자세한 설명과 해설이 독자의 마음을 사로잡기에 충분한 훌륭한 저작물입니다. 스포츠 기념우표는 한 종목의 스포츠가 보급되고 정착되어 가는 과정에서 그 나라의 문화와 어떻게 조화롭게 발전되어 가는지를 살펴볼 수 있는 소중한 문화 자료입니다. 스포츠 우표전이 올림픽 경기의 문화 행사로 정착된 이유가 바로 여기에 있습니다. 각국의 태권도 기념우표는 태권도가 세계화되어 그 나라의 문화로 정착되어 가는 과정을 조명하는 중요한 문화 소재로서 보존 가치성이 높을 뿐만 아니라 문화자산으로서 태권도의 위상을 드높이는데 크게 기여할 것입니다. 우리 재단은 앞으로 태권도 문화를 진흥시키는 역량 있는 분들에게 많은 성원을 해줄 것입니다. 그동안 간과되어 온 태권도 소재의 만화를 비롯한 서적, 영화, 음악, 미술 등 다양한 문화·예술 저작물을 발굴·수집할 뿐만 아니라 새롭게 창출하고 다듬어서 태권도 종주국의 위상에 걸맞는 수준 높은 문화를 정립하고자 합니다.

오랫동안 태권도 역사와 대중문화 분야에서 많은 연구 활동을 하고 있는 저자 김영선씨에게 찬사를 보냅니다. 앞으로 태권도계 다양한 분야에서 이와 같은 훌륭한 저작물이 많이 출간되기를 기대합니다.

Letter of Recommendation

Dr. Dai Soon Lee
Chairman, Taekwondo Promotion Foundation
Vice President, World Taekwondo Federation / President, Asian Taekwondo Union

 I would like to congratulate Mr. Kim Young-Sun for publishing his book, "The Evolution Taekwondo as Seen Through Postage Stamps." This special book is a collection of Taekwondo stamps printed by the governments of countries around the world. Due to the author's great effort and dedication, readers will be able to get a glance of the whole process in which Taekwondo has grown to become a world sport.
 Readers will be amazed to find a large collection of stamps in this book, approximately 145 stamps printed in 68 countries. They will be fascinated by the author's elaborate explanations about the design, historical background, and story of each stamp.
 Commemorative sports stamps are a precious cultural property of an individual country because they can serve as a record of how a particular sport has developed in harmony with a country's traditional culture, and how it has taken root and spread as well. This is why sports stamp exhibitions are widely accepted as a cultural event of the Olympic Games. Each country's commemorative Taekwondo stamps are worth keeping as important cultural material that sheds light on the historical process involved in the globalization of Taekwondo and blending into the country's mainstream culture. They will contribute significantly to boosting the image of Taekwondo as a cultural asset. The Taekwondo Promotion Foundation will actively support those who are capable of promoting Taekwondo culture in the days to come. The Foundation will explore and collect diverse cultural and artistic works related to Taekwondo, such as various publications including comic books, films, music, paintings and sculptures, which have been overlooked or disregarded. The Foundation also intends to establish a high to such a degree of Taekwondo culture that it fits the image of Korea as the birthplace of Taekwondo. I want to compliment Mr. Kim Young-Sun for his research achievements in the field of Taekwondo history and pop culture. I hope that many more outstanding publications like this one will be published in many other areas.

축사 강원식 (국기원 원장)

'태권도 종주국'이라 함은 단순히 '태권도 발생지'만을 의미하지는 않습니다. 태권도 철학, 기술, 문화 등 모든 분야에서 원천 지식과 활동 역량을 축적하여 세계 각국에 보급하고 선도하는 역할을 수행해야만 명실상부한 종주국이 되는 것입니다. 특히 21세기는 대중이 선호하는 문화적 가치와 결부된 태권도 흐름을 창안하고 주도하는 역할이 요청되는 시대입니다.

이 서적은 태권도 문화를 진작시키고 태권도 종주국의 위상을 강화시키는 훌륭한 저작물이 아닐 수 없습니다. 더욱이 각국 정부의 권위와 대중성이 실린 '우표'로서 '태권도 발전상'을 묘사한다는 점이 더욱 의의가 있습니다. 국기원에서는 수년 전부터 세계 각국에서 발행된 태권도 우표의 가치를 인식하고 홍보 사업을 시행한 바 있습니다. 2005년에 저자인 김영선씨의 참여로 '우표로 보는 태권도 역사'라는 국·영문 포스터를 제작하여 국내와 전 세계에 배포하여 큰 호응을 받았습니다.

그 이후 6년이 지나면서 68개국 145종에 달하는 태권도 우표들이 축적되어 멋진 책자로 빛을 보게 되어 전 세계적으로도 큰 반향을 불러일으킬 것입니다. 이 서적은 태권도 역사와 전통 뿐 아니라 최근 베이징과 런던 올림픽에 이르기까지 일목요연하게 정리되어 태권도 홍보 뿐 아니라 교육적 역할을 수행할 것입니다. 세계태권도 본부를 운영하는 국기원은 물론 전 세계 태권도인들과 함께 이 특별한 서적 발간을 경축합니다.

Congratulatory Message

Kang, Won Sik
President of Kukkiwon

The home of Taekwondo does not occur only where Taekwondo originated. The true home of Taekwondo should also accumulate and publicize the knowledge and capability of Taekwondo philosophy, skill and culture. Especially in the 21st century, Taekwondo connects with cultures for which public relations will also be required.

It is not much to say that this book greatly enhances the status in the birthplace of Taekwondo, Korea. Overall, it is more significant since it describes the development of Taekwondo through 'Taekwondo Stamps' which holds the authority and popularity of each nation's government. Years ago, the Kukkiwon recognized the value of the Taekwondo stamps from each nation and started public relations activities. In 2005, we have gained great relations all over the world by designing Korean and English posters titled 'Viewing the Taekwondo History through Stamps,' which the author of this book Young Sun Kim has contributed too.

After 6 years, over 145 Taekwondo stamps from 68 countries were collected and made into a book being issued over the world. This book not only carries the history and tradition of Taekwondo, but also will publicize and used for Taekwondo education based upon its quality. On behalf of the Kukkiwon, the World Taekwondo Headquarters and the world Taekwondo family, I express my deep congratulations to you on the publication of this precious book.

추천사 조 정 원 (세계태권도연맹 총재)

태권도의 전통과 발전 과정을 우표로 표현한 단행본 발간을 축하 드립니다.

칼라판 화보 형식으로 편집된 이 책자는 누구나 손쉽게 읽을 수 있으며, 또한 국내외 독자층을 배려하여 한글과 영어 두 개국 언어로 표기됨으로써 우표와 태권도에 관련된 상세한 정보를 제공하고 있습니다.

이 책은 태권도가 오늘날 올림픽의 이념을 실현하는 이상적인 경기 및 무술 스포츠로 우뚝 서기까지 그 상세한 과정을 68개 국가에서 발행한 145종의 태권도 우표로 표현함으로써 태권도의 위상을 잘 알 수 있게 합니다.

'한국이 세계에 준 선물' 인 태권도는 현재 192개국 약 7천만 명이 수련하고 있으며, 세계태권도연맹은 태권도를 단순한 스포츠를 넘어 인류 평화 증진에 기여하기 위한 일환으로, 2008년부터 "태권도평화봉사단원"을 해외에 파견하고 있습니다. "태권도를 통한 세계평화"라는 슬로건 아래 세계태권도연맹은 앞으로 아프리카 지역 회원국의 불우 청소년들에 대한 지원을 강화하여 이들에게 꿈과 희망을 주도록 할 것입니다.

태권도를 사랑하는 전 세계 사람들에게 이 책은 아주 소중한 자료가 될 것입니다.

Letter of Recommendation

Dr. Chungwon Choue
President
World Taekwondo Federation

On behalf of the world taekwondo family members, I would like to congratulate the publication of a book containing about 145 postage stamps on Taekwondo from 68 countries.

The book, in a color, picture-book format, provides the readers a brief history and the development of Taekwondo as a global martial art and an Olympic sport.

The book, written both in Korean and English, shows us the enhanced status of Taekwondo in the international sports circles as an ideal sport striving to realize the ideals of Olympism.

Taekwondo, Korea's gift to the world, is now practiced by about 70 million people in 192 countries. To take Taekwondo beyond a mere sport, the World Taekwondo Federation has dispatched since 2008, hundreds of members of Taekwondo Peace Corps abroad. Under the theme for the year 2011 of World Peace through Taekwondo, the W.T.F will expand its assistance to needy youths in the African region, thereby giving them dreams and hope.

This book will serve as a good guide to all the Taekwondo-loving people around the world.

축 사 홍 준 표 (대한태권도협회 회장)

이 서적은 68개국 145종의 태권도 우표를 활용하여 태권도의 발전상을 한 권으로 집대성한 경이로운 저작물입니다. 수 많은 태권도 우표를 주제별로 분류하고 시기에 따라 발전 단계를 보여줌으로써 태권도의 전통과 발전 과정을 한눈에 볼 수 있는 역사 자료로서의 기능을 충실히 감당하고 있습니다. 또한 시각성이 강조된 700여 장의 관련 이미지가 함께 실린 컬러판 화보 형식으로 제작되어 디자인 면에서도 우수하다고 판단됩니다.

이 서적의 탄생은 탁월한 지식과 역량을 토대로 오랜 세월 열정을 쏟아온 저자의 값진 땀방울이 있었기에 가능했습니다. 저자는 30여 년 가까이 대한태권도협회 기술전문위원회 임원으로 재임하면서 태권도 역사, 철학, 문화를 연구하고 저작 활동을 해 온 박식한 전문 연구가입니다. 태권도 관련 우표가 언제 어디서 발행되었는지조차 파악하기 쉽지 않는 상황에서 우표를 모으고 태권도 역사 자료로 정리해 내는 것은 새로운 분야를 개척하는 선구적 업적임이 틀림없습니다. 저자는 여러 차례 국제 태권도 행사에서 '태권도 우표 전시회'를 열었으며, 본 협회는 2006년 개최한 '코리아오픈국제태권도대회'에서 태권도 우표 전시회를 유치하여 저자의 활동을 지원했습니다.

이 서적은 태권도 역사와 가치를 담음으로써 다가오는 미래에 더욱 중요시 될 태권도 문화를 모든 태권도인들에게 일깨우는 데 기여할 것입니다. 아울러 태권도 위상을 높이는 홍보 자료집일 뿐 아니라 태권도장에서 수련자 교육용으로 활용될 수 있는 특별한 교재이기도 합니다. 이 성과를 기반으로 국내와 세계인의 사랑 받는 태권도가 더욱 널리 전파되어 지구상의 모든 나라에 흰색 도복 물결이 가득하길 기대해 봅니다.

Congratulatory Message

Hong, Joon Pyo
President of the Korea Taekwondo Association

 This book is a wonderful collection which culminates over 145 kinds of Taekwondo stamps from over 68 countries to portray the developmental aspect of Taekwondo in a single work. Numerous Taekwondo stamps have been categorized by topic and because they show the level of progress according to each era, this work is capable of functioning as a historically faithful resource that allows one to see the tradition and evolution of Taekwondo with only a glance. Furthermore, the album boasts an excellent design since the visual effect is emphasized through over 700 fully-colored images.

 The creation of this book can be attributed to the superior knowledge and competence gained from the author's enthusiasm, passion, and constant efforts over many years. While holding office for over 30 years in the Taekwondo Association's Technical Committee, the author became a well-informed, professional researcher through his study of Taekwondo history, philosophy, culture, and through his authoring of Taekwondo publications. In a situation where it is hard to even pin-point the origin of Taekwondo-related stamps, there is no doubt that the collection of stamps and their organization into a Taekwondo historical resource is a pioneering achievement and initiative into a completely new field.

 The author has held several Taekwondo Stamp Exhibitions internationally, and he received international support for his activities when his 'Taekwondo Stamp Exhibition' was opened and held by our association in 2006 at the Korea Open International Taekwondo Championships. This publication, which contains Taekwondo-related history and values, will contribute to the enlightenment of all Taekwondo practitioners as Taekwondo culture becomes more and more recognized. This collection is not being published to just increase the publicity of Taekwondo, but it is also being published to serve as a unique text to be used in the education of practitioners at Taekwondo Dojangs. The success of this work will lead to the spreading of the love of Taekwondo both domestically and internationally and, as Taekwondo becomes more popular around the world, the author awaits the day that every country will be full of waves of white Taekwondo uniforms.

발 간 사 저자 김 영 선

2000년 시드니올림픽이 열리던 해부터 필자가 열렬히 모은 태권도 우표가 68개국 145종에 달하게 되었습니다. 태권도 소재 우표가 한 장씩 발견될 때마다 마치 땅속에 묻혀있던 유물을 발굴해낸 것처럼 신나는 기분이었습니다. 지난 10년간의 결실로 이렇게 어엿한 책자로 펴내게 되어 감개무량할 따름입니다.

필자가 태권도 우표를 본격적으로 모으게 된 계기는 아이러니하게 월드컵 축구 우표 때문이었습니다. 2002년 월드컵 수년 전부터 주최국인 우리나라에서 나온 갖가지 멋진 축구 기념우표들을 접하면서 제가 몸담고 있는 태권도 분야를 생각하게 되었습니다. 그 시점이 바로 2000년 시드니올림픽 태권도 정식종목이 열린 직후였습니다. 당시 필자는 "이제 올림픽 정식종목으로 위상이 높아진 태권도 종목에 대해 분명히 세계 여러 나라에서 우표들이 나왔을지 모른다." 라는 막연한 짐작으로 태권도 테마 우표 수집에 발을 들여놓게 되었습니다. 그 때부터 인터넷을 통해 우표 경매사이트와 국제 우표 판매상은 물론 스포츠 우표 목록 등을 샅샅이 뒤지면서 오늘 이렇게 많은 나라들이 제공한 다채로운 태권도 우표들이 모이게 되었습니다.

'구슬도 꿰어야 보물' 이라고 했습니다. 수 많은 태권도 우표들을 발견하고 수집하는 데 그친다면 값진 보물을 방속 깊숙이 묻어두는 격이 되고 맙니다. 이제는 한국의 것이 아닌 세계 사람들이 관심 갖는 태권도를 소재로 각국의 정부 차원에서 발행한 우표들을 어떻게든 널리 알리고 자랑해야 합니다. 그러한 취지로 필자는 수년 전부터 국제태권도대회에서 전시회를 열기도 하고 국기원의 지원으로 국·영문 대형포스터를 제작하였으며, 이 포스터는 국내와 해외 태권도장에 배부되기도 했습니다. 이번에는 태권도 역사적 지식을 활용하여 태권도의 전통과 발전상을 간단한 우표 설명을 곁들여 한 권의 서적으로 엮어 보았습니다.

오늘날 태권도가 세계적 위상을 떨치기까지는 세계 곳곳에서 정열을 바친 수 많은 해외 사범님들의 노고가 바탕이 되었습니다. 이 책의 본문에는 우표가 발행된 나라와 관련된 그 분들의 존함을 실었습니다. 아울러 이처럼 많은 우표들이 발행되도록 태권도를 반석 위에 올려놓으신 김운용 전 세계태권도연맹 총재님께도 감사의 뜻을 전합니다. 태권도 세계화에 공헌하셨던 이금홍 전 세계태권도연맹 사무총장님(2010. 10월 작고하심)의 영전에 이 책을 바칩니다. 앞으로 언젠가는 200여 전세계 모든 국가들이 태권도 우표를 발행하는 날이 오기를 학수고대해 봅니다.

※ 저자 경력
· 태권도 8단
· 태권도 본질, 철학, 역사, 문화 분야에 대한 전문 연구가
· 연세대학교 체육교육학과 〈영어로 배우는 태권도〉 강사
· 연세대학교 평생교육원 태권도 최고지도자과정 전문강사
· 연세대 국제태권도아카데미 관장
· 국기원 학술담당전문위원회 인문과학연구원
· 대한태권도협회 기술심의회 임원
· 태권도진흥재단 자료수집위원회 위원

– Forward –

Kim, Young Sun

The author has amassed a collection of over 145 Taekwondo stamps from 68 countries since the 2000 Sydney Olympic Games. The discovery of each stamp was as joyous as unearthing a treasure buried and hidden deep within the arth. 10 years of work have been put into the publishing of this book and its release is accompanied by great joy and emotion.

The author began collecting Taekwondo stamps after seeing all the stylish stamps Korea had issued for the 2002 World Cup. These stamps were released right after the Sydney Olympics, which was the first Olympic Games to feature Taekwondo as an official event. During that time, the author had a thought: "Now that Taekwondo is finally an official Olympic event, countries all over the world just may begin to publish their own stamps featuring Taekwondo." Though it was a vague guess at the time, it was right on the money. From then on the author began to peruse internet auction sites, international postage stamp dealers, sports postage stamp catalogs and the like, continuously collecting to create the colorful display that he owns today.

The author has already collected a wide array of Taekwondo stamps, but to put them away in the cabinet would be like leaving treasure buried in the sand. The nations that have interest in and practice, Taekwondo can share and spread their love for the sport through the issuing of their postage stamps. It is the author's belief that Taekwondo was originally spread from the holding of international Taekwondo tournaments. Exhibitions were also held with great posters proclaiming support for Kukkiwon. This time though, the history of Taekwondo as well as its tradition and culture, have been weaved together with these postage stamps to create this book.

Today Taekwondo has reached a global status thanks to the hard work and labor of masters working overseas in various countries. This book honors the countries that issued Taekwondo stamps as well as the masters who taught there. In addition, the author would like to thank the former President of the World Taekwondo Federation Un Yong Kim for elevating Taekwondo to such a high level. The book is also dedicated to the memory of Geum Hong Lee, former Secretary General of the World Taekwondo Federation who passed away in October of 2010. His contributions aided in the globalization and international acceptance of Taekwondo. The author eagerly awaits, with the hope that the remaining countries of the world will also release their very own Taekwondo stamps.

※ Author's Career
· 8th dan Black belt
· Research Specialist on Taekwondo Essentials, Philosophy, History and Culture
· Special Lecturer on Taekwondo, Yonsei University Lifelong Education Center
· Lecturer on Taekwondo, Yonsei University Physical Education Department
· Headmaster of the International Taekwondo Academy, Yonsei University
· Research Member of the Human Science Kukkiwon Academic Committee
· Korea Taekwondo Association Technical Committee Member
· Committee Member of Material Acquisitions, Taekwondo Promotion Foundation

차 례 / TABLE OF CONTENTS

- 3 • 태권도의 가치 The Values of Taekwondo
- 4 • 추천사 Letters of Recommendation
- 8 • 발간사 Forward
- 12 • 일러두기 Remarks

13   I. 태권도의 전통
     The Traditions of Taekwondo

29   II. 한국의 국기(國技), 태권도
     Taekwondo, The Korean National Sport

45   III. 아시아에 전파된 새로운 무예스포츠, 태권도
     Taekwondo Spreads in Asia as a New Martial Sport

63   IV. 세계로 뻗어간 태권도
     The Worldwide Spread of Taekwondo

91   V. 태권도와 동양무예를 사랑했던 엘비스 프레슬리
     Elvis Presley, An Enthusiast of Taekwondo and
     Other Asian Martial Arts

95   VI. 태권도 발차기를 활용한 무술영화배우 부루스 리
     Bruce Lee, The Famous Martial Arts Movie
     Star Used Taekwondo Kicks

101   VII. 1988년 제24회 서울 하계 올림픽 시범종목 거행
     A Demonstration Sport at The 24th Olympiad
     – The 1988 Seoul Summer Olympic Games

113   VIII. 올림픽 정식종목을 향한 힘찬 발걸음
     The Critical Steps Toward Becoming an Official Olympic Sport

127 IX. 마침내 2000년 제27회 시드니 하계 올림픽에 정식종목으로 채택
At Long Last, the Adoption of Taekwondo as an Official Sport
- The 27th Olympiad - The 2000 Sydney Summer Olympic Games

145 X. 2004년 제28회 아테네 하계 올림픽 정식종목 거행
Taekwondo As an Official Sport at The 28th Olympiad
- The 2004 Athens Summer Olympic Games

161 XI. 2008년 제29회 베이징 하계 올림픽 정식종목 거행
Taekwondo As an Official Sport at The 29th Olympiad
- The 2008 Beijing Summer Olympic Games

183 XII. 2012년 제30회 런던 하계 올림픽 정식 종목 거행 예정
Taekwondo Will Be an Official Sport at The 30th Olympiad
- The 2012 London Summer Olympic Games

188 · 해설 I. 놀랄만큼 다채로운 '태권도 테마 우표'
Appendix I. The Amazing Variety of Taekwondo-Themed Stamps

192 · 해설 II. 이것이 최고의 '태권도 우표' - 지상우표갤러리
Appendix II. The Best Taekwondo Stamps - The Stamp Gallery

194 · 해설 III. 국가별 태권도 우표 발행 현황
Appendix III. Taekwondo Stamps Issued by Country

200 · 저자 우취 활동상 Author's Philatelic Activities
204 · 참고문헌 및 자료 References
206 · 국가별 찾아보기 Country Index

일러두기

1. '태권도 테마 우표'란 태권도를 소재로 각국 정부 소속 우정국에서 발행한 공식 우표를 말한다. 우표 중에는 태권도 특징이 뚜렷하지 않지만 동양무예를 포괄하는 이미지로 표현된 것도 '태권도 테마 우표'의 범주에 속한다.
2. 개인이나 태권도단체 차원에서 발행된 '나만의 우표'는 태권도 우표에서 제외되었다. '나만의 우표' 중 특별한 의미가 있는 것은 소개하기로 한다.
3. '제1장 태권도의 전통' 부분은 관련 한국 역사 관련 우표나 나만의 우표 이미지를 활용하여 태권도 역사를 시대 순으로 해설했다.
4. 68개국 124건 145종의 태권도 우표에 대해 식별하기 쉽도록 〈태권우표 표시번호〉를 붙였다.
5. 태권도 우표를 주제별로 12단락으로 나누고 각 쪽에 한 건의 태권도 우표를 배치하고 해당 나라의 국기를 넣었다.
6. 각 태권도 우표에 대해 ① 태권도가치성 ② 도안성 ③ 희귀성 등 세 가지 항목을 5단계 ★ 표시로 평가했다.

Remarks

1. A 'Taekwondo-Themed Stamp' is an official stamp issued by the post office department of a national government. Although some of the stamps included in this book do not seem to have a distinct Taekwondo character, instead depicting East Asian martial arts inclusively, I have included them as Taekwondo stamps.
2. I have excluded 'customized stamps' issued by individuals or organizations from the definition of Taekwondo stamps. However, particularly meaningful 'customized stamps' have been included.
3. The first chapter, The Tradition of Taekwondo, explains Taekwondo history chronologically through the use of relevant Korean history-related stamps and images on 'customized stamps.'
4. To help the reader to distinguish the 145 stamps in 124 different cases from 68 countries from one another, I have incorporated the "Taekwondo Stamp Recognition Number" designation.
5. I have divided Taekwondo stamps within 12 chapters, each according to the category it discusses, and placed one Taekwondo stamp on each page along with the national flag of its issuing country.
6. Each stamp was evaluated with a '5-star ★ Ranking System' according to the following three categories:
   ① Taekwondo Value ② Design ③ Rarity

태권도의 전통
The Traditions of Taekwondo

고려시대 맨손 격투무예
'수박희' 그림 (나만의 우표)
The illustration of the unarmed martial art in Koryo dynasty(A Customized Stamp)

오늘날 세계적 무예스포츠로 정착한 태권도는 한국의 무예 전통을 배경으로 성장 발달해왔다. 한반도에는 고대시대부터 수많은 전쟁을 치르면서 검술, 창술, 궁술 등 병기 무예 뿐 아니라 수박, 권법 등 맨손 격투술도 발달하여 이웃나라 일본에도 전파되기도 했다. 손으로 치고 발로 차는 맨손격투 무예는 고대에는 '수박' 또는 '수박희'라고 칭해졌고 군사무예의 일부였을 뿐 아니라 축제에서 용력(勇力)을 겨루는 경연 종목으로도 행해졌다. 조선시대에는 '권법(拳法)', '택견' 등의 맨손무예가 전승되면서 오늘날 태권도를 발달시킨 밑거름이 되었다. 이 장에서는 한국에서 발행된 우표들을 통해 반도에 존재했던 맨손 격투 무예들을 살펴보기로 한다.

These days, Taekwondo which has settled down as a world martial sport, grew and developed with Korean martial art tradition as its setting. As the Korean Peninsula went through many wars since ancient time, it developed not only armed martial arts such as the art of swordmanship, spearmanship and archery, but unarmed martial arts such as *Soobak, Soobakhee* (Traditional Unarmed Martial Arts) which later spread to Japan. The unarmed martial arts hitting with hands and kicking with feet was called 'Soobak' or 'Soobakhee' and was also a part of soldier military arts. In addition, it was conducted in a competitive environment to test the strength of the opponents during festivals. During the Chosun dynasty, the ancient martial arts transformed into 'Kwonbeop' and 'Taekkyeon' which eventually provided the fertile ground for the development of what Taekwondo is today. In this chapter, we will look at stamps related to these unarmed martial arts that existed on the Korean Peninsula.

I-1. 고대 군사 강국 고구려의 무사와 전투 무예
Goguryeo, The Ancient Military Kingdom and Martial Arts in War

고구려 장수들의 전투 광경이 담긴 우표 2종 (1982. Korea)
Two stamps designed for Goguryeo Warriors and troops against their enemies in war

고구려(BC.37~AD.668)는 지금의 북한과 중국 동남부 지역을 통치했던 강력한 한국의 고대 제국이었다. 고구려인은 험난한 지형을 이용하여 산성을 쌓고 왕에서 일반 백성에 이르기까지 막강한 전투 역량을 지녔다. 칼, 창 등 무기술 뿐 아니라 맨손 격투 무예에 능했던 그들은 무예 수련과 전투가 일상생활의 일부가 되었다. 고구려의 무사 집단인 '조의선인'은 농사를 짓지 않고 오로지 군사훈련이나 전투에만 종사하는 직업 무사로서 그 수가 3만 여명에 달할 정도였다.

Goguryeo (37 B.C.~668 A.D) was the Korean ancient military kingdom which governed over today's North Korean area and most of Manchuria including the Gilin province in China. The Goguryeo people built fortress walls on hills using the rough natural features and had a strong battle ability from the king to the common people. They had excellent ability not only in military art skills with a sword and spear, but unarmed martial arts as well. Their training martial arts and battle became a part of common life. 'Jo Ui Seon In', a soldier group in Goguryeo was a trained professional group of soldiers who did not work on farms like most other citizens. Instead they engaged in rigorous warrior training and combat drills, and the number of them was over 30 thousand.

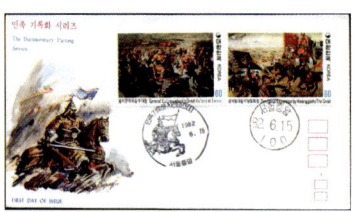 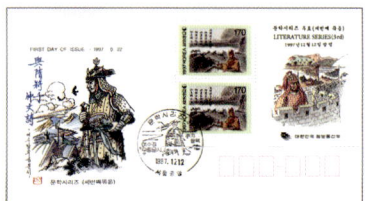

고구려 장수들이 도안된 초일봉투
The First Day Covers designed for Goguryeo Warriors

을지문덕, 연개소문, 양만춘 등 고구려 시대의 무사 영웅들이 모두 '조의선인' 출신이었고 고구려 발전의 견인차 역할을 하였다. 중국 깊숙이 진출하여 고구려 역사상 최대의 영토를 확장했던 광개토대왕은 무예를 수련했던 무인 군주였다. 고구려의 용맹한 무사들은 중국 수나라 113만 대군과 당나라의 40만 대군의 침입을 여러 차례 물리치는 공적을 세우기도 한다. 고구려인들의 생활과 무예가 묘사된 고분벽화 유적이 1,500년이 지난 오늘날까지 생생하게 전해진다.

Military heroes in Goguryeo including generals Ulji-Munduk, Yeongae-Somun, Yang Manchun etc, were the origin of 'Jo Ui Seon In (head of the special forces), and they played a great role in developing the Goguryeo Kingdom. Emperor Kwanggaeto-Daewang was a military lord trained in martial arts that gained vast territories, even into parts of south eastern China, extending the borders of Goguryeo. A courageous band of warriors in Goguryeo also fended off an enormous military invasion staged by 1,130,000 Sui Dynasty(589-618 A.D.) soldiers. Goguryeo was also able to defeat forces numbering 400,000 from the Tang Dynasty(618-907 A.D.) mulitple times throughout history. Many ancient frescos depicting the lifestyles of the Goguryeo people and martial arts, dating back to 1,500 years, have been handed down for generations.

용맹한 고구려 장수들의 기마 전투 장면이 담긴
우표 2종 (2005. Korea)
Two stamps designed for Goguryeo warriors in a fighting scene

 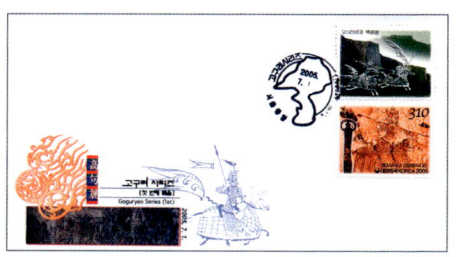

고구려 무사단의 우두머리 광개토대왕 우표와 고구려 무사 초일봉투 (2000 & 2005. Korea)
The Stamp and First Day Cover designed for the Goguryeo Emperor Kwanggaeto-Daewang and warriors

우표로 보는 태권도 발자취 The Evolution of Taekwondo as Seen Through Postage Stamps

I-2. 무예를 닦았던 고구려의 무인
The Ancient Martial Artist, The Goguryeo Warrior

전투 기술과 호연지기를 길렀던 고구려 무인들의 기마 사냥 모습이 담긴 우표.
Stamps designed for Goguryeo Warrior's horse riding martial arts. (1989 & 1999. Korea)

고대에는 칼, 창 등 무기로 싸우는 무예 그 자체가 전투 기술이었다. 맨손 무예는 전투 보조 기술로 포함되었다. 축제 기간에는 맨손 격투 무예인 수박 경기가 행해졌다. '수박(手搏)'은 무인들의 전투적 역량을 기르고 상무정신을 고양함으로써 무인들의 필수 과목으로 채택되었다. 사냥과 가무, 수박 등의 여러 경기에서 승리한 사람을 '선배'라 불렀고 이들은 국가에서 급료를 받아 생활하면서 무예와 학문을 갈고 닦았고 전쟁에서 정예군으로 활약했다.

In ancient times, martial art fighting with weapons like swords and spears was itself a battle skill. Unarmed martial arts were included among the skills of warfare. During festivals, competitions of the unarmed martial art of 'Soobak' was held. Soobak was chosen as an essential subject for warriors to develop their fighting ability and raise their militaristic spiritualism. Those who won competitions such as hunting, singing and dancing, Soobak, etc., were called 'Seonbae'. They lived on a salary from the state, trained in martial arts and academic arts, and were actively utilized as special forces in battles.

고구려 무사들의 마상무예
Stamps designed for Martial arts on the horse in the Goguryeo Dynasty

I-3. 고구려 무인(武人)의 맨손무예
The Unarmed Martial Arts of Goguryeo Warriors

태권도의 전통이 되는 고구려의 맨손 타격무예 '수박(手搏)'의 존재는 고분 벽화와 여러 기록을 통해 오늘날까지 전해진다. 수박은 고구려 고분 벽화를 통해 최초로 나타난 5세기 경부터 통일신라시대(676~936), 고려시대(918~1391), 조선시대(1392~1910) 중기에 이르기까지 장장 1,000년을 이어온 한국 토착무예로 정착했다. 수박은 상대와 맞잡고 넘어뜨리는 씨름과는 고대부터 분리되어 행해졌으며 일본 스모(相搏)와 유술(柔術)의 원류로 간주되고 있다.

Taekwondo's ancient predecessor, the traditional martial art of Soobak, has been handed down through the generations to today through many records and ancient frescos. Soobak was established as a Korean aboriginal martial art, and was practiced from the 5th century on for a thousand years throughout the unified Silla Dynasty(676~936 A.D.), the Goryeo Dynasty(918~1391 A.D.), up to the middle of the Josun Dynasty(1392~1500s A.D.). It was rediscovered through the excavation of ancient tombs in the 15th century. Soobak is distinct from 'Ssirum', which is regarded as the origin of 'Sumo'(Japanese traditonal wrestling) and 'Jujitsu'(the Japanese traditional unarmed martial art).

고구려 맨손격투 무예 수박을 도안한 우표자료인 미터스탬프 (1999. Korea)
A Meter-Stamp designed for Soobak, the unarmed martial art of the Goguryeo Dynasty

고구려 벽화에 나온 씨름 모습이 담긴 우표와 초일봉투 (2000, Korea)
A Stamp and the First Day Cover designed for 'Ssirum', the traditional wrestling in the Goguryeo Dynasty

I-4. 삼국통일을 이룬 신라의 무예
Silla's Martial Art Unified the Three Kingdoms

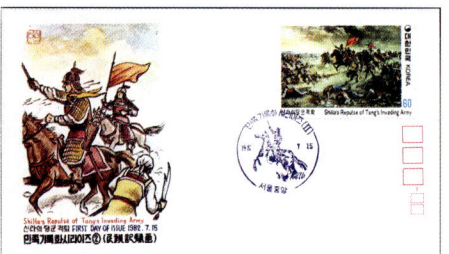

신라 군사가 당나라를 물리치는 민족기록화 우표와 초일봉투 (1982, Korea)
The Stamp and the First Day Cover designed for 'Silla's Repulse of Tang's Invading Army'

신라는 고구려, 백제에 비해 국력이 가장 약했지만 중국 당나라와 연합하여 고구려, 백제를 멸망시킨 후 삼국을 통일했다. 통일 직후 신라와 당나라 연합군 간에 분쟁이 생겼고 마침내 당나라 대군이 신라를 침공했다. 신라는 숫적으로 월등히 열세임에도 불구하고 수십만 당나라 대군에 맞서 대승을 거두었다. 당 대군을 물리친 원동력은 바로 무인(武人) 지도자들의 전투 역량에서도 비롯되었다. 오랜 기간동안 계속된 삼국 간의 전쟁은 자연히 무사와 무예 중심의 사회상을 형성시켰다. 무사들은 전투에 필요한 병장기 무예를 필수적으로 연마했을 뿐 아니라 맨손으로 적과 싸우는 격투 기법도 익혔다. 국가의 존망을 책임진 무사들은 병법에 통달하고 무예를 전문으로 수련함으로써 자연히 '무사인의 길'(무사도)을 추구하게 되었다

Silla was the weakest of the three nations overshadowed by Goguryeo and Baekje, during the three Kingdoms period. However, Silla was able to unite the three Kingdoms by creating an alliance with Tang China. After unification, complications arose between Silla and Tang China, resulting in armed conflicts between once friendly allies. Despite Silla's underpowered military force they were able to repel the attacks of several hundred thousand soldiers from Tang China. Silla was able to overcome such seemingly insurmountable odds by the excellent leadership abilities of their military commanders. The long lasting war among the Three Kingdoms gave rise to great military forces and a newly martial arts centered society. In preparation for battle, the warriors would practice not only the necessary weapon techniques, but unarmed hand-to-hand fighting techniques against their enemies. Each was responsible for the protection of his land and people, therefore each soldier was specially trained in martial arts and pursued 'The Way of the Warrior'(Moosa Do).

I-5. 신라 무인(武人)의 모습
The Silla Dynasty Warrior Statues

이 우표 이미지들은 신라의 무사의 모습을 보여주는 한국의 국보문화재 도제기마인물상(국보 제91호)이다. 신라 무인들은 자신들의 모습과 똑같은 도자기 술잔을 만들어 실생활에 사용했다. 장식이 화려한 고깔 삼각모를 쓴 갑옷 차림의 무사가 무장시킨 전투마를 타고 시종과 함께(별도의 시종 기마상이 함께 출토되었다.) 기품있게 나들이하는 모습이 재현되었다. 삼국을 통일한 신라의 무인들 대다수는 청소년 시절 화랑 출신이었다. 화랑도는 충성심과 용맹성을 배양하고 가무와 무예를 익히던 무사단으로서 국난을 극복하는 데 크게 기여하였다.

The image on this stamp is of a Korean treasure (National Treasure No. 91), the porcelain figure of a horseman which represents the image of a Silla warrior. Silla warriors used porcelain cups made in their images. This porcelain cup depicts a dignified warrior, on horseback and wearing a splendid conical hat, on an excursion accompanied by his servant (a separate servant horseman porcelain cup was excavated along with this warrior porcelain cup). The Silla Warriors who contributed to the unification of the three kingdoms were mostly young men from the elite 'Hwarang' Warrior clan. The 'Hwarang' were a group of warriors who trained both in dance and martial arts to build loyalty and courage, and they contributed tremendously in overcoming many national crises.

신라의 무인 토기
Three Stamps featuring porcelain art of a Silla Warrior

 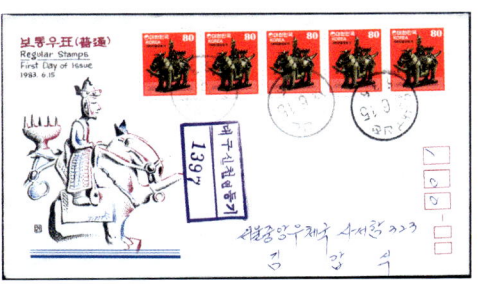

초일실체봉투   Used Cover of the First Day Issue

I-6. 무예정신의 정수, 화랑도의 세속오계
The Hwarangdo Warrior and the Five Commandments

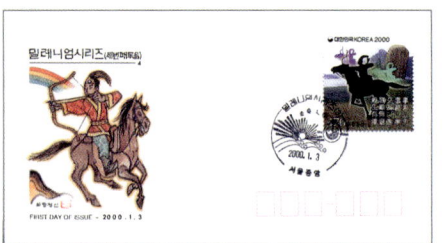

화랑도 기사(騎射; 말타고 활을 쏘는 무예) 무예와
세속오계를 담은 우표와 초일봉투 (2000, Korea)
The stamp and the First Day Cover designed for the
Hwarangdo Warrior and the five commandments

화랑도의 '세속오계'는 신라 무사단의 계율이자 실천 이념이었다. 첫째, 군주 (임금)에게 충성한다(사군이충;事君以忠), 둘째, 부모에게 효도한다(사친이효; 事親以孝), 셋째, 믿음으로써 벗을 사귄다(교우이신;交友以信), 넷째, 전투에서 물러서지 않는다(임전무퇴;臨戰無退), 다섯째, 살생을 하더라도 구별해서 한다 (살생유택;殺生有擇)이다. 세속오계는 화랑도의 신조가 되어 삼국통일의 기초를 이룩하게 하는 데 크게 기여하였다. 화랑도의 세속오계는 현대의 태권도 정신과 철학의 한 줄기가 되고 있다. "첫째, 나라를 사랑한다. 둘째, 부모님과 웃어른을 공경한다. 셋째, 약속을 잘 지킴으로써 믿을만한 사람이 된다. 넷째, 자신감 있고 굳센 마음을 가진다. 다섯째, 하찮은 생명체라도 존중한다." 등 태권도 정신의 바탕이자 태권도장 인성교육의 실천 덕목으로 큰 의미가 있다.

The five secular commandments of the Hwarangdo were the cannons and practical traits of the warriors: first, be loyal to the king; second, be loyal to your parents; third, maintain friendship with trust; fourth, never retreat in battle; and fifth, kill with deliberation. The five secular commandments served as the representative traits of the 'Hwarangdo' and contributed to the foundation of the state after the unification of the three kingdoms. They are also applied as elements of the principal philosophy of Taekwondo as follows: first, love one's own country; second, respect one's parents and elders; third, maintain trustful relationships with others by keeping one's word; fourth, carry a strong will with confidence; fifth, be mindful even of the tiniest inconsequential living creature.

I-7. 맨손무예의 상징, 신라의 금강역사상
The Statue of Keumgang Expresses Unarmed Martial Art.

금강역사상은 신라시대 유물로서 맨손무예 태권도의 주요 상징물이다. 신라의 수도 경주에 위치한 석굴암(국보 제24호. 774년 건립)내 조각된 예술작품이지만 당시 신라에서 맨손무예가 성행했음을 알려주는 주요 단서로도 볼 수 있다. 금강역사는 원래 부처님의 경호신장 역할로서 인도에서 유래했다. 일반적인 금강역사는 여러 가지 무기를 들고 있지만 석굴암 금강역사는 맨손무예를 취하는 점에서 이례적이었다. 삼국시대의 맨손 격투무예가 통일신라(676~936) 기간인 250년을 거쳐 고려시대로 전승된 것을 보면 당시 신라에서도 맨손무예가 성행된 사실을 짐작할 수 있다. 금강역사상의 동작은 태권도 품새의 금강막기 기술의 표본이 되고 있다.

The statue of 'Keumgang' is one of the major Taekwondo symbols from the Silla Dynasty. It is an artistic sculpture carved into the wall of a stone cave housing a Buddhist shrine named 'Seokguram' (National Treasure No. 24, established in 774), located in Gyungju, and is considered an important clue that unarmed martial arts were in vogue at that time. The image of the statue of 'Keumgang' (a deva king) originated in India, depicting a guardian of the Buddha. Usually, 'deva' kings are depicted holding various weapons, but the statue of 'Keumgang' in 'Seokguram' is unique because it is unarmed. We may assume that unarmed martial arts were popular during the Silla dynasty due to the fact that Silla unarmed martial arts were transmitted to the Goryeo Dynasty 250 years after the beginning of the unification era (676-936 A.D.). The gesture of the 'Keumgang Statue' image serves as the technical model of the 'Keumgang' 'poomsae' of Taekwondo.

신라 맨손무예의 유행을 상징하는 석굴암 금강역사상 우표 (1980 & 2010)
Stamps designed for the 'Keumgang Statue', the symbol of the 'Unarmed Martial Art' in Silla Dynasty

금강역사상이 도안된 초일 실체봉투(1980)
Used Cover of the First Day Issue (1980)

금강역사상을 도안한 소형쉬이트 (2010)
Souvenir Sheet of the Keumgang Stature (2010)

I-8. 고려시대에 성행한 맨손 격투무예
The Unarmed Martial Art Continued through the Goryeo Dynasty

고려시대 맨손무예 대가 '이의민' 나만의 우표
Eui-Min Lee, a famous martial artist in Goryeo

삼국시대 '수박'이라 불렸던 맨손 격투무예는 무인들이 오랜 기간 권력을 잡았던 고려시대(918~1392)에는 더욱 성행했다. 오늘날 이종격투기처럼 왕들과 귀족들이 어울려 관람하는 실전 격투경기는 당시 '수박희'라고 불렸다. 수박희는 당시 무인들이 정변을 일으켜 권력을 차지하는 중요한 계기가 되기도 한다. 수박희 경기에서 진 무인이 젊은 문인에게 뺨을 맞는 사건은 박대 받던 무인들이 많은 문인들을 죽이고 정권을 잡는 계기가 된 것이다. 미천한 신분에서 최고 집권자가 된 '이의민(?~1196)'은 수박희 실력이 출중했다고 한다. 고려 무인 중 '두경승(?~1197)'은 맨 주먹으로 벽을 뚫을 정도로 위력적인 무예가로 전해진다

The unarmed martial arts of the Three Kingdoms period, collectively referred to as 'Soobak,' became more popular when the warriors class reigned during the Goryeo Dynasty (918~1392 A.D.). Just like today's mixed martial arts fighting championships, unarmed fighting tournaments were held at the time called 'Soobakheui.' Soobakheui also served as a major opportunity for a coup d'etat by the members of the warrior class. A group of warriors who had been badly mistreated by the high ranking scholar-officials began killing members of the scholar-official class during a 'Soobakheui'-led uprising (the 1170 A.D. Rebellion of General Joong-Boo Jeong). Eui-Min Lee (~1196 A.D.), who was born into the lowest class, was an expert in Soobakheui tournaments and took the top position of political power. It is also recorded that Gyeong-Seung Doo, a Goryeo martial artist, was so powerful that he could punch through a wall with his bare fists.

외적의 침입을 물리친 고려 강감찬 장군이 나온 우표와 초일봉투 (1982)
A stamp and the First Day Cover for General Gam-Chan Gang of the Goryeo Dynasty (1982)

I-9. 오키나와에 전래된 고려 삼별초의 무예
Sambyeolcho Contributions to Okinawan Martial Culture

고려시대의 무인들이 가라테의 본고장으로 알려진 오키나와에 건너가서 중세 국가의 기초를 세웠다는 최근의 학설이 신빙성 있게 받아들여지고 있다. 13세기 칭기스칸이 세운 대제국인 몽골의 침략을 받자 고려 무인정권은 강화로 천도하여 40여 년간 강경하게 저항하였다. 무인정권이 무너지고 몽골과 강화가 성립되자, 정예부대였던 삼별초는 진도를 거쳐 제주도에서 끝까지 저항하다 진압되었는데, 일부 병력이 오키나와로 건너갔다는 내용이다. 당시 선사시대에 머물던 오키나와는 삼별초가 건너가 고려의 축성, 건축 기술, 고려의 정예 군사들의 체제 등을 전하여 류큐왕국이 건설되는 데에 결정적인 영향을 주었던 것으로 보인다. 오키나와의 기와 등 유적과 문화 양식들이 고려의 그것과 비슷한 것이 증거로 제시되었다. 그렇다면 오키나와 전통무예의 성립에도 고려의 수박희가 영향을 미쳤을 가능성도 높다. 오키나와는 일본 규슈 남서쪽에서 타이완에 이르는 방대한 1,200km의 열도 가운데에 있는 섬으로서 지리적으로 남중국, 한국, 일본 등 삼국과 교류했다. 오랫동안 류큐왕국으로서 독특한 특색과 문화를 유지하다가 19세기에야 일본 영토로 편입되었다.

A new theory has emerged, that a group warriors of the Goryeo Dynasty emigrated to Okinawa, the birthplace of Karate, in order to establish the foundation for building the state during the middle of the era. For 40 years, the Goryeo warrior-based government held back invasions by the Mongols, whose empire had been established by Genghis Khan in the 13th century. According to this theory, once the tide turned toward the Mongol's favor, some of the elite troops, referred to as 'Sambyeolcho', went to Okinawa to escape oppression. Artifacts such as roof tiles, wall fortifications, architecture, martial arts and cultural modes of expression are presented as proof of the transmission of the Goryeo military system to Okinawa. If this is true, there is a possibility that Goryeo Soobakheui influenced the formation of Okinawan traditional martial arts. Okinawa is one of the islands in the 1,200 km. Japanese archipelago, ranging from the southern part of Kyushu to Taiwan. Okinawa maintained trade relations with Southern China, Korea and Japan. It kept its unique characteristics and culture for a long time, as the Ryuku Kingdom, until it was incorporated into Japan in the 19th century.

삼별초 관련 자료가 실린 나만의 우표
Customized stamps of the Sambyeolcho

우표로 보는 태권도 발자취 The Evolution of Taekwondo as Seen Through Postage Stamps

I-10. 조선시대 민간 무예의 흔적
Civilian Martial Arts in the Joseon Dynasty

16세기 조선시대의 도적 임꺽정의 무예, 돌려차기가 만화로 그려진 우표와 초일봉투 (1999)
A Cartoon Stamp and the First Day Cover featuring a 'Roundhouse Kick' by Gguk-Jeong Im, the Famous Outlaw of the Joseon Dynasty in the 16th Century(1999).

원래 무술이란 상대를 굴복시키거나 죽이기 위해 사용하는 물리적인 투쟁 기술이다. 무술을 사용하는 주체는 주로 직업적으로 전쟁을 수행하는 군사들이었다. 조선시대에는 범죄자를 잡기 위하여 설치한 관청(포도청)에 소속된 포졸(경찰)들이 무예를 익혔다. 그 외에도 정적(政敵)이나 도적들의 공격으로 부터 무장(武裝)을 할 필요성이 있는 계층들이 적지 않았다. 유력 정치가의 사병(私兵), 양반에 귀속된 무예전문 경호원(술사), 귀중품을 싣고 해외 무역을 하는 상선의 선원, 등짐 운반 상인인 보부상(褓負商), 재력 있는 불교 사원의 무술 승려(武僧) 등은 생명과 재산을 지키기 위해 일단의 무장력을 갖추기 위해 조직적으로 무술을 수련했다. 다른 사람의 재물을 강탈하는 도적들 또한 무술가 집단이다. 조선시대 18세기경 민간 청소년들이 격투 무예를 익힌 사례도 아래 민화 '나만의 우표'를 통해 알 수 있다.

Originally, martial arts were physical fighting skills used to subdue or kill an opponent. Those who used martial arts were warriors who fought in wars as professionals. During the Joseon Dynasty, the police who were charged with arresting criminals practiced martial arts. In addition, there were quite a few classes who needed protection from their political enemies and bandits. Private soldiers of powerful politicians, body guards of nobles, wealthy overseas trade merchants, peddlers and Buddhist monks in wealthy monastic-estates practiced martial arts in order to protect their lives and properties and to arm themselves. Bandits who robbed passers-by of their belongings are also considered among the group referred to as martial artists. We can also see, through this 'customized stamp' of a folk painting, that civilian youths also practiced fighting arts in the 18th century.

무예 수련 장면이 나온 민화 (나만의 우표)
A Customized stamp of a folk painting of martial art

I-11. 오키나와에 전승된 홍길동의 무예
Gildong Hong, The Legendary Outlaw Who Moved to Okinawa

도적 무리가 오키나와로 이주하여 축성과 무예 등 군사문화 발달에 기여했다는 학설이 공개되었다. 15세기 조선시대 의적 홍길동은 영웅소설 속의 주인공일 뿐 아니라 실재 인물로서 활동했던 흔적들이 전남 장성군과 오키나와 현지에서 발견되었다. 홍길동은 도술과 무예에 능하여 양반이나 관청의 재물을 빼앗아 가난한 사람들에게 나누어준 도적 세력의 우두머리였다. 조선 관청의 진압을 피해 부하들을 이끌고 오키나와 이시카키섬에 이주하여 호족 세력으로 활동하며 가면극, 축제, 놀이, 기와, 맨손무예 등 오키나와 전통 문화와 무예 발달에도 영향을 주었다고 한다.

A new theory recently presented to the public is that a group of bandits from Joseon emigrated to Okinawa and contributed to the development of warfare, by introducing such things as new fortifications of castle walls (castellations) and martial arts. While we know of Gildong Hong, the Robin Hood of Joseon, as a character in a novel, the recent discovery of traces of his activity in Jang Sung Gun of Cholla Namdo (South Cholla Province) in Korea and in Okinawa show that he was actually an historical figure. Gildong Hong was an expert in Taoist magic and martial arts, as well as the bandit chief who took the riches from nobles and government officials and distributed them to the poor. The theory claims that he emigrated to Okinawa with his troops due to the suppression of the Goryeo government, and influenced the development of aspects of traditional culture and martial arts in Okinawa such as mask plays, festivals, games, roof tiles, unarmed martial arts, etc.

홍길동 우표와 일부인 (1999)
A stamp and a date seal for Gildong Hong, the legendary outlaw(1999)

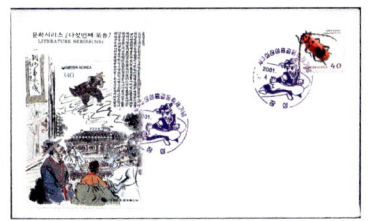
홍길동 초일봉투 First Day Cover

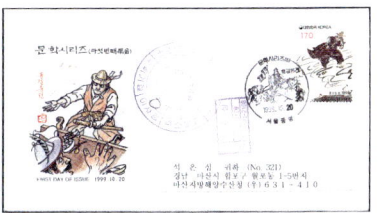
초일실체봉투 Used Cover of the First Day Issue

우표로 보는 태권도 발자취 The Evolution of Taekwondo as Seen Through Postage Stamps

I-12. 무예를 중흥한 정조대왕과 무예의 전당, 화성(華城)
The Great King Jeongjo Promoted the Martial Art and Built Hwaseong Castle.

18세기말 조선시대의 정조대왕은(1776~1800) 문무겸비한 천재적 군주로서 무예를 부흥시켰다. 전란에 대비하여 군사무예교범인 '무예도보통지'를 편찬케 하고 손수 머리말을 붙였다. '무예도보통지'는 당시 중국, 일본 등 방대한 무술 기법들을 망라하여 24종목으로 분류하여 4권짜리 책으로 집대성된 동양 최대의 재래식 군사 무예서이다. 무술 기법과 동작에 대해 조선 풍속화의 대가 김홍도의 세밀한 그림과 상세한 해설이 붙어 있다.

King Jeongjo (1776~1800 A.D.) was a ruler-genius who promoted martial arts with both the pen and the sword. He ordered the publishing of 'Mooyedobotongji,' a military field manual on how to fight in battle and wrote the preface to the book himself. Mooyedobotongji was the most thorough traditional military field manual in East Asia at that time. It referenced military techniques from China and Japan, and is divided into 24 techniques in four volumes. A detailed description and illustration drawn by the great folk painter, Hong Do Kim, are attached here for a look at the techniques and movements.

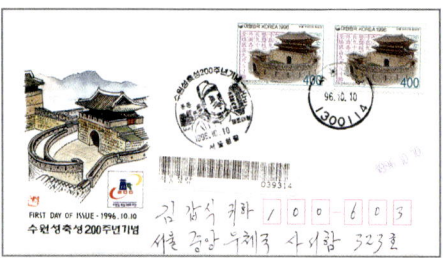

수원 화성 축성 200주년 기념우표와 초일실체봉투 (1996)
The stamp and the Used Cover of the First Day issued for the Bicentennial Anniversary of Hwaseong

무예도보통지 (나만의 우표)
Muyedobotongji, the Textbook for Martial Arts (customized stamps)

1796년 정조의 왕명에 따라 지어진 수원 화성은 5,000여명의 장용영 군사들이 주둔하며 무예를 연마했던 성이나. 정예군으로 편성된 장용영 군사들은 24반 무예를 익히며 국왕 호위 업무를 수행했다. 각종 전투용 병장기 무술은 물론 맨손 무예인 권법을 연마하며 전투력을 배양했다. 정조 사후(死後) 장용영 군사 조직이 해체되어 우두머리이자 무예전문가 백동수(白東脩)를 비롯한 수많은 장용영 군사들이 지방으로 뿔뿔이 흩어졌다. 이들이 전국 각지로 퍼지면서 지방 곳곳으로 무예가 전파되는 계기가 될 수 있었다. 무예 중 무기를 쓰지 않는 맨손무예 권법은 호신 무예가 절실히 필요한 상인이나 승려, 민간인에게 전승되기도 했다

The Hwaseong Castle of Suwon, established by the order of Jeongjo, is a castle where 5,000 Jangyongyoung soldiers (king's guards) resided to practice martial arts. Jangyongyoung soldiers consisted of elite troops who practiced 24 types of martial arts and held the responsibility of protecting the king. They practiced not only various forms of weaponry techniques but also 'Kwonbup', or unarmed martial arts, to develop their fighting skills. After the death of Jeongjo, Jangyongyoung was disbanded and most of the Jangyongyoung soldiers, including the chief of the organization, the professional martial artist Dong Soo Baek, scattered among various regions. Their dispersion contributed to the promotion of martial arts in various areas. Kwonbup, or unarmed martial arts, was thus transmitted to those who urgently needed protection; merchants, Buddhist monks and civilians.

유네스코 세계문화유산 기념우표, 화성 (2002)
The Stamp and the First Day Cover for Hwaseong, The World Cultural Heritage adopted by UNESCO (2002)

화성 초일봉투
First Day Cover

우표로 보는 태권도 발자취   The Evolution of Taekwondo as Seen Through Postage Stamps

I-13. 태권도의 고전 형태, 택견
The Traditional Form of Taekwondo, Taekkyun

Taekwondo Stamp No. 001

☞ 국가명 : 한국. 2002
　　Nation : South Korea

☞ 자료 평가 Evaluation :
① 태권도가치성 Taekwondo Value ★★★★★
② 도안성 Design ★★★★★
③ 희귀성 Rarity ★★★☆☆

☞ 우표 구성 : 기념우표 22종 중 1종
　　Stamp Composition : 1 of 22 stamps

발기술을 주로 사용하는 민족 고유무예이자 축제 경연종목으로서 태권도의 고전 형태이다. 우표에는 한 사람이 호쾌한 발차기로 상대를 공격하는 모습이 담겨있다. 택견은 삼국시대부터 유래된 씨름과 더불어 마을의 민속 격투 경기로서 오랫동안 전승되었다. 일제강점기(1910~1945)에는 택견과 같은 민족 저항정신을 띤 무예는 금지되었다가 해방 이후 택견의 기술 내용이 되살아나게 되었다. 택견 경기에서 발로 상대방 얼굴을 차거나 다리를 걸어 넘기면 승부가 결정된다. 택견은 1983년 대한민국 중요무형문화재 76호로 지정되었다. 태권도의 기술 원리와 경기 방법이 택견에서 착안되었다.

Taekkyun is an old style of Taekwondo consisting mainly of leg movements and kicks that was performed in competitions at festivals and special events. This stamp displays a man fiercely attacking his opponent with a leaping kick. Ssirum (Korean style wrestling) and traditional folk fighting tournaments held within villages have been traced all the way back to Korea's Three Kingdoms period. During the Japanese occupation of Korea (1910~1945 A.D.) Taekkyun was banned by the Japanese for its characteristics of being a fighting technique. After Korea's liberation Taekkyun enjoyed a warm revival. Scoring in Taekkyun competitions was done by either kicking the face or succesfully taking an opponent down to the ground. In 1983, Taekkyun was designated the 76th Important Intangible Cultural Asset of Korea. The technical principles of Taekwondo and competition style were derived from Taekkyun.

초일실체봉투 Used Cover of First Day Issue

택견 초일봉투 First Day Cover

한국의 국기(國技), 태권도
Taekwondo, The Korean National Sport

정부가 선정한 한국 10대 문화 주요상징물,
태권도 (나만의 우표)
Taekwondo, one of Ten Major Symbols of Korean Culture adopted by the Government (customized stamp)

태권도는 1996년 한국 정부에 의해 한복, 한글, 김치, 불고기 등과 더불어 한국 10대 문화상징물로 공식 선정되었다. '역동적인 한국(Dynamic Korea)' 이미지에 부합되는 태권도는 앞으로도 더욱 부각될 전망이다. 2008년 국내 외국인들을 대상으로 한 설문 조사에서 '긍정적인 한국의 대표 이미지'로 삼성, 현대 등 국내기업 브랜드에 이어 태권도가 2위에 오르기도 했다. 한국의 국기(國技)이자 세계 수 많은 사람들이 애용하는 무예스포츠로서 태권도의 위상을 확인하게 한다. 이 단원에서는 태권도의 발전 과정을 담은 9종의 한국 공식우표와 함께 중국과 세인트피에르앤드미켈론 등 외국 우표 2종이 추가되었다. 총 43종의 태권도 우취 자료를 통해 한국이 태권도의 본산지임을 보여주고 있다.

In 1996, the Korean government officially assigned Taekwondo, along with the 'Hanbok' (Korean traditional clothes), 'Hangeul' (Korean language), Kimchi and Bulgogi(Korean traditional food), as one of the top ten cultural symbols of Korea. Taekwondo is undoubtably further progressing under its corresponding representation as 'Dynamic Korea'. A 2008 survey addressing foreigners residing in Korea even ranked Taekwondo as the second 'best representation of Korea' right after major corporations such as Samsung and Hyundai. This is key evidence backing Taekwondo's prestige as the Korean national sport and as a globally acknowledged martial art practiced worldwide.

우표로 보는 태권도 발자취　The Evolution of Taekwondo as Seen Through Postage Stamps

II-1. 국내 태권도 경기 개최 및 태권도 행정 조직의 정비
Holding a Taekwondo Tournament Setting Up an Administrative Organization

Taekwondo Stamp No. 002

- 국가명 : 한국. 1969
  Nation : South Korea
- 자료 평가 Evaluation :
  ① 태권도가치성 Taekwondo Value ★★★★★
  ② 도안성 Design ★★★★★
  ③ 희귀성 Rarity ★★★☆☆
- 우표 구성 : 5종 중 1종
  Stamp Composition : 1 of 5 stamps

세계 최초의 태권도 소재 우표이다. 1969년 제50회 전국체육대회에서 태권도 종목을 포함한 각종 스포츠 경기가 개최되었다. 태권도 경기는 1962년 제43회 전국체육대회 시범 종목으로 열린 후 1963년 제 44회 전국체육대회부터 정식 종목이 되었다. 당시 8x8m 정방형 경기장에서 주먹으로 얼굴 공격을 금지하며 발로는 하체 공격을 금지하는 등의 득점 및 감점 규칙에 따라 발 공격은 2점, 주먹공격은 1점을 배정했다. 초기에는 보호대 없이 진행되었으나 곧 대나무로 만들어진 보호대가 사용되었다. 태권도의 경기화는 상대와 직접 겨루는 실전적 스포츠 경기 체제를 도입함에 따라 엄청난 변화와 발전을 이룩했다. 전국체육대회 채택을 계기로 수많은 태권도 경기가 창설되어 저변 확대에 박차를 가하게 되었다.

This is the very first instance of a Taekwondo postage stamp in the world. The 1969 National Athletic Games featured Taekwondo along with various other events. Taekwondo was selected to be a demonstration sport at the 43rd National Athletic Meet, and became an official sport ever since the 44th National Athletic Meet in 1963. During this time period, the 8x8m quadrate stadium devised a demerit point system for athletes who violated the rules. Attacking the face with fists and kicking the lower parts of body with feet were strictly forbidden, doing so would result in point deduction; 2 points for kicking, 1 point for fist attacks. Although the games proceeded without any protective equipment, the athletes soon began wearing protective guards made of bamboo. Combining combat techniques into the martial art, Taekwondo evolved further and advanced as a major sporting event. Various titles of Taekwondo competition were establised and spread all over the nation thanks to the adoption by the National Athletic Games.

국제 초일 실체봉투
An International Used Cover of the First Day Issued

- 태권도 행정단체 창립과 주요 사건이 담긴 4종의 '나만의 우표'를 통해 발전 과정을 살펴본다.
  These four customized stamps show important events of Taekwondo's organization and Taekwondo's modern development.

- 1961 대한태권도협회 창립
  Founding of 'Korea Taekwondo Association'
- 1963 대한체육회 가맹 승인
  Approval of 'Korea Sport Committee'
- 1963 제44회 전국체육대회 정식종목 개최
  Adoption as an official event at the 44th National Athletic Games.

- 1971년 박정희 전대통령 '국기태권도' 휘호 하사.
  국가 수반인 대통령이 태권도를 한국 국기로 공식 승인함
  The title 'Taekwondo, the Korean National sport' was bestowed by former President Park signifying official approval by the authorized government.

- 1972년 태권도 중앙도장 국기원 준공.
  각종 태권도 경기와 심사 등 태권도 행사가 열리고 세계 태권도 행정 업무에 착수했다.
  The Kukkiwon, the World Taekwondo Headquaters, was built in 1972. Taekwondo events, competions, and promotion tests are regularly held here.

- 1973년 한국의 서울에서 제1회 세계태권도선수권대회가 개최된 후 세계 태권도연맹(초대 총재 김운용)이 창설되었다.
  The World Taekwondo Federation was established in 1973 right after the 1st World Taekwondo Championships in Seoul, Korea.

우표로 보는 태권도 발자취 The Evolution of Taekwondo as Seen Through Postage Stamps

II-2. 1974년 제1회 서울 아시아태권도선수권대회
The 1st Asian Taekwondo Championships in Seoul in 1974

Taekwondo Stamp No. 003

국제 태권도대회를 기념한 최초의 태권도 우표이다. 1974년 아시아 최초의 국제 태권도 대회가 서울 국기원에서 열렸다. 호주, 싱가폴 등 아시아 10개국에서 130여명이 참가하여 남자부 8체급에 걸쳐 사흘간의 열전을 벌였다. 주최국 한국은 전 체급에서 금메달을 획득하여 종합우승을 달성했고 대만이 종합 2위, 캄보디아가 종합 3위를 차지했다. 이 대회는 2년마다 열리며 아시아태권도연맹에 의해 주관된다. 우표에는 헤드기어 없이 몸통보호대와 낭심보호대만 착용한 당시의 경기 모습이 담겨있다. 우표 중앙에는 경기 장소인 국기원이 그려져 있다.

This is the first Taekwondo stamp commemorating an international Taekwondo Championship. The 1st Asian Taekwondo Championships were held at the World Taekwondo Headquarters, the Kukkiwon in 1974. For four days, 130 athletic delegates from 10 countries, including Australia and Singapore, participated in eight male weight classes. The host country Korea, had the honor of winning the championship by acquiring Gold medals for every weight class, followed by Taiwan and Cambodia respectively. Superintended by the International Taekwondo Federation, the competition is still held every two years. The stamp depicts the athletes without head gear, only wearing body protectors and groin guards. At the center of the stamp is the World Taekwondo Headquarters, where the competition took place.

☞ 국가명 : 한국. 1974
　Nation : South Korea

☞ 자료 평가 Evaluation :
① 태권도가치성 Taekwondo Value ★★★★★
② 도안성 Design ★★★★★
③ 희귀성 Rarity ★★★☆☆

☞ 우표 구성 : 기념우표 1종
　Stamp Composition : single stamp

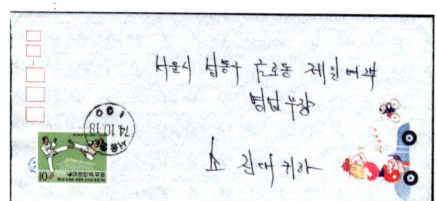

한국 국내 실체봉투
A Domestic Used Cover of Korea

국제 초일 실체봉투
An International Used Cover of the FDC

II-3. 1975년 제2회 세계 태권도 선수권대회
The 2nd World Taekwondo Championships in 1975

1975년 8월 25일부터 9월 1일까지 서울에서 개최된 제2회 세계태권도 선수권대회 기념우표이다. 1973년 거행된 제1회 세계대회가 있은 지 2년 지나서 30개국 165명의 선수가 참가하여 국기원과 장충체육관에서 나흘간의 열전을 벌였다. 한국은 8체급 전체급을 석권하여 종합우승했고 대만이 종합2위, 멕시코가 종합 3위를 기록했다. 우표는 태권도 겨루기 대회 기념우표로는 적합해 보이지 않는다. 태권도 수련자가 겨루기 시합용 보호대를 착용하고 태권도 품새에 나오는 앞굽이 얼굴지르기 동작을 행하고 있다. 얼굴지르기는 품새 기술이지만 겨루기에서는 반칙 기술이다. 태권도 기술을 잘 모르는 당시 우표 도안사가 겨루기와 품새를 섞어서 도안하여 어색한 태권도 우표 이미지가 되었다.

This stamp commemorates the 2nd World Taekwondo Championships held in Seoul from August 25th to September 1st, 1975. Two years after the 1st World Championships, 165 athletic delegates from 30 different countries competed against one another at the World Taekwondo Headquarters and Chang Chung Gymnasium for four consecutive days. The Republic of Korea swept the competition, winning the championship by acquiring Gold medals for every weight class, followed by Taiwan and Mexico. Though this stamp does contain solid Taekwondo value, it is not a very suitable commemorative stamp for a sparring competition. The athlete, wearing competition protective gear, is performing a Taekwondo 'Poomsae' (Form) technique called a 'High Punch' with a 'Forward Stance'. The problem is that this move is illegal during sparring. The stamp designer's lack of understanding between 'Sparring' and 'Poomsae' is clearly shown by the ironic design choice for the stamp.

- 국가명 : 한국. 1975
  Nation : South Korea
- 자료 평가 Evaluation :
  ① 태권도가치성 Taekwondo Value ★★★★★
  ② 도안성 Design ★★★★☆
  ③ 희귀성 Rarity ★★★☆☆
- 우표 구성 : 대회기념우표 1종
  Stamp Composition : 1 single stamp

기념 초일봉투
The First Day Cover

우표로 보는 태권도 발자취 The Evolution of Taekwondo as Seen Through Postage Stamps

II-4. 1986년 제10회 서울 아시아경기대회 성공
The Success of the 10th Seoul Asian Games

공식 태권도 테마 우표는 아니지만 1986년 아시안게임 소형시트 테두리에 태권도 픽토그램과 금메달 7개를 뜻하는 7자가 표기된 중요한 태권도 자료이다. 태권도가 국제스포츠대회에서 최초로 정식종목으로 채택된 것은 바로 이 우표 자료인 1986년 서울아시안게임에서이다. 태권도 경기에서 남자부만 총 8체급이 거행되었는데 한국은 이란 선수가 우승한 밴텀급을 제외한 7체급에서 우승했다. 이 소형시트는 서울아시안게임에서 중국에 이어 종합 2위를 달성한 기념으로 발행되었다. 서울아시안게임 개막식에서 1,001명이 펼친 집단 태권도시범 '약동(안무 이규형, 강형구)'은 큰 찬사를 받았다. 아시안게임 태권도 경기는 선수의 안전을 위해 헤드기어, 전광판, 바닥용 매트를 사용한 최초의 국제경기였다.

At the 1986 Asian Games in Seoul, Taekwondo was finally adopted by the Olympic Council of Asia (O.C.A.) as an official sport. This souvenir sheet was issued to celebrate South Korea's achievements at the Seoul Asian Games. Korea ranked second place during the competition right behind China. In the upper right corner, the number 7 along with the Taekwondo pictogram is displayed representing the seven gold medals. The numbers listed along the border of the souvenir sheet represent the gold medals won by the national team in all the events. The large group demonstration of Taekwondo, titled 'Yakdong'('Stir'- choreography : Kyu Hyung Lee & Hyung Ku Kang), was presented by 1,001 members at the opening ceremony of the ASIAD and received warm and generous applause. The Taekwondo event was the first international game to utilize head gear, a score board, and a floor mat for the safety and security of the athletes during the competition. Of the eight male weight divisions, Korea won 7 golds, the remaining being won by an Iranian athlete in the Bantam weight division.

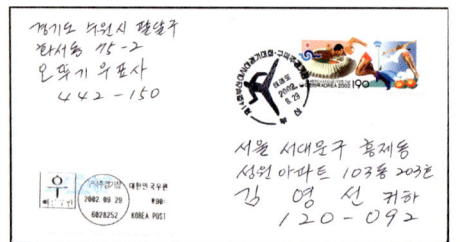

태권도 일부인이 찍힌 2002년
서울아시안게임 초일 실체봉투
A Used FDC for the 2002 Seoul Asian Games

II-5. 국제 스포츠 우표 전시회
The International Exhibition of Sports Philately

1988 서울올림픽대회를 경축하는 문화행사의 일환으로 올림필렉스 '88 국제 스포츠우표전시회가 1988년 9월 19일부터 28일까지 서울의 한국종합전시장(KOEX)에서 개최된 기념으로 발행된 우표이다. 국제올림픽위원회(IOC), 국제올림픽우취연맹(FIPO)의 후원 및 국제우취연맹(FIP)의 협찬으로 진행된 이 행사에는 세계 각국으로부터 1,400여 틀의 각종 스포츠 우취 작품이 출품되어 올림픽 및 스포츠를 주제로 한 단일 테마 우표전시회로는 최대 규모의 전시회가 되었다. 올림픽 성화를 상징하는 불꽃 속에 태권도 픽토그램이 포함되어 다른 올림픽 종목과 함께 도안되었다.

As a cultural event celebrating the 1988 Seoul Olympics, OLYMPHILEX88, an International Exhibition of Olympic and Sports Philately, was held at the Korea Exhibition Center (COEX), Seoul, September 19-28, 1988. The exhibition, held under the patronage of IOC and FIPO and with the auspices of FIP, was the worlds single largest postage stamp show ever held, displaying more than 1,400 frames of philatelic art of sports submitted from all over the world. The Ministry of Communications issued this commemorative postage stamp as a token of expectation that OLYMPHILEX88 would serve to promote friendship and understanding among all the philatelists of the world, going beyond national and ideological differences. The Taekwondo pictogram is contained within the Olympic flame along side other official Olympic sports.

기념 초일봉투
A First Day Cover

☞ 국가명 : 한국. 1988
　Nation : South Korea

☞ 자료 평가 Evaluation :
① 태권도가치성
　Taekwondo Value ★★★★☆
② 도안성 Design ★★★★★
③ 희귀성 Rarity ★★★☆☆

☞ 우표 구성 : 우표 및 소형시트 각 1종씩
　Stamp Composition :
　single stamp & souvenir sheet

우표로 보는 태권도 발자취 The Evolution of Taekwondo as Seen Through Postage Stamps

II-6. 1988년 제24회 서울올림픽 경기대회 시범종목으로 거행된 태권도 경기

Taekwondo Stamp No. 006

☞ 국가명 : 한국, 1988
  Nation : South Korea

☞ 자료 평가 Evaluation :
① 태권도가치성 Taekwondo Value ★★★★★
② 도안성 Design ★★★★★
③ 희귀성 Rarity ★★★☆☆

☞ 우표 구성 : 우표 및 소형쉬트 각24종 중 1종
  Stamp Composition : 1 of 24 stamps & souvenir sheets

1988년 서울올림픽대회에서 태권도가 시범종목으로 채택되어 발행된 기념 우표이다. 두 선수가 헤드기어와 몸통보호대를 착용하고 겨루기 경기를 하는 장면이 도안되었다. 서울올림픽에서 태권도가 시범종목으로 채택된 이유는 인내, 예의 등 바람직한 정신 덕목을 기반으로 한 호신 무예일 뿐 아니라 세계 각국의 호응을 받는 합리적 경기 스포츠로 인정되었기 때문이었다. 한민족 역사상 최대의 축제인 서울올림픽은 태권도가 올림픽 정식종목이 되는 관문이 되었고 대회 개최는 성공적으로 마무리되었다.

This is the commemorative stamp for the adoption of Taekwondo as a one of the demonstration sports at the 1988 Olympic Games in Seoul, Korea. The stamp is presenting the image of two athletes, wearing head-gear and protective chest gear, practicing sparring techniques. Taekwondo was selected as a demonstration sport not only because of its martial arts basis of philosophy, discipline, and code of ethics, but also due to its recognition as a global sport that has gained an international reputation. Taekwondo's later inclusion as an official sport in the Olympics was made possible by the incredible success of one of Korea's most significant historical events - the 1988 Olympic Games in Seoul.

맥시멈카드 A Maximum Card

정부공식 맥시멈카드
An Official Government-Issued Maximum Card

Taekwondo as a Demonstration Sport in the 24th Seoul Summer Olympic Games in 1988

서울올림픽 시범경기인 태권도 종목에는 남자 32개국 120명, 여자 16개국 63명 등 총 183명의 선수가 참가했다. 남녀 각각 8체급에 걸쳐 경기가 진행되었고 남자부 종합우승은 금메달 7개를 딴 한국이 차지했고 여자부는 금메달 3개를 딴 미국이 종합 우승했다. 태권도 최초의 올림픽 행사인 만큼 국내에서 수 많은 우표, 엽시, 동전 등 수집 자료들이 발행되었다.

Taekwondo was first staged at the Olympics as one of the demonstration sports at the 24th Olympic Games. 120 male and 63 female athletes from 34 countries competed in eight weight divisions each, with a total of 16 for both male and female. Korea took first place with seven gold medals in the male division, and the USA took first in the female division earning 3 gold medals. Because of Taekwondo's adoption as an official event in Korea, various postage stamps, post cards, and coins were designed and published.

서울올림픽을 기념하여 한국에서 발행된 은화 1종
A Commemorative Coin made from silver for the Seoul Olympics (front and back)

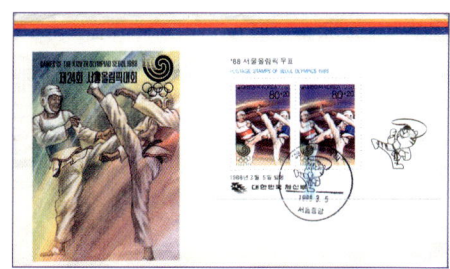

서울올림픽 태권도 초일봉투 2종 (1988, Korea)
Two First Day Covers of Taekwondo for the Seoul Olympics

서울올림픽 기념 엽서 2종
서울올림픽 공식 마스코트 호돌이와 엠블렘 위에 태권도 기념 일부인이 찍혀있다.
Postcards featuring the mascot and emblem published in commemoration of the Seoul Olympics (stamped with the date)

초일실체봉투
Used Cover of the First Day Issue

II-7. 2000년 제27회 시드니 올림픽에서 태권도 종목이 정식종목으로 채택

Taekwondo Stamp No. 007

☞ 국가명 : 한국. 2000
　　Nation : South Korea

☞ 자료 평가 Evaluation :
① 태권도가치성 Taekwondo Value ★★★★★
② 도안성 Design ★★★★★
③ 희귀성 Rarity ★★★☆☆

☞ 우표 구성 : 우표 1종
　　Stamp Composition : single stamp

1994년 9월 프랑스 파리에서 열린 제103차 I.O.C 총회에서 태권도는 2000년 시드니올림픽 정식종목으로 선정되었다. 태권도계의 최대의 숙원 목표인 올림픽 정식종목 진출의 위업이 달성된 역사적 순간이었다. 태권도는 일본의 유도에 이어 아시아 무술 중 두 번째 올림픽 정식종목으로 등록되었다. 한국 정부는 시드니올림픽 개막일에 맞춰 기념우표 1종 200만장을 발행했다. 고구려 무용총 벽화의 겨루기 모습을 배경으로 시드니올림픽 로고와 태권도 경기 장면을 담고 있다.

In September 1994, Taekwondo was adopted as an official sport of the Sydney 2000 Olympic Games at the 103rd I.O.C. Session in Paris, France. It was a historical moment for Taekwondo, obtaining the ultimate goal of becoming a part of the Olympic Games as an official program. Among Asian sport disciplines, Taekwondo was second to be selected as an official sport in the Olympics after Japanese Judo. The Korean government printed two million of the commemorative stamp shown above to coincide with the date of the Sydney Olympics opening ceremony. The stamp features a Taekwondo sparring scene overlaying a traditional Korean unarmed martial art fresco.

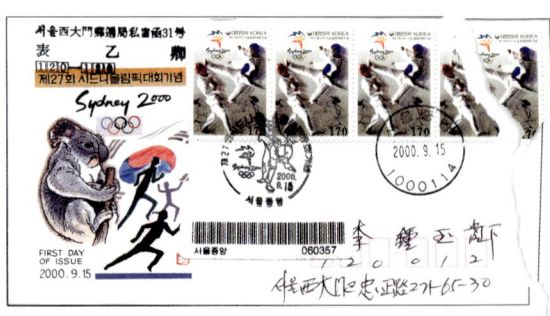

초일 실체봉투
A Used Cover of the First Day Issued

Taekwondo Adopted as an Official Sport at the 27th Sydney Summer Olympic Games in 2000

시드니올림픽 태권도 경기에서 남녀 각 4체급씩 총 8개의 금메달이 배정되었다. 남자부는 39개국 55명, 여자부는 32개국 48명 등 총 103명의 남녀 선수가 참가했다. 시드니 본선 티켓을 획득한 나라는 모두 44개국이며 이 가운데 한국, 필리핀, 타이완, 쿠바, 미국, 스페인 등 6개국이 남녀 두 체급 모두 출전권을 확보했다. 한국이 남자 1체급, 여자 2체급 등 총 3개의 금메달을 차지했고 미국, 호주, 그리스, 중국, 쿠바 등 국가가 각 한 개의 금메달을 획득했다. 베트남도 여자 선수가 은메달을 따냄으로서 올림픽 첫 메달을 따내는 쾌거를 올렸다.

A total of 8 Taekwondo gold medals were assigned to four male and four female weight classes at the Sydney Olympics. 55 male athletes from 39 nations and 48 female athletes from 32 nations totalling 103 participants competed in Taekwondo. Among the 44 nations that acquired entry to the main event, only 6 nations: the Republic of Korea, the Philippines, Taiwan, Cuba, the United States, and Spain secured spots for multiple weight classes in both the male and female divisions. The Republic of Korea attained a total of 3 Gold medals, one from the male division and two in the female weight classes; while the United States, Australia, Greece, China, and Cuba each received one Gold medal. Also, a Vietnamese female athlete had the honor of acquiring a Silver medal, obtaining Vietnam's first Olympic medal.

맥시멈카드
A Maximum Card

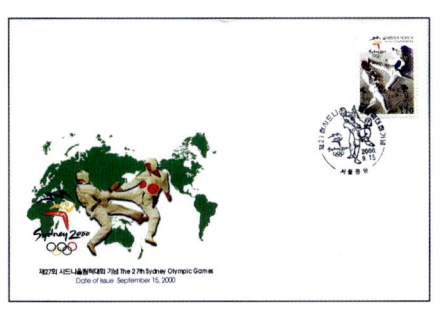

초일봉투
The First Day Cover (2000, Korea)

기념 우표첩
A Commemorative Booklet

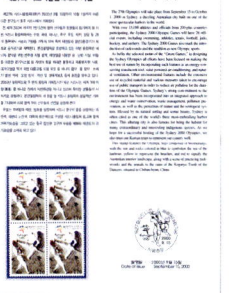

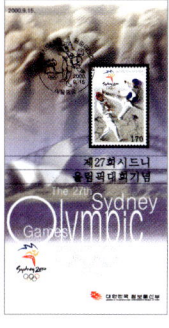

우표 안내장
Information for the Stamp

II-8. 한국·중국 국민교류 10주년. 한국 우표
The 10th Year of the People's Exchange between Korea and China

☞ 국가명 : 한국. 2002
　　Nation : South Korea

☞ 자료 평가 Evaluation :
① 태권도가치성 Taekwondo Value ★★★★★
② 도안성 Design ★★★★★
③ 희귀성 Rarity ★★★☆☆

☞ 우표 구성 : 한·중 국민교류기념 2종 중 1종
　　Stamp Composition : 1 of 2 stamps

한국과 중국 간의 정식 수교 10주년 기념으로 태권도와 우슈를 소재로 한 기념 우표이다. 태권도와 우슈는 양국의 대표적인 문화 상징물로 선정되어 우표에 도안되었다. 우표에는 오른쪽 사람이 옆차기로 상대의 얼굴을 공격하고 왼쪽 사람은 품새의 한손날 바깥막기로 얼굴을 방어하는 기술이 표현되어 있다. 품새 태극3장과 5장에 나오는 한손날 바깥막기는 몸통을 방어하지만 여기서는 얼굴을 방어하는 응용 동작으로 볼 수 있다. 단 서기는 통상 뒷굽이에서 행해지는데 뒷굽이 기준에서 보면 우표 도안에서는 두 발의 보폭이 너무 넓게 설정되어 있다.

This is the commemorative stamp for the 10th anniversary of the establishment of Sino-Korean diplomatic relations. This joint stamp was designed to represent Korea's martial art Taekwondo and China's martial art Wushu, both the chief cultural representatives of each nation. On the stamp, the person on the right is attacking the other's face with a side kick, while the person on the left is utilizing a single hand knife block, a 'Poomsae'(Form) technique. Although the single hand knife block of the 'Poomsae' in 'Taegeuk' 3 and 5 is used to protect the body, the person on the stamp is applying the technique to defend his face. The demonstrator's feet on the left of the stamp are too far apart, not clearly reflecting the actual execution of the Back Stance.

한국 우표전지
A Full-sheet of Korean Stamps

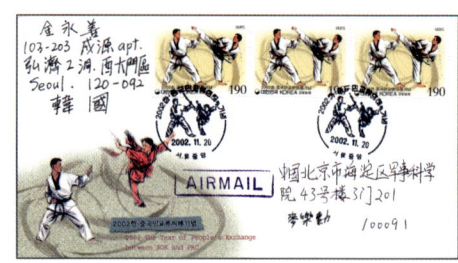

초일 실체봉투
A Used Cover of the First Day Issued

II-9. 중국・한국 국민교류 10주년. 중국 우표
The 10th Year of the People's Exchange between China and Korea

2002년 '한・중 국민교류의 해를 기념해 양국 정부가 발행한 공동 우표로서 양국의 문화 중 태권도와 우슈가 선택되었다는 것은 특별한 의미가 있다. 명실상부한 한국의 대표적인 무예스포츠이자 올림픽 정식 종목으로서 태권도의 위상을 확인할 수 있다. 1994년 태권도가 올림픽 정식종목으로 확정되자 중국은 태권도가 메달 획득에 유망한 종목으로 판단하고 본격적으로 태권도를 보급하기 시작했다. 세계태권도연맹 파견 사범인 양진방 교수를 비롯하여 이승국 교수, 김종삼, 강신영, 최영복, 이대성, 정근표, 배상준 등 사범이 중국 태권도 발전에 기여했다. 1995년에 중국태권도협회가 창설되었고 그 해 북경에서 중국 최초의 태권도 대회가 열렸다. 2001년 제9회 중국체육대회에서 태권도가 정식종목으로 채택되었다. 현재 쿠이 다렌 씨가 회장직을 맡고 있다.

This joint stamp holds great significance, representing Chinas martial art Wushu and Koreas martial art Taekwondo and it was designed in commemoration of 'The 10th Year of Peoples Exchange between Korea and China' in 2002. Through this event Taekwondo once again proved its considerable role as Korea's representative martial art and an official sport of the Olympics. As Taekwondo was adopted as an official sport in the year 1994, China had decided to actively proliferate Taekwondo for it being a solid chance for the nation to medal at the Olympics. Professor Jin Bang Yang, who was the first Taekwondo instructor dispatched by the Korean government, Professor Seung Kook Lee, and Masters Jong Sam Kim, Shin Young Kang, Young Bok Choi, Dae Sung Lee, Geun Pyo Chung, Sang Joon Bae, etc. all played great roles in developing Taekwondo in China. The Chinese Taekwondo Association (President Mr. Cui Dalin) was established in 1995 and the first Taekwondo Tournament was held the same year in Beijing. Taekwondo was adopted as an official sport for the 9th Chinese Sports Games in 2001.

☞ 국가명 : 중국. 2002
　Nation : China

☞ 자료 평가 Evaluation :
① 태권도가치성 Taekwondo Value ★★★★★
② 도안성 Design ★★★★★
③ 희귀성 Rarity ★★★☆☆

☞ 우표 구성 : 중・한 국민교류기념 2종 중 1종
　Stamp Composition : 1 of 2 stamps

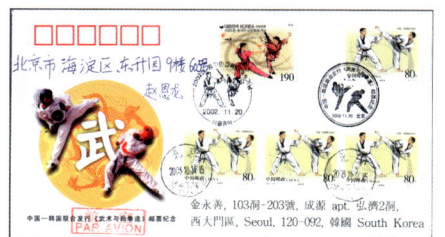

초일실체봉투　Used Cover of the First Day Issued

중국 우표전지
A Full-sheet of Chinese Stamps

우표로 보는 태권도 발자취 The Evolution of Taekwondo as Seen Through Postage Stamps

II-10. 태권도 공원 기공식 및 태권도의 날
The Formation of the Taekwondo Park & Taekwondo Day

- ☞ 국가명 : 한국. 2009
  Nation : South Korea

- ☞ 자료 평가 Evaluation :
  ① 태권도가치성
     Taekwondo Value ★★★★★
  ② 도안성 Design ★★★★★
  ③ 희귀성 Rarity ★★★☆☆

- ☞ 우표 구성 : 기념우표 1종
  Stamp Composition : single stamp

1994년 9월 4일 시드니올림픽 정식종목으로 채택이 확정된 날짜를 기념한 '태권도의 날'을 기해 태권도공원 기공식을 가졌는데, 이를 기념한 우표이다. '태권도의 날'은 2006년 7월 베트남 호치민시에서 세계태권도연맹 정기총회에서 처음으로 지정되었다. 그 해 9월 4일 서울에서 열린 '제1회 세계품새선수권대회' 개막식에서 '태권도의 날' 선포식과 심벌이 공개되었다. 우리나라는 2007년 12월 국회에서 '태권도진흥및태권도공원조성등에관한법률'이 제정됨에 따라 2008년부터 국가 법정 기념일이 되었다. 해마다 9월 4일이면 국기원, 세계태권도연맹, 태권도진흥재단, 대한태권도협회 등 태권도 주요 4단체장들이 함께 모여 '태권도의 날' 공식 행사를 개최하고 있다.

This is the commemorative stamp for September 4th, 1994, the date in which the 103rd Paris Olympic Assembly decided to include Taekwondo as an official sport in the 2000 Sydney Olympic Games. The Taekwondo Park was also built to celebrate the momentous occasion. 'Taekwondo Day' was designated at the regular general meeting of World Taekwondo Federation in Ho Chi Minh City, Vietnam, in July 2006. The same year, 'The First World Poomsae(form) Championships' in Korea promulgated 'Taekwondo Day' and announced its symbol. 'Taekwondo day' became a legal national holiday in 2008, after the Korean National Assembly legislated 'the Law for Taekwondo Promotion and the formation of the Taekwondo Park, etc.' in December 2007. The four leaders of major organization in Taekwondo, Kukkiwon, World Taekwondo Federation, Taekwondo Promotion Foundation and Korea Taekwondo Association gather on September 4th to host 'Taekwondo Day' as an annual event.

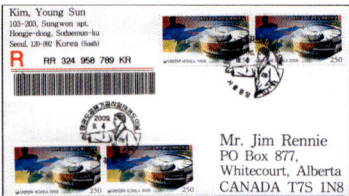

국내 및 국제 초일 실체봉투
Used Domestic and International Covers of the First Day Issued

태권도공원은 전라북도 무주군 설천면 소천리 일원 231만4천㎡에 2천361억 원이 투입되어 태권도 경기장과 수련장, 연구소, 태권도 전시관, 세계태권도마을 등 다양한 시설을 갖추고 2013년 개관될 예정이다. 태권도공원 조성사업을 추진하고 있는 태권도진흥재단(www.tpf.kr)은 2005년에 창립되어 태권도 관련 교육 및 문화 행사들을 주관하고 있다. 태권도진흥재단은 태권도 전문 포털사이트인 타고라(www.tagora.kr)를 개설하고 '세계 청소년 태권도캠프', '태권도 기술동작 3D 프로그램', '태권도 디지털 영상 및 사진 공모전', 등 사업을 비롯하여 영상, 사진, 만화, 음악, 미술 등 전 세계인이 즐기는 태권도 대중문화 콘텐츠도 개발하고 있다.

The Taekwondo Park is located in the Muju District of the Northern Jeolla Province and its facilities include: a Taekwondo arena, a research and training institute, an exhibition hall, a global Taekwondo village, etc. and will total an area of 2,314,049㎡. Construction began in 2009 and is scheduled to be completed in 2013. The Taekwondo Promotion Foundation(www.tpf.kr), responsible for the management and administration of the Taekwondo Park, was incorporated in 2005 and is supervising Taekwondo-related education as well as various cultural events. The Taekwondo Promotion Foundation has established an official Taekwondo portal website, the Tagora(www.tagora.kr), and plays a great role in the development of the Taekwondo society through activities including: the 'World Youth Taekwondo Camp', a '3D Program on Taekwondo Techniques', 'Digital Video and Picture Contests of Taekwondo' and a variety of other entertaining cultural events shared globally. The park will produce media relating to Taekwondo in the public including videos, pictures, comics, music, and art.

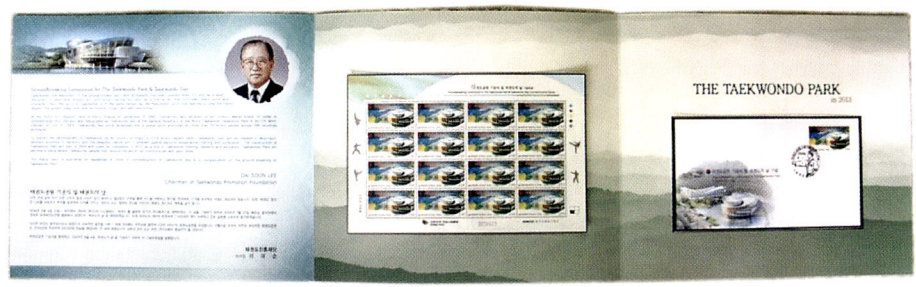

기념 우표첩 앞면과 뒷면
a Booklet (front and back)

우표로 보는 태권도 발자취　The Evolution of Taekwondo as Seen Through Postage Stamps

II-11. 태권도와 태극기를 도안한 외국 우표
A Foreign Taekwondo Stamp with the Korean Flag

캐나다 동부 뉴펀들랜드 인근의 프랑스령 섬나라인 '세인트 피에르 앤드 미켈론'에서 태권도와 태극기를 도안한 기념우표가 발행되었다. 외국 우표가 이 단원에 포함된 것은 태권도와 한국의 상징성이 우표에 잘 표현되었기 때문이다. 한국이 아닌 다른 나라에서 태권도를 소재로 하여 독립된 기념우표가 발행되는 것은 아주 보기 드문 사례이며 태권도인으로서 경축할 만한 일이다. 태권도가 지구 구석진 나라까지 뻗어간 것은 인종, 국가, 종교를 넘어서서 그 나라 사람들에게 바람직한 가치성이 인정되었기 때문일 것이다. 많은 사람들에게 태권도는 멋진 발차기 기술과 더불어 심신의 강건함과 호신 목적을 추구하는 철학성이 깃든 동양적 운동 문화로 각광받는 것이 아닐까 생각된다.

A commemorative stamp designed with Taekwondo and the Korean Flag was published in 'St. Pierre & Miquelon'. St. Pierre & Miquelon is located near Newfoundland, Canada. This specific foreign stamp has been included in this chapter because of its accurate portrayal of Taekwondo and its symbolic representation of Korea. Finding a separated commemorative stamp in a country other than Korea is quite a rare and celebrated case as a Taekwondoist. The fact that Taekwondo has reached even the furthest edges of the globe must be due to the global acknowledgement and acceptance of the martial art, extending beyond the scope of ethnicity, nationality, and religion. Its immense popularity must be a result of the various developments of the martial art into several domains including self-defense techniques, mainly dynamic kicks, and even Asian philosophical exercise.

☞ 세인트피에르 앤드 미켈론(프랑스령), 2008
　Saint Pierre & Miquelon(French)

☞ 자료 평가 Evaluation :
① 태권도가치성 Taekwondo Value ★★★★☆
② 도안성 Design ★★★★★
③ 희귀성 Rarity ★★★☆☆

　☞ 우표 구성 : 기념우표 1종
　　Stamp Composition : single stamp

맥시멈카드　A Maximum Card

아시아에 전파된 새로운 무예스포츠, 태권도
Taekwondo Spreads in Asia as a New Martial Sport

한국이 속해 있는 아시아에 있는 여러 나라들은 가까운 지리적 여건상 태권도가 활발히 보급되었다. 한국 이외의 나라에서 발행된 태권도 우표는 1981년 싱가포르에서 최초로 선보였다. 이후 1986 서울아시안게임, 1988 서울올림픽이 열리면서 아시아 여러 나라에서 태권도 우표들이 속속 나오기 시작했다. 초창기 태권도 우표는 가라테 등 다른 동양무술과 크게 구별되지 않았으나 곧 태권도 특징이 뚜렷이 도안된 우표들이 발행되었다. 이 장에 소개된 아시아 국가 태권도 우표는 총 12개국 16종이다.

한국의 유명 화가 김기창씨가 그린
태권도 붓그림 (나만의 우표)
A Taekwondo picture with caligraphy
by famouse artist, Gi Chang Kim
(a Customized stamp)

In East Asia, Korean Taekwondo spread rapidly due to geographical proximity. The first Taekwondo stamp outside of Korea appeared in Singapore in 1981. Following this stamp, many more were released after the 10th Asian Games in Seoul in 1986, and the 1988 Summer Olympics, also held in Seoul. Early Taekwondo stamps were not very different from Karate or other East Asian Martial Arts. Distinctive Taekwondo stamps began to be published one by one after the 1988 Seoul Olympics. 16 Taekwondo stamps from 12 Asian countries are introduced in this chapter.

우표로 보는 태권도 발자취   The Evolution of Taekwondo as Seen Through Postage Stamps

III-1. 싱가포르 인기 스포츠가 된 태권도
Taekwondo as a Popular Sport in Singapore

외국 최초의 태권도 우표는 스포츠를 대중적 여가 활동으로 권장할 목적으로 1981년 싱가포르에서 발행되었다. 태권도, 가라테, 킥복싱 등을 함께 모아 대중적인 격투스포츠로 소개했다. 싱가포르에서 첫 태권도 외국 우표가 나오게 된 연유는 오래 전부터 태권도 보급 활동이 활발했기 때문이었다. 싱가포르에서는 1963년부터 김복만, 이병무, 이성수, 이상구 등 사범들이 활약하며 태권도를 보급했다. 싱가포르 태권도협회는 1975년 세계태권도연맹에 등록되었으며 현재 밀란 크위 씨가 회장을 맡고 있다

The first Taekwondo stamp from outside of Korea was issued by Singapore in 1981 for the purpose of promoting recreational martial sports. Not only Taekwondo stamps but also those of Karate and Kick Boxing introduced these popular fighting sports. The reason for the appearance of Taekwondo stamps is the long time promotion of Taekwondo by Masters such as Bok Man Kim, Byung Moo Lee, Sung Soo Lee, and Sang Ku Lee, all of who had promoted Taekwondo in Singapore since 1963. The Singapore Taekwondo Association was established in 1975. Currently, Mr. Milan Kwee is serving as President.

☞ 국가명 : 싱가포르 I. 1981
　　Nation : Singapore I

☞ 자료 평가 Evaluation :
① 태권도가치성 Taekwondo Value ★★★★☆
② 도안성 Design ★★★☆☆
③ 희귀성 Rarity ★★★☆☆

☞ 우표 구성 : 3종 중 1종
　　Stamp Composition : 1 of 3 stamps

함께 나온 우표세트
accompanied stamp set

III-2. 싱가포르 대중 문화 요소인 태권도
Taekwondo as Public Culture in Singapore

싱가포르에서 나온 두 번째 태권도 우표이다. 우표에서는 태권도복을 입은 수련자가 태권도 시범을 하는 장면을 담고 있다. 태권도도 싱가포르 대중들에게 다른 문화 종목과 함께 주요한 여가 활동으로 정착했음을 나타내고 있다.

싱가포르에서는 1982년 제5회 아시아태권도선수권대회가 개최되어 태권도 보급 열기가 고조되었다. 1993년 제17회 동남아시아대회 태권도 경기가 싱가포르에서 개최되었다. 2010년 8월에는 제1회 하계 청소년 올림픽에 태권도 종목이 포함되어 열리기도 했다. 청소년 올림픽은 청소년들이 스포츠를 통해 건강과 자신감을 얻게 한다는 취지로 창설되었다. 전 세계 204개국 3천600여 명의 청소년 선수들이 스포츠 경기 뿐 아니라 문화·교육 프로그램도 함께 참여했다

Taekwondo Stamp No. 013

This is the second stamp issued by Singapore. This stamp depicts an image of a Taekwondo demonstration by figures in Taekwondo uniforms. It shows that Taekwondo had become established as a leisure sport along with other cultural activities. In 1982, the 5th Asian Taekwondo Championship was held in Singapore. The rapid promotion of Taekwondo was making it into a hot item. In 1993, the 17th Southeast Asian Games Taekwondo Championship was also held in Singapore. In August of 2010, Taekwondo was included in the first Summer Youth Olympics, officially known as the Singapore 2010 Youth Olympic Games. The Summer Youth Olympics were established for the purpose of promoting health and confidence among the youth through sports. 3,600 young athletes from 204 countries participated in this event, not simply as a sport's competition, but also as a cultural and educational program.

- ☞ 국가명 : 싱가포르 II. 1985
  Nation : Singapore II
- ☞ 자료 평가 Evaluation :
  ① 태권도가치성 Taekwondo Value ★★★★☆
  ② 도안성 Design ★★★★☆
  ③ 희귀성 Rarity ★★★☆☆
- ☞ 우표 구성 : 4종 중 1종
  Stamp Composition : 1 of 4 stamps

기념 초일봉투
First Day Cover

우표로 보는 태권도 발자취 The Evolution of Taekwondo as Seen Through Postage Stamps

III-3. 말레이시아 스포츠대회 태권도 경기
Taekwondo in Malaysia's Sports Games

말레이시아에서 열린 스포츠 대회를 기념하여 나온 우표에 태권도의 모습이 나타난다. 우표에는 태권도 돌려차기 모습의 픽토그램으로 표현되었다. 말레이시아에는 1962년 최홍희씨가 첫 발을 디뎠고 뒤를 이어 윤영구, 양우엽. 김용호 사범이 활약하여 태권도를 성공적으로 보급했다. 양우엽 사범은 1973년 한국에서 열린 제1회 세계태권도대회에 팀코치로 참가했다. 김용호 사범은 1974년 세계태권도연맹 파견사범이었다. 1992년 말레이시아 수도 쿠알라룸푸르에서 제10회 아시아태권도선수권대회가 열렸다. 1974년 말레이시아 태권도협회가 창설되었고 툰쿠 임란 왕자가 회장이다.

Stamps featuring Taekwondo figures were issued to commemorate the Sports Games held in Malaysia. This stamp depicts a figure doing a roundhouse kick. In 1962, General Hong Hee Choi began promoting Taekwondo in Malaysia, and Masters Young Ku Yoon, Woo Yup Yang, and Yong Ho Kim succeeded him. Master Woo Yup Yang participated in the 1st World Taekwondo Championships held in Korea as the team coach. Master Yong Ho Kim was designated as an Instructor by the World Taekwondo Federation in 1974. The 10th Asian Taekwondo Championship was held in the capital city Kuala Lumpur of Malaysia in 1992. The Malaysia Taekwondo Association was established in 1974 and H.R.H. Prince Tunku Imran is currently the president.

☞ 국가명 : 말레이시아. 1986
　　Nation : Malaysia

☞ 자료 평가 Evaluation :
① 태권도가치성 Taekwondo Value ★★★★☆
② 도안성 Design ★★★★★
③ 희귀성 Rarity ★★★★☆

☞ 우표 구성 : 3종 중 1종
　　Stamp Composition : 1 of 3 stamps

함께 나온 우표세트
accompanied stamp set

III-4. 타이완 국민운동회 종목, 태권도
Taekwondo in Taiwan's National Games

1993년 타이완 전국체육대회 기념우표로 태권도가 체조와 함께 2종으로 발행되었다. 타이완은 1967년부터 태권도가 보급되어 태권도의 인기가 높다. 특히 겨루기 경기에서 여자부는 한국을 능가할 정도의 기량을 보유하여 올림픽 등 각종 대회에서 훌륭한 성적을 올림으로써 국민적 성원을 받고 있다. 우표에 여자 선수가 돌려차기를 하는 모습이 담긴 것도 그러한 연유 때문임을 알 수 있다. 1974년 타이완태권도협회가 창설되었고 김사옥, 홍성인, 노효영, 정지수, 홍상래, 김영인 등 수많은 사범들의 노력으로 태권도가 활성화되었다.

Two kinds of the commemorative Taekwondo stamps were issued to celebrate the 1993 Taiwan National Athletic Championships, along with gymnastics. Taekwondo has been growing in Taiwan since 1967 and is very popular today. Especially, the women's sparring ability in competition has often exceeded that of Korean athletes. Taiwanese female Taekwondo competitors have also received great public support nationwide by obtaining good results in various championships, including the Olympic Games. One can easily understand why simply by seeing the woman executing a 'Roundhouse Kick' on the stamp. In 1974, the Chinese Taipei Amateur Taekwondo Association was formed and it was run by the efforts of Korean masters such as Sa Ok Kim, Seong In Hong, Hyo Yoeong Noh, Ji Soo Jeong, Sang Rae Hong, and Young In Kim.

Taekwondo Stamp No. 015

기념 초일봉투
First Day Cover

☞ 국가명 : 타이완, 중국 I , 1993
　Nation : Chinese Taipei I
☞ 자료 평가 Evaluation :
① 태권도가치성 Taekwondo Value ★★★★★
② 도안성 Design ★★★★★
③ 희귀성 Rarity ★★★☆☆
☞ 우표 구성 : 2종 중 1종
　Stamp Composition : 1 of 2 stamps

우표로 보는 태권도 발자취 The Evolution of Taekwondo as Seen Through Postage Stamps

Ⅲ-5. 이란 국민체육대회 태권도 경기
Taekwondo in Iran's National Games

Taekwondo Stamp No. 016

☞ 국가명 : 이란 I . 1993
   Nation : Iran I

☞ 자료 평가 Evaluation :
① 태권도가치성 Taekwondo Value ★★★★☆
② 도안성 Design ★★★★★
③ 희귀성 Rarity ★★★☆☆

☞ 우표 구성 : 3종 중 1종
   Stamp Composition : 1 of 3 stamps

실체봉투   a Used Cover

1993년 이란 체육대회기념으로 태권도가 레슬링과 함께 도안되어 우표로 발행되었다. 수 많은 태권도 사범들이 양성되어 160만 명에 이르는 이란인들이 배우는 인기 무예종목이 바로 태권도이다. 국제 태권도 대회에서 한국팀이 경계하는 주요 경쟁국도 이란이다. 이란이 오늘날 태권도 최강국으로 우뚝 서게된 것은 여러 가지 이유가 있다. 초창기 태권도는 이란에서 효과적인 맨손격투술로서 군인들과 경찰들이 배움으로서 중동 국가 중에서도 태권도 발전 속도가 가장 빨랐다. 김수련, 송상근, 김병운, 김정훈, 함광식 사범이 군인들에게 태권도를 전수하며 초창기 태권도 활동을 전개했다. 민형근 사범(캐나다 거주)은 경찰 간부들을 교육했고 박정호 사범은 경호실에 태권도를 보급했다. 혁명 이후 1985년 세계태권도연맹 파견으로 이란에 건너가 국가대표선수단을 양성하고 수준 높은 지도자 교육을 시행한 강신철 사범의 활약상이 이란 태권도 발전에 큰 기여를 했다. 이란태권도협회는 1975년 등록되었고 세예드 모하메드 풀럇갸르 씨가 회장이다.

In 1993, a Taekwondo stamp was issued, along with a wrestling stamp, to celebrate the National Athletic Championships in Iran. Taekwondo became a popular discipline that fostered numerous masters, and about 1.6 million Iranians practice it today. One of the national teams that the Korean team is keeping a close eye on is Iran's. The promotion of Taekwondo in Middle Eastern countries, including Iran, fell behind due to Karate's advantage of arriving earlier, as well as the areas differences from Korea in climate, religion, and customs. Early in the introduction and promotion of Taekwondo, soldiers and the police learned efficient unarmed self-defense techniques. Today, Taekwondo in Iran is growing the fastest among countries in the Middle East. Its reputation as one of the strongest Taekwondo countries is due to the active role of masters such as Soo Ryeon Kim, Sang Guen Song, Byung Woon Kim, Jeong Hoon Kim, Kwang Sik Ham, Hyung Guen Min and Jung Ho park. Master Shin-Chul Kang was dispatched by the World Taekwondo Federation in 1985 and had a great role in Iranian Taekwondo promotion. Iran's Taekwondo Federation was enrolled in 1975 and Mr. Seyed Mohammad Pouladgar is the leader of the federation.

III-6. 1993년 제17회 시게임 태권도 경기
Taekwondo in the 17th Southeast Asian (SEA) Games in 1993

1993년 싱가포르에서 열린 제17회 동남아시아경기대회(시게임) 기념으로 베트남에서 태권도 우표를 발행했다. 1장짜리 기념우표에 태권도 종목만을 도안한 것은 태권도에 대한 특별 배려가 아닐 수 없다. 베트남은 총 6종의 태권도 우표를 발행하여 종주국 한국에 이어 두 번째 많은 종류의 태권도 우표를 발행했다. 베트남이 적극적으로 태권도 우표를 발행하는 것은 태권도에 대한 국민적 성원과 무관하지 않다. 베트남은 1959년 한국에서 파견된 국군태권도교관단에 의해 태권도가 전파된 최초의 외국 국가이기도 하다. 당시 태권도는 군인과 경찰 격투술 훈련과목으로 중시되었다.

To commemorate the 17th Southeast Asian Games held in Singapore in 1993, a Taekwondo postage stamp was issued by Vietnam. It was a special treat for Taekwondo to have an exclusive Taekwondo-only design on a stamp. Presently, Vietnam has issued six different Taekwondo stamps, and is ranked as the second most Taekwondo stamp-issuing country after Korea. The fact that Vietnam is so prolific in issuing Taekwondo stamps is closely related to its national support for Taekwondo. Vietnam is the first country where Taekwondo was introduced by the Korean Army Taekwondo Instructors Team, who visited and settled there. At that time, Taekwondo was considered an important combat drill course for both the army and the police.

Taekwondo Stamp No. 017

☞ 국가명 : 베트남 I. 1993
  Nation : Vietnam I

☞ 자료 평가 Evaluation :
① 태권도가치성 Taekwondo Value ★★★★★
② 도안성 Design ★★★★★
③ 희귀성 Rarity ★★★☆☆

☞ 우표 구성 : 기념우표 1종
  Stamp Composition : single stamp

기념 초일봉투
First Day Cover

우표로 보는 태권도 발자취   The Evolution of Taekwondo as Seen Through Postage Stamps

III-7. 제3회 베트남 전국 스포츠 대회
Vietnam's 3rd National Games

☞ 국가명 : 베트남 II. 1995
  Nation : Vietnam II

☞ 자료 평가 Evaluation :
① 태권도가치성 Taekwondo Value ★★★★☆
② 도안성 Design ★★★★★
③ 희귀성 Rarity ★★★☆☆

☞ 우표 구성 : 기념우표 1종
  Stamp Composition : single stamp

베트남에서 발행된 1995년 제3회 전국 스포츠 경기대회 기념우표에 태권도가 나왔다. 우표의 하단부에 두 가지 태극품새 동작이 태권도 이미지를 나타낸다. 베트남에 태권도 동호인 수가 1천만 명에 달한다고 하면 지나친 과장일지 모르지만 베트남 태권도 보급 역사가 정확히 반 세기를 넘어서고 있고 지금까지 6종에 달하는 태권도 우표를 발행한 것을 보면 납득될 수 있다. 베트남에서는 대도시는 물론 농촌 마을까지도 태권도복을 입은 청소년들이 진지하게 태권도를 수련하는 광경을 흔히 볼 수 있다고 한다. 2010년에 제1회 한국대사배 베트남 전국대회가 하노이에서 개최되었다. 이번 대회에는 전국에서 선발된 40개 팀 소속 선수들과 중국 광저우 아시안게임에서 은메달을 딴 국가대표급 선수들이 대거 참가해 기량을 겨루었다.

This is the second Taekwondo stamp issued by Vietnam. It appears to be a commemorative stamp of the 3rd National Games held in 1995, as a preparatory step for the Olympic Games. At the bottom of the stamp are two 'Taegeuk Poomsae'(form) designs. In Vietnam, saying that there are close to ten million practitioners would be a gross over exaggeration, but the half century history of Taekwondo development and its issuing of six kinds of Taekwondo stamps make it easier to believe the incredibly large, though not quite ten million, number of Taekwondo practitioners in the country. It is common to see young adults wearing their uniforms and practicing Taekwondo even in small villages. In 2010, the first Korean Ambassador's Cup Taekwondo Tournament was held in Hanoi. Competitors from 40 of the best national level club teams from all over Vietnam, including the silver medalist from the 2010 Asian Games, participated in the tournament.

기념 초일봉투 First Day Cover

III-8. 1998년 제13회 아시안게임
The 13th Asian Games in 1998

1998년 제13회 방콕아시안게임 기념으로 인도네시아에서 발행한 3종짜리 기념 우표 중 1종에 태권도가 나왔다. 우표에는 역동적인 태권도 동작이 잘 표현되었지만 세밀히 살펴보면 태권도 기술을 혼동한 도안사의 실수가 나타난다. 겨루기 보호대를 착용하고 품새 태극5장의 옆차지르기 기술을 표현함으로써 어색한 태권도 도안이 되었다. 태권도 경기는 겨루기와 품새 경기가 각각 구분되어 열리므로 태권도 도안도 기술 내용에 따라 명확히 구별해서 사용되어야 한다. "인도네시아에서 태권도는 30년 이상 인기스포츠로 자리 잡았고 현재 수련 인구는 약 60만 명 정도 된다"라고 2007년 한국을 방문한 인도네시아 유도요노 대통령이 언급했다. 최오영, 허영, 이종남, 오일남 사범이 태권도 보급에 기여했다. 인도네시아 태권도 협회는 1975년 창립되었고 에드윈 수도노 씨가 회장이다.

Among the three stamps issued in commemoration of Bangkok's 13th Asian Games in 1998, you can find a Taekwondo stamp. At first glance, you may think that a dynamic Taekwondo move is being depicted. However, look closer and you will notice a mistake by the designer, who confuses Taekwondo techniques. The design shows a competitor needlessly wearing a chest protector and head gear while performing a side kick from 'Taegeuk 5-jang'(Taegeuk form 5). In Taekwondo, 'Kyuruki'(sparring) and 'Poomsae'(form) competitions are held separately. As such, Taekwondo designs must depict the proper techniques according to the competition. President Susilo Bambang Yudhoyono of Indonesia said during his visit to Korea in 2007, "Taekwondo has kept its place in Indonesia for 30 years as a popular sport. About 600,000 people are currently practicing Taekwondo." Masters Oh-Young Choi, Young Huh, Jong Nam Lee, and Il Nam Oh have contributed to the spread of Taekwondo in Indonesia. The Indonesian Taekwondo Association was established in 1975 and Lieutenant Gen. Erwin Sudjono is current president.

☞ 국가명 : 인도네시아. 1998
　Nation : Indonesia

☞ 자료 평가 Evaluation :
① 태권도가치성 Taekwondo Value ★★★★★
② 도안성 Design ★★★★★
③ 희귀성 Rarity ★★★☆☆

☞ 우표 구성 : 종 중 1종
　Stamp Composition : 1 of 3 stamps

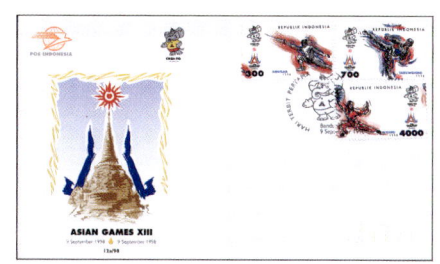

기념 초일봉투　First Day Cover

우표로 보는 태권도 발자취 The Evolution of Taekwondo as Seen Through Postage Stamps

III-9. 1999년 제20회 브루나이 시게임
The 20th SEA Games in Brunei in 1999

☞ 국가명 : 브루나이. 1999
　　Nation : Brunei

☞ 자료 평가 Evaluation :
① 태권도가치성 Taekwondo Value ★★★★☆
② 도안성 Design ★★★★★
③ 희귀성 Rarity ★★★★☆

☞ 우표 구성 : 10종 중 1종
　　Stamp Composition : 1 of 10 stamps

1999년 브루나이에서 열린 제20회 시게임 기념우표에 태권도가 포함되었다. 동남아시아 국가들이 2년에 한번씩 개최하는 시게임에서 태권도는 1985년 제14회 시게임 때부터 정식종목이 되었다. 시게임을 주최한 브루나이는 인구 40만의 작은 나라이지만 풍부한 석유자원과 천연가스로 인해 세계에서 가장 부유한 나라의 하나이다. 양우엽, 심상술, 박원하 사범이 브루나이에 태권도를 뿌리내리게 했다. 심상술 사범은 1993년부터 5년간 브루나이에서 태권도 국가대표팀 감독과 왕실 사범을 지내기도 했다. 심 사범은 그 후 도예가가 되어 우리 전통도자기 기법으로 태권도를 소재로 한 작품을 제작하며 도자기를 통한 태권도 홍보에 매진하고 있다. 브루나이는 1973년에 세계태권도연맹에 가입했으며 현재 아왕 하이지씨가 회장을 맡고 있다.

Here you see a Taekwondo stamp issued to commemorate the 20th Southeast Asian Games held in Brunei in 1999. In the Asian Games, held every two years in East Asia, Taekwondo has been a compulsory sport since the 14th Asian Games in 1985. Brunei, which hosted the Southeast Asian Games, is a small country of only 400,000 people, but is one of the richest countries in the world due to its abundant petroleum and natural gas reserves. Masters Woo Youp Yang, Sang Sool Shim, and Won Ha Park planted the roots of Taekwondo in Brunei. Master Sang Sool Shim taught the national Taekwondo team head coach and the royal family for 5 years from 1993. Soon thereafter Master Shim became a porcelain and a traditional Korean ceramic artist, promoting Taekwondo by his ceramic works. Brunei joined the World Taekwondo Federation in 1973 and its association is lead by Mr. Awang Haji.

기념 초일봉투
First Day Cover

III-10. 2001년 제3회 일본 오사카 동아시아대회
The 3rd East Asian Games in Osaka, Japan in 2001

일본 오사카에서 열린 제3회 동아시아 경기대회 기념으로 태권도 우표가 나왔다. 태권도 겨루기 경기 장면을 도안하였다. 무도(武道)의 강국 일본에서 나온 최초의 태권도 우표라서 가치가 높다. 유도, 검도, 아키도, 가라데 등 다양한 종목을 보유한 일본은 중국, 한국과 더불어 세계 무술계를 주도하고 있다. 1964년 일본 토오쿄오(東京)에서 아시아 국가로서는 처음 올림픽이 열렸고 유도가 정식종목에 포함되었다. 일본의 가라테(空手)와 중국 우슈(武術)는 현재 아시안 게임 정식종목으로서 올림픽 종목 채택을 경쟁적으로 추진하고 있다. 김천구, 이기도, 김한노, 장명삼, 김용성 사범이 일본 태권도 발전에 공헌했다. 일본 태권도협회는 1981년에 창립되었고 노부로 가네하라 씨가 회장직을 맡고 있다.

Japan issued a Taekwondo stamp to commemorate the 3rd East Asian Games held in Osaka in 2001. It shows a Taekwondo sparring scene. It has a high value for being the first Taekwondo stamp issued in Japan, which is a powerful martial arts country. Japan, with its variety of martial arts including Judo, Kendo, Aikido, and Karate, leads the martial arts world along with China and Korea. Japan hosted the first Summer Olympic Games in Asia, Tokyo in 1964, and Judo was adopted as an optional sport. Japanese Judo and Chinese Wushu are official sports in the Asian Games, and are pushing ahead competitively to be adopted as official sports in the Olympics. Masters Chun Ku Kim, Ki Do Lee, Han Noh Kim, Myung Sam Jang, and Yong Sung Kim have contributed to the development of Taekwondo in Japan. The Japan Taekwondo Association joined the World Taekwondo Federation in 1981 and Mr. Noboru Kanehara is currently the president

초일 실체봉투
a Used Cover of the First Day Issued

- 국가명 : 일본. 2001
  Nation : Japan

- 자료 평가 Evaluation :
  ① 태권도가치성 Taekwondo Value ★★★★★
  ② 도안성 Design ★★★★★
  ③ 희귀성 Rarity ★★★☆☆

- 우표 구성 : 4종 중 1종
  Stamp Composition : 1 of 4 stamps

우표로 보는 태권도 발자취   The Evolution of Taekwondo as Seen Through Postage Stamps

III-11. 타이완 전국운동회, 태권도 경기
Taekwondo in the Taiwanese National Games

Taekwondo Stamp No. 022

☞ 국가명 : 타이완, 중국 II. 2001
　Nation : Chinese Taipei II

☞ 자료 평가 Evaluation :
① 태권도가치성 Taekwondo Value ★★★★☆
② 도안성 Design ★★★★☆
③ 희귀성 Rarity ★★★☆☆

☞ 우표 구성 : 2종 중 1종
　Stamp Composition : 1 of 2 stamps

2001년 제90회 전국운동회 기념우표에 태권도가 포함되어 타이완 내에 태권도의 위상을 잘 알 수 있다. 1967년 태권도가 보급된 이래 타이완태권도협회 집계에 의하면 전국에 800개 도장과 동호회에 9만 명의 유단자가 있는 것으로 추산하고 있다. 1980년 제4회 아시아태권도선수권대회가 타이페이에서 개최되었고 남자부 미들급에서 타이완선수가 한국선수를 누르고 우승하기도 했다. 지난 2004년 아테네올림픽에서 타이완 선수가 금메달을 획득한 이후 태권도에 대한 관심이 날로 높아지고 있다. 초 · 중 · 고등학교에서 태권도가 정식 수업으로 채택되어 일찍이 청소년 태권도 저변확대가 이루어 졌다. 태권도는 인기 스포츠인 야구에 버금가는 타이완의 국민 체육으로 자리잡고 있다. 타이완태권도협회는 1974년 창립되었으며 첸 치엔 핑 씨가 회장을 맡고 있다.

We can ascertain the status of Taekwondo in Taiwan by looking at the stamp issued to commemorate the 90th National Games in 2001. Since the dissemination of Taekwondo in 1967, it is estimated that there are now 800 Taekwondo schools and 90,000 black belts in Taiwan. In 1980, at the 4th Asian Taekwondo Championships held in Taipei, a Taiwanese competitor won his match against a Korean in the male middle weight division. Since the 2004 Athens Olympic Games, in which a Taiwanese competitor won a gold medal, the interest in Taekwondo has further increased. Taekwondo has been adopted as a credit course in elementary, middle, and high schools, enlarging interest in Taekwondo among the youth. Taekwondo maintains its place as a national sport next to the popular sport, baseball. The Taiwanese Taekwondo Association was established in 1974 and Chien Ping Chen leads the association.

초일실체봉투
a Used Cover of the First Day Issued

III-12. 2005년 제4회 마카오 동아시아대회
The 4th East Asian Games in Macao, China in 2005

2005년 제4회 마카오 동아시아경기대회 기념으로 태권도 우표가 나왔다. 마카오가 발행한 두 번째 태권도 우표이다. 태권도 경기가 열리는 실내체육관과 함께 태권도 뛰어차기를 역동적으로 표현한 우표의 도안이 돋보인다. 이 대회 태권도 경기 결과는 한국이 금 6개로 우승, 대만이 준우승, 중국이 3위를 하였고, 마카오도 은1, 동3개로 주최국의 체면을 세웠다. 2006년 태권도를 소재로 한 액션무대극인 점프(Jump)가 마카오에서 공연되어 전회가 매진되는 큰 호응을 얻기도 했다. 마카오는 국가올림픽위원회(NOC)가 없어 그동안 준회원에 머물렀으나 2010년 세계태권도연맹 임시총회에서 지난 15년간의 활발한 태권도 활동과 기여를 인정받아 정회원으로 승격되었다.

In 2005, a Taekwondo stamp was issued to commemorate the 4th East Asian Games in Macao. This is the second Taekwondo stamp issued by Macao, featuring an eye catching design depicting a dynamic Taekwondo 'Jump Kick' by a stylized figure set to the picture of an arena in the background. The results of the Taekwondo tournament in these games were Korea winning with six gold medals. Second place was taken by Chinese Taipei followed by China in third place. Though the host country did not win any gold medals, Macao was honored at the Games by receiving one silver and three bronze medals. In 2006 the martial art action-comedy stage show based on Taekwondo, named 'Jump', was performed in Macau and elicited a huge response. Macau was originally an Associate Member of the World Taekwondo Federation because they do not have a National Olympic Committee. However, in 2010 the World Taekwondo Federation approved Macau as a Regular Member due to their enthusiastic fifteen year contribution to Taekwondo society.

Taekwondo Stamp No. 023

☞ 마카오(중국령) II. 2005
　Chinese Macao II

☞ 자료 평가 Evaluation :
① 태권도가치성 Taekwondo Value ★★★★★
② 도안성 Design ★★★★★
③ 희귀성 Rarity ★★★☆☆

☞ 우표 구성 : 6종 중 1종
　Stamp Composition : 1 of 6 stamps

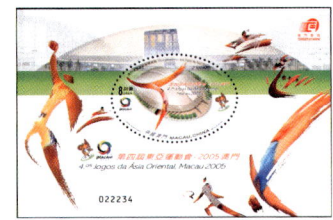
소형쉬이트 a Souvenir Sheet

기념 초일봉투 First Day Cover

우표로 보는 태권도 발자취 The Evolution of Taekwondo as Seen Through Postage Stamps

III-13. 2006년 제15회 카타르 도하 아시안게임
The 15th Doha Asian Games In Qatar in 2006

Taekwondo Stamp No. 024

☞ 국가명 : 카타르. 2006
   Nation : Qatar

☞ 자료 평가 Evaluation :
① 태권도가치성 Taekwondo Value ★★★★★
② 도안성 Design ★★★★★
③ 희귀성 Rarity ★★★☆☆

☞ 우표 구성 : 10종 중 1종
   Stamp Composition : 1 of 10 stamps

중동의 산유국 카타르의 수도 도하(Doha)에서 열린 제15회 아시안게임 기념 우표이다. 아시안게임 종목인 겨루기 경기 장면 대신 두 사람이 발차기 하는 모습을 우표에 담았다. 보호대를 착용하고 겨루는 경기의 특성을 도안에 반영했으면 하는 아쉬움이 있다. 태권도 경기는 남녀 각 8체급씩 총 16개의 금메달을 배정받았다. 카타르 선수인 압둘카데르 샤르한은 남자 웰터급에서 강호 이란 선수를 물리치고 아시안게임 사상 처음으로 금메달을 따서 주최국의 명예를 드높였다. 카타르 언론들은 금메달을 딴 선수 못지 않게 한국인 지재기 감독의 지도력을 높게 평가했다. 오래 전부터 허영, 나종열, 신재근 사범의 활약으로 카타르에서 태권도 가 꽃필 수가 있었다. 카타르태권도협회는 1977년에 등록되었고 모하메드 아메드 알 술라이티씨가 회장이다.

This stamp commemorates the 15th Asian Games in which Taekwondo is an official event, held in Doha, Qatar, a petroleum-rich country in the Middle East. It depicts a sparring scene where two people are kicking each other. However, the design should have included a scene depicting the true characteristics of sparring, like the wearing of sparring gear. The Taekwondo competition event was allotted 16 medalsc in 8 different divisions for both men and women. Abdulqader Hikmat garnered honor for the organizing country by gaining Qatar's first gold medal in the Asian Games, in the men's welter weight division. The Qatar news media lavishly praised Korean Master Jae Ki Ji's leadership as well as the gold medal winner. Thanks to the long time effort and exploits of Masters Young Huh, Jong Yeol Nah and Jae Keun Shin, Taekwondo in Qatar has blossomed. Qatar Taekwondo Association was enrolled in 1977 and Mr. Mohamed Ahmad Al-Sulaiti is the President.

기념 초일봉투
First Day Cover

III-14. 네팔의 국위를 선양한 태권도
The Enhancement of Nepal's Prestige by Taekwondo

도하아시안게임에서 3개의 동메달을 따낸 네팔이 국가적 경사를 기념하기 위해 태권도 우표를 발행했다. 네팔 태권도 지도자인 신재균, 권혁중 사범의 열정이 빚어낸 결과다. 네팔의 태권도 붐에 발맞추어 2009년 국기원은 람 바란 야다브 네팔 대통령에게 '명예 9단'을 수여했다. 야다브 네팔대통령은 태권도를 네팔의 국기(國技)로 추진하고 태권도 학과를 설치하는 등 태권도에 대한 열성과 공로를 인정받았다. "태권도를 통해 네팔 국민들이 큰 희망을 얻는다. 앞으로 태권도가 네팔 전 국민이 즐기는 무도스포츠가 되기를 바란다"라고 야다브 네팔 대통령이 언급했다. 네팔태권도협회는 1983년 등록되었고 프라카쉬 슘세르 라나 씨가 회장이다.

Nepal issued three Taekwondo stamps to commemorate the national event of earning 3 bronze medals in the 15th Doha Asian Games in 2006. It was the result of the passionate leadership of Masters Jae Kyun Shin and Hyuk Joong Kwon. In accordance with the boom of Taekwondo in Nepal, the Kukkiwon awarded an honorary 9th degree black belt to President Ram Baran Yadav of Nepal. President Yadav strived to make Taekwondo a national sport and established a Taekwondo department at the university level. Kukkiwon recognized his enthusiasm for and achievement in Taekwondo. President Yadav mentioned that Nepalese people were encouraged by Taekwondo, and that he hoped that Taekwondo would become a martial art loved by all Nepalese people. Nepal Taekwondo Association was enrolled in 1983 and Mr. Prakash Shumsher Rana leads the association

Taekwondo Stamp No. 025

- 국가명 : 네팔 I. 2007
  Nation : Nepal I
- 자료 평가 Evaluation :
  ① 태권도가치성 Taekwondo Value ★★★★★
  ② 도안성 Design ★★★★★
  ③ 희귀성 Rarity ★★★☆☆
- 우표 구성 : 2종 중 1종
  Stamp Composition : 1 of 2 stamps

기념 초일봉투
First Day Cover

우표로 보는 태권도 발자취   The Evolution of Taekwondo as Seen Through Postage Stamps

III-15. 2009 타이페이 청각장애자 올림픽
The 2009 Summer Deaflympics in Taiwan

Taekwondo Stamp No. 026

☞ 국가명 : 타이완, 중국 III. 2009
　　Nation : Chinese Taipei III

☞ 자료 평가 Evaluation :
① 태권도가치성 Taekwondo Value ★★★★☆
② 도안성 Design ★★★★★
③ 희귀성 Rarity ★★★☆☆

☞ 우표 구성 : 2종 중 1종
　　Stamp Composition : 1 of 2 stamps

타이완에서 세 번째로 나온 태권도 우표로서 장애자올림픽 여성 장애인 선수가 도안된 기념우표이다. 2009년도 타이완에서 열린 장애자올림픽에서 태권도 경기가 개최되면서 태권도 우표도 발행되었다. 태권도가 일찍이 보급된 타이완에서는 자녀들의 인성 교육은 물론 심신 수양을 위해 태권도가 인기를 끌면서 사회적으로 긍정적인 역할을 수행하고 있다. 아울러 일반인들뿐 아니라 장애인 등 특수 계층에도 태권도 보급이 이루어짐으로써 획기적 발전 단계를 맞고 있다. 타이완태권도협회의 노력으로 장애인에게도 '희망과 즐거움 주는 태권도'가 성공적인 반응을 얻고 있다.

This is the third Taekwondo stamp issued by Taiwan with a design depicting a female competitor performing a side kick. This Taekwondo stamp was issued to celebrate Taekwondo competition as a part of the Paralympic Games held in Taiwan in 2009. In Taiwan, where Taekwondo has been growing for a long time, Taekwondo has been enacting a positive role in the society and gaining popularity as a way to cultivate the mind and body. Today, it is facing an innovative development phase through its dissemination not only among the general public but also special classes, such as the handicapped. Thanks to the efforts of the Chinese Taipei Taekwondo Association, Taekwondo is successfully getting a favorable response by also providing hope and enjoyment to the handicapped.

기념 초일봉투
First Day Cover

III-16. 2009년 제5회 홍콩 동아시아게임
The 5th East Asian Games in Hong Kong in 2009

2009년 홍콩 동아시아 대회 기념우표로서 태권도 등 격투경기가 여러 가지 종목과 더불어 포괄적으로 도안되었다. 태권도 경기는 남녀 8체급씩 총 16개의 금메달이 배정되었다. 홍콩은 은1, 동2를 획득하는 성과를 올렸다. 홍콩에는 오래 전부터 각종 무술이 성행했으며 격투영화의 본고장이다. 권격영화스타 이소룡이 어릴적부터 활동한 곳이기도 하다. 2010년 홍콩에서 촬영 중인 로맨틱액션영화 '진심화대모험'은 태권도를 중요 소재로 삼고 있어 많은 관심을 끌고 있다. 주인공인 '마오퓨'는 여자 태권도 사범 역을 맡아 열연 중이다. 김복만, 승강용, 봉석근 사범은 홍콩에 태권도를 전파한 지도자들이다. 홍콩 태권도협회는 1978년에 공식 등록되었고 현재 칼 멘키칭 씨가 회장을 맡고 있다.

These are the stamps designed by Hong Kong in 2009 to commemorate the 5th East Asian Games, which included Taekwondo along with other martial arts. 16 gold medals were allocated for Taekwondo, 8 divisions each for men and women. Hong Kong enjoyed the successful achievement of earning 1 silver medal and 2 bronze medals. Hong Kong has promoted a variety of martial arts for a long time, and it is the Asian capital of action movies, especially those of the martial arts genre. It is also the hometown of action movie star, Bruce Lee, and the place where he made his movies. A romantic Taekwondo action movie is being filmed in Hong Kong in 2010 and is attracting much public attention. The main character, played by Miao Pu, is a passionate female Taekwondo master. Masters Bok Man Kim, Kang Yon Seung, and Seok Keun Bong are the leaders who spread Taekwondo in Hong Kong. The Hong Kong Taekwondo Association officially enrolled in 1978 and is led by Dr. Carl Men Ky Ching.

☞ 국가명 : 홍콩, 중국. 2009
　 Nation : Hong Kong, China

☞ 자료 평가 Evaluation :
① 태권도가치성 Taekwondo Value ★★★★☆
② 도안성 Design ★★★☆☆
③ 희귀성 Rarity ★★★☆☆

☞ 우표 구성 : 6종 중 1종
　 Stamp Composition : 1 of 6 stamps

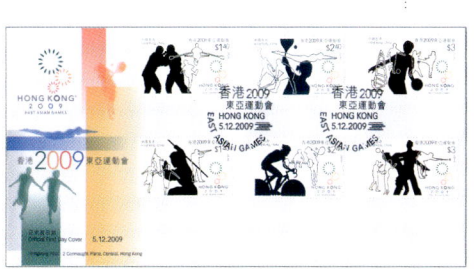

기념 초일봉투　First Day Cover

우표로 보는 태권도 발자취 The Evolution of Taekwondo as Seen Through Postage Stamps

 쉼터 · Break Time

1982년 제3회 인도 전국태권도대회
The 3rd National Taekwondo Championship in India in 1982

1982년 인도 캘커타에서 제3회 전국태권도대회기념으로 발행된 기념봉투이다. 1982년 12월 2일 날에 거행된 태권도 행사 일부인과 까세가 선명히 나와 있다. 태권도 정식 우표는 아니지만 이른 시기 인도 태권도 현황을 보여주는 희귀한 우취자료이다.

This is a memorial envelope issued to commemorate the 3rd National Taekwondo Championships held in Calcutta, India showing Taekwondo sparring scenes. A portion of the Taekwondo events were held on December 2nd, 1982. Though this is not an actual Taekwondo stamp, it is a great testimonial to the development of Taekwondo at the time in India.

IV

세계로 뻗어간 태권도
The Worldwide Spread of Taekwondo

세계로 뻗어 나간 태권도 (나만의 우표)
Taekwondo Extended to the World (a customized stamp)

태권도가 세계 많은 나라에 보급됨에 따라 태권도 소재 우표들도 속속 등장하였다. 세계 스포츠 종목 중 수련자 수로 볼 때 축구 다음엔 태권도가 인기를 구가하고 있다. 태권도는 '보는 스포츠' 라기 보다는 직접 몸으로 행하는 심신수양의 무예 종목으로 인기가 높다. 특히 자라나는 청소년들의 관심을 끌어 초, 중, 고등학교, 대학교에서 태권도 과목이 생겨 활발히 보급되고 있다. 오래 전에는 외국 사람들이 태권도를 잘 몰라 '코리안 가라테' 라고 했다. 반세기가 지난 지금은 '태권도' 는 알지만 '한국' 을 모르는 외국 사람들도 있다. 이제 '태권도' 하면 '한국' 이 연상될 정도가 되었다. 태권도는 올림픽을 계기로 더욱 활성화되어 지구 곳곳에 퍼져 나가 세계화의 꽃을 피웠다. 이 장에서는 아시아 국가들을 제외한 18개국 28종의 태권도 우표를 소개한다.

Taekwondo stamps have continued to appear as Taekwondo has spread throughout the world. In terms of the sheer number of participants, Taekwondo is the second most popular sport in the world, behind soccer. Taekwondo's popularity is due to it being a martial art for cultivating one's mind and body through practice, rather than merely a sport to watch. Taekwondo has especially attracted the attention of the youth, and it is adopted as a credit course in elementary, middle, and high schools as well as universities in order to be actively disseminated. Up until fairly recently, people outside of Korea did not know much about Taekwondo, and it was even often called 'Korean Karate'. A half a century later, people in many countries may not know much about Korea, but they do know Taekwondo. Nowadays, when people hear about Taekwondo, they can associate it with Korea. In this chapter, I will introduce 29 stamps from 18 countries outside of Asia.

우표로 보는 태권도 발자취   The Evolution of Taekwondo as Seen Through Postage Stamps

IV-1. 니제르 동양무예 축제 행사 종목인 태권도
As an Item of a Martial Art Festival in Niger

Taekwondo Stamp No. 028

☞ 국가명 : 니제르, 1982
　 Nation : Niger

☞ 자료 평가 Evaluation :
① 태권도가치성 Taekwondo Value ★★★★☆
② 도안성 Design ★★★★☆
③ 희귀성 Rarity ★★★★☆

☞ 우표 구성 : 3종 중 1종
　 Stamp Composition : 1 of 3 stamps

1982년 아프리카 니제르에서 나온 최초의 태권도 관련 우표이다. 우표에서 도복을 입은 두 사람이 발차기 공격과 막기를 하는 무술 공방 장면이 그려져 있다. 우표에 나온 글자를 봐서는 축제 행사 종목인 동양무술을 통칭해서 발행한 기념우표이다. 니제르는 프랑스 식민지였던 관계로 프랑스 주재 태권도 사범들에 의해 초창기 태권도가 전파되었을 것으로 추정된다. 이후 조형구 사범이 니제르에 정착하여 태권도 발전에 큰 기여를 했다. 세계태권도연맹 산하 아프리카태권도연합(AFTU)이 1979년에 창설되었지만 20년 후인 1999년에 와서 니제르태권도협회가 정식 등록되었다. 2009년 세계태권도연맹 집행위원회에서 니제르 태권도협회장 이데 이사카 씨가 아프리카 대륙을 대표한 집행위원으로 선출되었다.

This is the first Taekwondo-related stamp issued by the African country of Niger in 1982. The design in this stamp depicts two men in martial arts uniforms executing kicking and defensive moves. By observing the words "Arts Martiaux" in the stamp, we can say that this stamp was issued to celebrate and represent all martial arts during the festival. Niger was formerly a French territory and I assume that Korean Masters residing in France may have contributed to the earlier spread of Taekwondo there. Later, Master Hyung Gu Cho moved to Niger and played a great role in developing Taekwondo. Even though the African Taekwondo Union was established in 1979, the Niger Taekwondo Federation only joined the Union in 1999. In the 2009 executive meeting of the W.T.F. General Assembly in Copenhagen, Denmark, Mr. Ide Issaka from Niger was elected as a Council Member to represent the African continent.

실체봉투
a Used Cover

IV-2. 유럽태권도대회 기념우표 2종
The European Taekwondo Championships

지중해에 위치한 북사이프러스(터키계)가 유럽태권도대회를 기념하여 2종의 태권도 우표를 발행했다. 우표는 터키계 북사이프러스에 위치한 '키레니아'란 도시에서 1984년 6월 5일에 열린 대회를 기념하여 발행되었다. 이 대회는 세계태권도연맹이 아닌 다른 단체에서 주관한 대회로 보인다. 세계태권도연맹이 주관한 유럽태권도대회는 같은 해인 1984년 8월 26일 독일의 슈트가르트에서 제5회 대회가 열린 바 있다. 인구 85만명이 사는 섬나라 사이프러스는 터키계와 그리스계 원주민들이 분열되어 북쪽(터키계)과 남쪽(그리스계)으로 영토가 둘로 나뉘어져서 현재 국제사회로부터 남키프러스만 독립국가로 인정받고 있다. 1965년 터키에 건너간 조수세 사범 등 터키 본토 주재 사범들이 사이프러스에 태권도를 전파한 것으로 알려져 있다.

Northern Cyprus, located in the Mediterranean Sea, issued 2 stamps to commemorate the European Taekwondo Championships. The tournament was held on June 5th, 1984 at Kyrenia, a town on the northern coast of Cyprus, but was not sanctioned by the World Taekwondo Federation. The 5th official European Taekwondo Championship organized by the W.T.F. was held in Stuttgart, Germany on October 26, 1984. Cyprus, with a population of 850,000, is divided into 2 parts: the northern (Turkish) and the southern (Greek). Only the south is recognized as an independent nation by the international community. Masters such as Soo Se Jo went to Turkey in 1965, spread Taekwondo in North Cyprus.

Taekwondo Stamp No. 029 & 030

☞ 북사이프러스(터키계) I. 1984
  Northern Cyprus (Turkish)

☞ 자료 평가 Evaluation :
① 태권도가치성 Taekwondo Value ★★★★☆
② 도안성 Design ★★★★★
③ 희귀성 Rarity ★★★☆☆

☞ 우표 구성 : 2종 중 2종
  Stamp Composition : 2 of 2 stamps

기념 초일봉투
First Day Cover

우표로 보는 태권도 발자취 The Evolution of Taekwondo as Seen Through Postage Stamps

IV-3. 청소년 교육 수단으로서 태권도
Taekwondo as a Means of Youth Education

Taekwondo Stamp No. 031

☞ 국가명 : 기니비사우 I. 1985
　Nation : Guinea-Bissau I

☞ 자료 평가 Evaluation :
① 태권도가치성 Taekwondo Value ★★★★★
② 도안성 Design ★★★★☆
③ 희귀성 Rarity ★★★☆☆

☞ 우표 구성 : 소형시트 1종
　Stamp Composition : 1 Souvenir Sheet

아프리카 서부 해안에 위치한 기니비사우는 태권도, 가라테 등 동양무예를 망라하여 '국제 청소년의 해' 기념우표를 발행했다. 제34회 유엔총회(1979년)는 청소년이 사회의 개발·발전과 평화의 실현을 위하여 보다 적극적으로 참여하도록 1985년을 '청소년(15~24세)의 해'로 선정했다. 기니비사우는 인라인, 스케이팅보드, 행글라이딩, 파라슈팅, 윈드서핑 등 청소년들이 선호하는 스포츠 종목 우표 7종과 함께 동양무예를 강조한 소형시트 1종을 발행했다. 기니비사우 우정국은 동양무예가 청소년 교육에 차지하는 역할을 비중 있게 다루었다. 태권도와 같은 무예는 단순히 즐기기 위한 스포츠가 아니라 청소년의 심신 수양의 수단임을 상징하는 우표이다.

The Republic of Guinea-Bissau issued stamps of martial arts including Taekwondo and Karate to commemorate the 'International Year of Youth'. The 34th session of the United Nations General Assembly adopted 1985 as the International Year of Youth (for ages between 15 to 24) to encourage the youth to participate in the development of societies and the peace movement. The Republic of Guinea-Bissau issued a small sheet of stamps representing East Asian martial arts, including seven different stamps depicting the sports that youngsters enjoy, such as in-line skating, skateboarding, hang gliding, parachuting, and wind surfing. The stamp authority of the Republic of Guinea Bissau saw great importance in the role of East Asian martial arts in the education of the youth. This sheet of stamps symbolically represents the fact that a martial art such as Taekwondo is not a sport merely for watching but an instrument for youngsters to cultivate their minds and bodies.

IV-4. 과테말라 유니버시아드 대회
The Guatemalan University Games

1990년 과테말라에서 열린 중앙아메리카 지역 유니버시아드 대회 기념우표로서 태권도가 포함되었다. 과테말라에서 나온 유일한 태권도 우표로서 이 대회 캐릭터의 태권도 발차기 모습이 담겨있다. 과테말라의 태권도 보급은 지금부터 50년 이전으로 거슬러 올라간다. 1962년 유학생으로 과테말라로 출국했다가 전문 태권도 지도자가 된 김용덕 사범이 최초로 태권도의 씨를 뿌렸다. 과테말라에서 태권도 동향은 활발하지 못해 아직도 개척되어야 할 황무지로 여겨진다. 태권도 활동은 오래되었지만 과테말라태권도협회가 세계태권도연맹에 공식 등록된 해는 1991년이고 마리아 로자리오 버렐로 카스틸로 여사가 세계태권도연맹 집행위원 겸 과테말라태권도협회 회장을 맡고 있다. 2009년 아제르바이잔에서 열린 제1회 W.T.F 세계장애인태권도대회 58kg급에서 과테말라 선수인 헤르손 메히아 알베레스가 은메달을 따냈다.

Taekwondo Stamp No. 032

Taekwondo was included in the commemorative stamps issued to celebrate the 1990 University Games in Guatemala. This is a unique stamp issued in Guatemala and depicts the toucan mascot of the event performing a kick. The initial promotion of Taekwondo in Guatemala dates back 50 years. Master Yong Duk Kim, who went to Guatemala as a foreign student in 1962, planted the seed of Taekwondo in Guatemala. However, Taekwondo promotion is currently not very active, and the country is considered very challenging for the growth of Taekwondo. Even though Taekwondo has had a long history there, it was only finally registered by the World Taekwondo Federation in 1991. Ms. Maria Rosario Borello Castillo is serving as a member of the Executive Council of the W.T.F. and also leads the Guatemalan Taekwondo Federation. At the 1st W.T.F. World Para-Taekwondo Championships held in the Republic of Azerbaijan (in 2009), Mejia Alvarez Gersson Josue of Guatemala won the silver medal in the male 58kg division.

☞ 국가명 : 과테말라. 1990
　Nation : Guatemala

☞ 자료 평가 Evaluation :
① 태권도가치성 Taekwondo Value ★★★★★
② 도안성 Design ★★★★★
③ 희귀성 Rarity ★★★★☆

☞ 우표 구성 : 7종 중 1종
　Stamp Composition : 1 of 7 stamps

IV-5. 제11회 쿠바 팬아메리칸 대회 태권도 경기
The 11th Pan American Games in Cuba

쿠바의 수도 하바나에서 열린 제11회 팬암대회 기념 우표에 태권도가 포함되었다. 두 선수가 겨루는 태권도 경기 장면이 기념 우표로 도안되었다. 이 태권도 경기에서 주최국 쿠바는 총 8체급 중 페더급, 라이트급, 헤비급 등 3개 체급을 석권하여 금메달 2개를 딴 베네수엘라를 제치고 종합 우승했다. 태권도 경기는 1987년 제10회 미국 인디아나폴리스(Indianapolis) 팬암대회 정식종목으로 채택되었다. 쿠바태권도협회는 1993년에 세계태권도연맹에 정식 등록되었고 마즈밀리아노 곤잘레스 디아즈 씨가 회장직을 맡고있다.

This Taekwondo stamp was included in the 11th Pan American Games held in Havana, the capital of Cuba, in 1991. A competition scene of two competitors sparring is depicted in the commemorative stamp. In this Taekwondo Championships, the organizing country, Cuba, earned 3 gold medals in the Feather, Light, and Heavy weight divisions, and won in the overall medal standings by beating Venezuela, which had won 2 gold medals. The Taekwondo competition was adopted as an official sport at the 10th Pan-American Games (in 1987) held in Indianapolis, USA. The Cuban Taekwondo Federation was registered by the W.T.F. in 1993, and is today led by President Maximiliano Gonzalez Diaz.

Taekwondo Stamp No. 033

☞ 국가명 : 쿠바. 1991
　 Nation : Cuba
☞ 자료 평가 Evaluation :
　① 태권도가치성 Taekwondo Value ★★★★★
　② 도안성 Design ★★★★★
　③ 희귀성 Rarity ★★★☆☆
☞ 우표 구성 : 10종 중 1종
　 Stamp Composition : 1 of 10 stamps

함께 나온 우표세트
accompanied stamp set

IV-6. 제14회 이스라엘 하포엘경기
The 14th Hapoel Games in Israel

이스라엘에서 열린 국제 스포츠경기인 하포엘경기 기념으로 나온 우표이다. 1923년에 설립된 하포엘은 마카비아와 더불어 주요 체육단체로서, 세계 각지에서 온 이스라엘 운동선수들을 모아 4년마다 한번씩 경기를 주최한다. 이스라엘 태권도 인구 수는 1만명 정도이며 해마다 숫자가 늘고 있는 추세이다. 태권도 선수들은 년간 5회 정도의 국, 내외 태권도 대회에 참가하고 있다. 남성복 사범의 활약으로 이스라엘 태권도협회는 1981년에 등록되었고 세계태권도연맹 집행위원인 미셸 마다르씨가 회장을 맡고 있다.

This is a commemorative stamp to celebrate the international Hapoel Games held in Israel. Hapoel, established in 1923, is a major athletic group that organizes the Games every 4 years by gathering Israeli athletes from all over the world. The Taekwondo population in Israel is about 10,000, and the number is increasing every year. Israeli Taekwondo competitors are participating in national or international tournaments an average of five times a year. Thanks to Master Sung Bok Nam, the Israel Taekwondo Federation was enrolled in 1981, and is today led by President Michel Madar, who is also serving in the W.T.F. as a Council Member.

Taekwondo Stamp No. 034

☞ 국가명 : 이스라엘 I . 1991
　 Nation : Israel I

☞ 자료 평가 Evaluation :
① 태권도가치성 Taekwondo Value ★★★★★
② 도안성 Design ★★★★★
③ 희귀성 Rarity ★★★☆☆

☞ 우표 구성 : 3종 중 1종
　 Stamp Composition : 1 of 3 stamps

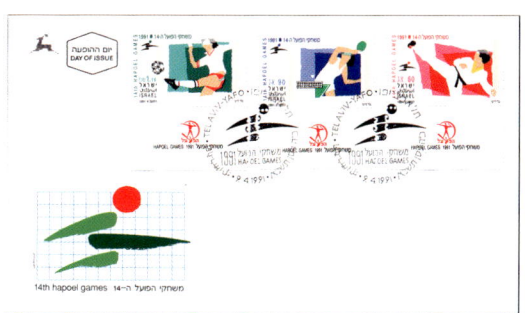

기념 초일봉투
First Day Cover

우표로 보는 태권도 발자취 The Evolution of Taekwondo as Seen Through Postage Stamps

IV-7. 제5회 아프리카 경기대회
The 5th All-African Games in Cairo, Egypt

Taekwondo Stamp No. 035

☞ 국가명 : 이집트 Ⅰ. 1991
　　Nation : Egypt Ⅰ

☞ 자료 평가 Evaluation :
① 태권도가치성 Taekwondo Value ★★★★☆
② 도안성 Design ★★★★★
③ 희귀성 Rarity ★★★★☆

☞ 우표 구성 : 6종 중 1종
　　Stamp Composition : 1 of 6 stamps

1991년 이집트의 수도 카이로에서 열린 전아프리카 경기대회 기념우표에 태권도 이미지가 포함되었다. 태권도 도안으로 1986 서울아시안게임에서 제작된 태권도 발차기를 표현한 픽토그램을 채택했다. 이집트는 오래 전부터 태권도 강국으로 위세를 떨쳤다. 1988년 서울올림픽 시범종목인 태권도 경기에서 은메달 1개를 따내 종합5위를 차지했다. 정기영 사범이 태권도 전파에 큰 역할을 했고 임한수 사범은 1995년 이집트 국립경찰대학에 전 학년의 필수과목으로 태권도가 채택되도록 하는 성과를 올렸다. 노승옥 사범은 이집트 최고의 명문대학인 카이로대학에서 태권도를 정규과목으로 채택시키는데 큰 기여를 했다. 김승주 사범도 이집트 태권도 보급에 기여했다.

A Taekwondo image is included in the commemorative stamps celebrating the All-Africa Games held in Cairo, Egypt in 1991. The pictogram depicting the Taekwondo kick design used for the 10th Asian Games in Seoul in 1986 was adopted. The Arab Republic of Egypt has maintained itself as a Taekwondo power country for a long time. Egypt took 5th place in the overall medal count by earning a silver medal in the Taekwondo Championships at the 1988 Seoul Summer Olympics. Master Ki Young Chung played an influential role in promoting Taekwondo in Egypt, while Master Han Soo Lim made a great achievement by helping the Egyptian National Police Academy adopt Taekwondo as a compulsory credit course for all officer grades in 1995. In addition, Master Seung Ok Noh contributed to the process of adopting Taekwondo as a credit course at Cairo University, the most prestigious university in Egypt. Master Seong Ju Kim also contributed Taekwondo promotion in Egypt.

기념 초일봉투
First Day Cover

IV-8. 제12회 팬암경기대회
The 12th Pan American Games

1995년 제12회 팬암대회는 아르헨티나에서 열렸지만 도미니카공화국이 대회 기념 태권도 우표를 발행했다. 우표에는 팬암 대회 글자를 배경으로 뛰어 차기를 하는 태권도 동작이 도안되었고 영문으로 태권도 글자가 선명하게 표기되었다. 도미니카공화국은 2003년 수도 산토도밍고에서 제14회 팬암대회를 개최했다. 도미니카 태권도 선수인 가브리엘 메르세데스는 2008 베이징올림픽 은메달을 획득하여 조국으로부터 열렬한 환영을 받았다. 1980년대 이준구 재미태권도 사범이 도미니카공화국을 방문하여 태권도를 지도한 활동이 알려져 있다. 도미니카공화국 태권도협회는 1983년에 등록되었고 프란시스코 호세 카마초 리바스씨가 회장을 맡고 있다.

Even though the 12th Pan American Games were held in Argentina in 1995, the Dominican Republic still issued their own Taekwondo stamp. The stamp depicts a Taekwondo jump kick, and is designed with a background showing the title Pan American Games, with Taekwondo inscribed clearly in English. The Dominican Republic held the 14th Pan American Games in its capital, Santa Domingo, in 2003. A Dominican Republic competitor named Gabriel Mercedes won a silver medal in the Taekwondo competition at the 2008 Summer Olympic Games in Beijing. Joon Rhee, an American Taekwondo master, visited the Dominican Republic to teach Taekwondo in 1980. The Dominican Republic Taekwondo Federation was enrolled 1983 and is currently led by President Francisco Jose Camacho Rivas.

Taekwondo Stamp No. 036

- 국가명 : 도미니카공화국 I. 1996
  Nation : Dominican Republic I
- 자료 평가 Evaluation :
  ① 태권도가치성 Taekwondo Value ★★★★★
  ② 도안성 Design ★★★★★
  ③ 희귀성 Rarity ★★★★☆
- 우표 구성 : 2종 중 1종
  Stamp Composition : 1 of 2 stamps

기념 초일봉투
First Day Cover

우표로 보는 태권도 발자취 The Evolution of Taekwondo as Seen Through Postage Stamps

IV-9. 제6회 온두라스 중앙아메리칸게임
The 6th Central American Games in Honduras

☞ 국가명 : 온두라스 I. 1997
　Nation : Honduras I

☞ 자료 평가 Evaluation :
① 태권도가치성 Taekwondo Value ★★★★★
② 도안성 Design ★★★★★
③ 희귀성 Rarity ★★★★☆

☞ 우표 구성 : 30종 중 1종
　Stamp Composition : 1 of 30 stamps

1997년 제6회 중미경기가 7개국이 참가하여 온두라스에서 열렸다. 태권도와 가라테가 경기 종목으로 포함되어 기념우표도 함께 발행되었다. 태권도 우표는 대회 마스코트인 도마뱀이 보호대를 착용하고 발차기하는 모습을 담고 있다. 온두라스는 태권도 불모지였으나 1977년 이민간 송봉경 사범(2008년 작고)이 처음으로 도장을 열었다. 송봉경 사범은 지난 30년간 태권도를 보급하여 온두라스가 중미 태권도 강국으로 부상하게 된 공로를 인정받아 2006년 온두라스 국회에서 체육 공로훈장을 수상했다. 1986년 당시 법무장관이던 포르피리오 로보 소사 씨는 송사범의 절친한 제자로서 국기원 공인 2단을 획득했고 국회의장을 거쳐 2010년에 온두라스 대통령으로 취임했다. 온두라스태권도협회는 1979년에 세계태권도연맹에 등록되었고 현재 오브둘리오 로미오 파체고 바네가스 씨가 회장이다.

The 6th Central American Games were held in Honduras in 1997, with seven countries participating. Taekwondo and Karate were included in the games and commemorative stamps were issued for both disciplines. The Taekwondo stamp depicts an image of the games' mascot, a lizard, wearing sparring gear and performing a kick. Honduras had been a difficult country for Taekwondo to enter, but Master Bong Kyung Song immigrated there in 1977 (recently deceased in 2008) and opened the first school. Mr. Porfirio Lobo Sosa earned a 2nd degree black belt in 1986 when he was the minister of law, and through the position of Prime Minister, he is now serving as the country's president. The Honduras Taekwondo Federation was enrolled in 1979 and Mr. Romeo Pacheco Vanegas is the current president.

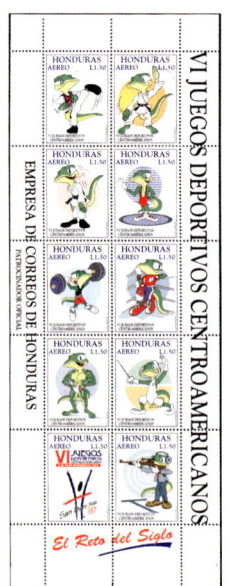

함께 나온 우표세트　accompanied stamp set

IV-10. 제6회 에콰도르 남미경기
The 6th South American Games in Ecuador

1998년 제6회 남미경기는 14개국이 참가하여 에콰도르에서 열렸다. 우표에 도복을 입고 발차기하는 도안이 태권도인지 가라테인지 분명치는 않지만 양쪽을 다 포괄하는 것으로 보인다. 태권도는 1986년 3회 대회부터 남미경기 정식종목이 되었고 가라테는 1994년 5회 대회에서 채택되었다. 에콰도르는 태권도가 일찍이 보급된 남미 태권도 강국으로 1982년 제5회 세계태권도대회를 주최했을 뿐 아니라 금1, 은1 로 종합2위를 달성했다. 1970년 장철웅 사범이 에콰돌로 이주하여 최초로 태권도를 전파했다. 1973년 에콰도르 태권도협회가 세계태권도연맹에 등록되었고 에르네스토 파비안 클라비조 블라쉬케 씨가 회장을 맡고 있다.

The 6th South American Games were held in Ecuador in 1998, and 14 countries participated. It is unclear whether the figure in the stamp wearing a uniform and performing a kick represents Karate or Taekwondo. The image seems to inclusively represent both disciplines. Taekwondo has been an official sport since the 3rd South American Games in 1986, while Karate was adopted in the 5th South American Games in 1994. Ecuador is a powerful Taekwondo country, and it hosted the 5th World Taekwondo Championships in 1982, where it placed second in the total medal count by earning one gold medal and one silver medal. Master Chul Woong Jang emigrated to Ecuador and introduced Taekwondo there. The Ecuador Taekwondo Federation joined the W.T.F. in 1973 and today is led by President Ernesto Fabian Clavijo Blaschke.

Taekwondo Stamp No. 038

☞ 국가명 : 에콰도르 II. 1998
　Nation : Ecuador II

☞ 자료 평가 Evaluation :
① 태권도가치성
　Taekwondo Value ★★★★☆
② 도안성 Design ★★★★☆
③ 희귀성 Rarity ★★★☆☆

☞ 우표 구성 : 3종 중 1종
　Stamp Composition : 1 of 3 stamps

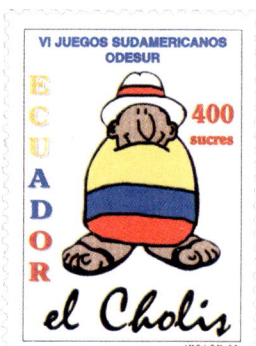 

함께 나온 우표세트
accompanied stamp set

IV-11. 짐바브웨 스포츠 장려
Zimbabwe's Sport Promotional Activities

☞ 국가명 : 짐바브웨. 2000
　　Nation : Zimbabwe

☞ 자료 평가 Evaluation :
① 태권도가치성 Taekwondo Value ★★★★★
② 도안성 Design ★★★★★
③ 희귀성 Rarity ★★★☆☆

☞ 우표 구성 : 6종 중 1종
　　Stamp Composition : 1 of 6 stamps

새천년을 맞아 아프리카 짐바브웨에서 발행한 스포츠 장려 기념우표 6종에 태권도가 포함되었다. 빨간띠를 맨 한 여성이 발차기를 하는 장면과 태권도 영문 글씨가 함께 새겨졌다. 이 우표는 여성들이 자기 방어 호신술을 겸해 날씬해 지려는 미용 운동 목적으로 하는 태권도를 상징한다. 짐바브웨는 대부분의 아프리카 나라들처럼 태권도 보급이 늦었지만 1995년에 제6회 전 아프리카태권도대회를 주최했다. 2009년 로버트 무가베 짐바브웨 대통령은 권택일 아프리카태권도연맹(ATU) 부회장이 배석하여 명예6단을 수여받기도 했다. 이병호 사범이 짐바브웨 태권도 보급에 큰 역할을 했다.

Taekwondo is included in the 6 commemorative stamps for the promotion of sports in the new millennium in Zimbabwe, Africa. The stamp depicts a woman wearing a red belt and kicking, with Taekwondo in English emblazoned on it. This stamp symbolizes women's interest in learning Taekwondo for self-defense as well as an exercise to enhance beauty. Similar to other African countries, Taekwondo has been promoted only recently in Zimbabwe. The nation organized the 6th African Taekwondo Championships in 1995. The nation's President, Mr. Robert Mugabe, was awarded an honorary 6th degree black belt in 2009 at a ceremony by Master Taek Il Kwon, Vice President of the African Taekwondo Union. Master Byung Ho Lee also played a great role to promote Taekwondo in Zimbabwe.

기념 초일봉투
First Day of Issue Cover

IV-12. 에콰도르 제5회 세계태권도대회 20주년
The 20th Anniversary of the 5th World Championships from Ecuador

태권도 단일 행사인 세계태권도대회를 기념하는 첫 외국 태권도 우표가 2002년 에콰도르에서 나왔다. 에콰도르가 주최한 제5회 세계태권도대회(1982년 거행됨) 20주년을 기념한 1장짜리 우표이다. 우표에는 5회 대회 금메달리스트 호세 세데노 선수(핀급)와 은메달리스트인 더반 캉가 선수(라이트미들급) 인물 사진과 함께 세계태권도연맹 로고가 도안되었다. 태권도는 양국 관계 우호 증진에도 큰 역할을 한다. 라파엘 코레아 델가도 에콰도르 대통령이 2010년 한국을 방문했을 때 양국 정상회담장에서 태권도 시범을 관람하고 태권도에 대한 찬사와 관심을 아끼지 않았다고 한다.

The Republic of Ecuador issued the first foreign Taekwondo stamp commemorating the World Taekwondo Championships, a single sport tournament, in 2002. This was to celebrate the 20th anniversary of the 5th World Taekwondo Championship (held in 1982) organized by Ecuador. This stamp includes the pictures of Mr. Jose Cedeno, gold medalist in the fin weight division, and Mr. Duvan Canga, silver medalist in the light middle weight division, along with the W.T.F. logo in the background. Taekwondo has played a big role in promoting friendship between Korea and Ecuador. When the Ecuadorian president, Mr. Rafael Vicente Correa Delgado, visited Korea in 2010, he observed a Taekwondo demonstration and lavishly praised Jose Cedeno and Duvan Canga's Taekwondo, showing great interest in it.

Taekwondo Stamp No. 040

☞ 국가명 : 에콰도르 Ⅲ. 2002
  Nation : Ecuador Ⅲ

☞ 자료 평가 Evaluation :
① 태권도가치성 Taekwondo Value ★★★★★
② 도안성 Design ★★★★★
③ 희귀성 Rarity ★★★★☆

☞ 우표 구성 : 기념우표 1종
  Stamp Composition : single stamps

기념 초일봉투
First Day of Issue Cover

우표로 보는 태권도 발자취　The Evolution of Taekwondo as Seen Through Postage Stamps

IV-13. 태권도 지도자 박정태 사범 추모
The Memorial Stamp for Master Jung Tae Park

태권도 지도자를 소재로 한 우표가 지중해 북사이프러스(터키계)에서 발행되었다. 2002년 터키에서 활동했던 박정태 사범(1944~2002)이 그 주인공이다. 우표에는 그의 발차기 모습과 함께 '현대 태권도의 아버지, 박정태 대사범을 추모하며'라는 글귀가 함께 인쇄되어 있다. 그는 한때 국제태권도연맹(I.T.F) 임원으로 1981년 북한을 방문하여 태권도 보급에 앞장섰다. 차후 북한과 너무 밀착한 국제태권도연맹과 결별하고 1990년 글로벌태권도연맹(G.T.F)을 창립하여 독자적인 태권도 활동을 전개하였다.

Northern Cyprus issued a stamp with a Taekwondo leader as its subject. The hero of the stamp is Master Jung Tae Park (1944-2002) who promoted Taekwondo in Turkey up to 2002. The stamp depicts him kicking along with the inscriptions, 'In memory of Grand Master Park Jung-Tae' and 'Father of modern Taekwon-do'. He visited North Korea in 1981 as a member of the I.T.F.(the International Taekwondo Federation) and promoted I.T.F. style Taekwondo. Later, he broke away from the I.T.F., which was too closely related to North Korea, and established the Global Taekwondo Federation (G.T.F.) in 1990 in which he developed his own Taekwondo activities.

- 북사이프러스(터키계) III. 2002
  Northern Cyprus(Turkish) III
- 자료 평가 Evaluation :
  ① 태권도가치성 Taekwondo Value ★★★★☆
  ② 도안성 Design ★★★★★
  ③ 희귀성 Rarity ★★★☆☆
- 우표 구성 : 2종 중 1종
  Stamp Composition : 1 of 2 stamps

기념 초일봉투
First Day Cover

IV-14. 제19회 중미 및 캐리비안경기
The 19th Central American and Caribbean Games

2002년 엘살바돌에서 열린 '제19회 중미 및 캐리비안 경기'를 기념하는 우표이다. 우표 왼편에 보이는 도복 차림의 이미지가 태권도인지 가라테인지 분명치는 않지만 양쪽을 다 포괄하는 것으로 보인다. 태권도는 1990년 16회 대회부터 정식종목이 되었고 가라테는 3년 후 1993년 17회 대회에 채택되었다. 1920년에 창립된 이 대회는 31개국 7,000명의 선수가 37개 종목에서 경쟁하는 큰 규모의 대회이다. 1966년 엘살바돌로 이주한 최병호 사범은 당시 대통령에게 태권도를 지도한 특별사범으로 예우받았고 육군사관학교, 군 정예부대를 지도하며 태권도를 심었다.

This stamp commemorates the 19th Central American and Caribbean Games held in El Salvador in 2002. It is hard to tell if the figure wearing a uniform in the left corner of the stamp represents Taekwondo or Karate. It would seem to represent both disciplines. Taekwondo has been an official sport since the 16th Games in 1990, and Karate since the 17th Games in 1993, three years after the adoption of Taekwondo. These Games, established in 1920, are a large scale event in which 7,000 competitors from 31 countries in 37 different disciplines compete. Master Byung Ho Choi, who emigrated to El Salvador in 1966, taught the President at that time, and promoted Taekwondo by teaching in the military academy and the elite unit of the army.

Taekwondo Stamp No. 042

- 국가명 : 엘살바도르 I. 2002
  Nation : El Salvador I
- 자료 평가 Evaluation :
  ① 태권도가치성
    Taekwondo Value ★★★☆☆
  ② 도안성 Design ★★★☆☆
  ③ 희귀성 Rarity ★★★☆☆
- 우표 구성 : 4종 중 1종
  Stamp Composition : 1 of 4 stamps

함께 나온 우표세트
accompanied stamp set

우표로 보는 태권도 발자취 The Evolution of Taekwondo as Seen Through Postage Stamps

IV-15. 그레나다 테디베어 인형
The Teddy Bear from Grenada

손바느질로 만든 곰인형인 테디베어(Teddy Bear)를 소재로 한 무술 우표가 그레나다에서 발행되었다. 테디베어는 미국 루스벨트 대통령의 애칭을 따서 곰인형의 보통명사가 되어 전세계적으로 사랑받는 완구가 되었다. 테디 베어의 매력은 남녀노소 누구나 친근감을 느낄 수 있다는 데 있다. 마찬가지로 태권도가 속한 동양무술이 농구, 야구와 더불어 성별과 연령에 상관없이 누구나 친숙해졌음을 그레나다 우표를 통해 알 수 있다. 그레나다 태권도협회는 1995년 등록되었고 니콜 알렉시스 여사가 회장을 맡고 있다.

A martial arts stamp with a handmade teddy bear on it as the subject was issued by Grenada. The teddy bear has become a doll loved by many people worldwide. The name is also the nickname of an American President, Theodore Roosevelt. The attraction of the Teddy Bear transcends age and gender, and everyone is familiar with it. Also through this Grenadan stamp, it can be seen that East Asian martial arts such as Taekwondo are also familiar to people regardless of age and gender, just like basketball and baseball. The Grenada Taekwondo Association was registered in 1995 and is led by its President, Mr. Fronzie Charles.

☞ 국가명 : 그레나다. 2002
   Nation : Grenada

☞ 자료 평가 Evaluation :
① 태권도가치성 Taekwondo Value ★★★★☆
② 도안성 Design ★★★★☆
③ 희귀성 Rarity ★★★★☆

☞ 우표 구성 : 4종 중 1종
   Stamp Composition : 1 of 4 stamps

예쁜 소형쉬이트
a Souvenir Sheet

IV-16. 경기 스포츠가 된 동양무술
Martial Arts Becomes a Competitive Sport.

태권도, 중국무술, 검도, 무에타이 등 동양무술 특별 우표가 아프리카 기니비사우에서 선보였다. 우표에는 태권도복을 입은 두 수련자가 태권도 겨루기를 시연하는 장면이 실렸다. 기니비사우는 포르투갈 언어권 나라에 속하는 나라들과 함께 루소포니아 경기 대회에 참가한다. 제1회 대회는 2006년 마카오에서 열렸고 2회 대회는 12개국 1,300명이 참가하여 2009년 포르투갈에서 열렸다. 태권도는 남녀 모두 정식종목으로 거행되며 타격 격투기 종목으로는 유일하다. 올림픽 선배 종목인 유도보다 앞서 채택되어 태권도의 위상을 실감케 한다. 루소포니아 대회는 영연방 경기대회(Commonwealth Games)나 스페인 문화권 국가의 프랑코포니 경기대회(Francophone Games)와 유사한 취지의 대회이다.

East Asian martial arts stamps that include Taekwondo, Chinese martial arts, Kendo, and Muai Thai were issued by Guinea Bissau. This stamp depicts a sparring scene of a couple of practicioners in Taekwondo uniforms. Guinea-Bissau participates in the Lusophony Games along with other Portuguese speaking countries. The first Lusophony Games was held in Macau in 2006, and the 2nd in Portugal, with 1,300 participants from 12 countries, in 2009. In these games, Taekwondo is an official sport for men and women, and is the only martial art to be included. The prestige of Taekwondo in Portuguese speaking countries is realized from its adoption into the Lusophony Games before Judo, which had been adopted into the Olympics long before Taekwondo. The Lusophony Games is similar to the Commonwealth Games of the Commonwealth Nations and the Francophone Games of Spanish speaking countries.

Taekwondo Stamp No. 044

☞ 국가명 : 기니비사우 II. 2003
　　Nation : Guinea-Bissau II

☞ 자료 평가 Evaluation :
① 태권도가치성 Taekwondo Value ★★★★★
② 도안성 Design ★★★★★
③ 희귀성 Rarity ★★★☆☆

☞ 우표 구성 : 6종 중 1종
　　Stamp Composition : 1 of 6 stamps

함께 나온 우표세트
accompanied stamp set

우표로 보는 태권도 발자취 The Evolution of Taekwondo as Seen Through Postage Stamps

IV-17. 나이지리아 제8회 올아프리카게임
The 8th All-Africa Games in Nigeria

Taekwondo Stamp No. 045

☞ 국가명 : 나이지리아 II. 2003
　　Nation : Nigeria II

☞ 자료 평가 Evaluation :
① 태권도가치성 Taekwondo Value ★★★★★
② 도안성 Design ★★★★★
③ 희귀성 Rarity ★★★★☆

☞ 우표 구성 : 4종 중 1종
　　Stamp Composition : 1 of 4 stamps

2003년 나이지리아에서 열린 제8회 올아프리카 경기를 기념한 태권도 우표이다. 우표에는 태권도 뛰어차기로 격파를 하는 장면과 태권도 영문 글씨가 새겨져 있다. 올아프리카경기는 1965년 창립되었고 태권도가 7회 대회부터 정식종목으로 거행되고 있다. 박희원 목사(공인9단)가 이끄는 국제선교태권도연맹은 태권도 유단자인 선교사를 나이지리아에 보내 태권도를 전파하고 있다. 2010년에는 제1회 한국대사배 나이지리아 태권도대회가 열려 태권도 보급이 더욱 활성화되고 있다. 나이지리아 태권도협회는 1988년 등록되었고 현재 조나단 냐지 씨가 회장이다.

This stamp was issued to commemorate the 8th All-Africa Games in Nigeria in 2003. In this stamp, you can see a breaking scene using a Taekwondo jump kick and the English inscription of Taekwondo. The All-Africa Games were established in 1965 and Taekwondo has been an official sport since the 7th Games. The International Mission Taekwondo Union led by Pastor Heui Won Park (9th degree black belt) is dispatching black belt missionaries to Nigeria in order to further spread Taekwondo. In 2010, the 1st Korean Ambassador's Cup International Taekwondo Championships were held in Nigeria. It is clear that Taekwondo is actively being promoted there. The Nigeria Taekwondo Federation was enrolled in 1988 and is led by President Jonathan Nnaji.

소형쉬이트
a Souvenir Sheet

IV-18. 니카라과 스포츠경기대회
The Sports Games in Nicaragua

2004년 니카라과 수도 마나구아에서 스포츠경기대회 기념으로 나온 우표로서 유도와 발차기 동작이 그려져 있다. 대회 관련 상세 정보를 확인할 수 없지만 우표에 있는 아래쪽 그림이 태권도와 가라테를 포괄적으로 표현한 이미지로 보인다. 미주 지역의 각종 국제스포츠 경기대회에서 태권도와 가라테가 함께 정식종목으로 거행되지만 태권도가 가라테보다 더 먼저 채택되었다. 올림픽 종목에서 동양무술 중 유도와 태권도만이 정식종목이므로 당연한 현상으로 보인다. 니카라과 태권도협회는 1991년 공식 등록되었고 현재 프랑코 실바 얼비나 씨가 회장이다.

This is a stamp issued to commemorate the Sports Games in Nicaragua held in the capital, Managua, in 2004. It depicts a Judo movement and Taekwondo kicking. It is impossible to find specific details of the Games, but the stamp seems to inclusively represent Taekwondo and Karate. Although Taekwondo and Karate are both official disciplines at various international sporting events in Pan-America, Taekwondo was the first to be adopted, long before Karate. It seems fitting since Judo and Taekwondo are the only official medal sports in the Olympics. The Nicaraguan Taekwondo Association was enrolled in 1991, and is headed by current President Frank Ramiro Silva Urbina.

- 국가명 : 니카라과. 2004
  Nation : Nicaragua
- 자료 평가 Evaluation :
  ① 태권도가치성 Taekwondo Value ★★★★☆
  ② 도안성 Design ★★★☆☆
  ③ 희귀성 Rarity ★★★☆☆
- 우표 구성 : 3종 중 1종
  Stamp Composition : 1 of 3 stamps

함께 나온 우표세트
accompanied stamp set

우표로 보는 태권도 발자취   The Evolution of Taekwondo as Seen Through Postage Stamps

Ⅳ-19. 제10회 엘살바도르 청소년경기대회
The 10th Central American Youth Games in El Salvador

Taekwondo Stamp No. 047

☞ 국가명 : 엘살바도르 Ⅱ-1. 2005
   Nation : El Salvador Ⅱ-1

☞ 자료 평가 Evaluation :
① 태권도가치성 Taekwondo Value ★★★★★
② 도안성 Design ★★★★★
③ 희귀성 Rarity ★★★☆☆

☞ 우표 구성 : 4종 중 1종
   Stamp Composition : 1 of 4 stamps

2005년 엘살바도르에서 열린 제5회 중미경기 청소년 대회를 기념하는 우표 1종과 소형시트에 태권도가 나왔다. 태권도 우표를 살펴보면 우표 도안사의 실책을 엿볼 수 있다. 우표와 소형시트 도안은 틀림없이 태권도 겨루기 경기 장면을 실었음에도 불구하고 우표의 오른편에 조그만 글씨로 가라테라고 표기했다. 아직도 세계 많은 사람들이 태권도와 가라테의 차이를 잘 구별 못하는 사례로 보인다. 엘살바도르의 이 우표류는 종이 재질이 스티커형으로 제작된 현대식 우표로서 사용하기 간편하게 되어 있다. 엘살바도르의 태권도에 대한 관심은 남미 중에서 특히 각별하다.

You can find Taekwondo on a stamp and a small sheet issued to commemorate the 10th Central American Youth Games in El Salvador in 2005. Upon closer inspection of the stamp, a blatant error made by the designer can be found. The design on the stamp and the small sheet depicts a Taekwondo sparring scene, but "Karate-do" is written in small letters on the right side of the stamp. This is a telling example that many people still cannot differentiate Taekwondo from Karate. This stamp issued by El Salvador is a modern sticker type and is easy to use. El Salvadorian interest in Taekwondo is quite unique compared to that of other Central American countries.

함께 나온 우표세트
accompanied stamp set

최병호 대사범이 엘살바도르 대통령과 경호실, 사관생도 등에게 1966년부터 태권도를 보급하기 시작했다. 최병호 사범이 미국으로 이주한 이후 1999년부터 윤진영 사범이 유일한 한국인 태권도사범으로 활동하고 있다. 엘살바도르 협회는 1987년 공식 등록되었으며 오스카 리카르도 피네다 로메로씨가 회장을 맡고 있다. 협회는 청소년 태권도대회를 통해 청소년 수련자층을 확대하고 유망선수를 육성할 계획이다. 또한 자국 올림픽위원회와 협력하여 2012년 런던 올림픽에서 금메달을 획득하겠다는 목표를 세웠다.

Grandmaster Byung Ho Choi began teaching Taekwondo to the President of El Salvador and his security guards, as well as the Military Academy, in 1966. After Grandmaster Choi immigrated to the U.S., Master Jin Young Yun became the only Taekwondo master in the country. The Salvadoran Taekwondo Association was established in 1987 and is led today by the President, Mr. Oscar Ricardo Pineda Romero. The Association plans to develop quality competitors and build a wider competitor base by hosting Taekwondo championships for the youth population. In addition, The Association has set a goal to earn gold medals at the London Olympics in 2012, in cooperation with its National Olympic Committee.

기념 초일봉투
First Day of Issue Cover

Taekwondo Stamp No. 048

☞ 국가명 : 엘살바도르 II-2. 2005
　Nation : El Salvador II-2
☞ 자료 평가 Evaluation :
① 태권도가치성 Taekwondo Value ★★★★★
② 도안성 Design ★★★★★
③ 희귀성 Rarity ★★★☆☆
☞ 우표 구성 : 소형시트 1종
　Stamp Composition : single souvenir sheet

IV-20. 멕시코 전국 유니버시아드대회
The National University Games in Mexico

☞ 국가명 : 멕시코. 2005
　　Nation : Mexico

☞ 자료 평가 Evaluation :
① 태권도가치성 Taekwondo Value ★★★★☆
② 도안성 Design ★★★☆☆
③ 희귀성 Rarity ★★★☆☆

☞ 우표 구성 : 기념우표 1종
　　Stamp Composition : single stamp

2005년 멕시코 전국 대학생스포츠대회 기념으로 나온 1장짜리 우표이다. 도복을 입은 수련자의 발차기가 태권도인지 가라테인지 분명치 않지만 태권도 우표류에 포함시켜 소개한다. 멕시코는 일찍이 태권도가 보급되어 베이징올림픽 태권도 경기에서 금메달 2개를 획득한 태권도 강국이다. 1969년 멕시코에 정착한 문대원 대사범을 비롯한 박상권, 방영인 등 사범들의 활약이 두드러졌다. 문사범은 부루스리와 함께 미국 무술 시합에 종종 초대되어 같은 방에서 지내면서 무술 교류를 했다. 문사범의 태권도 발차기 실력은 홍콩무술스타 이소룡의 무술에 영향을 주었다. 그는 인격 면에서도 많은 사람들의 존경을 받는 '진정한 무도인'으로 손꼽힌다. 한국인 사범진들의 노력으로 1978년 멕시코시티에서 팬암연맹(회장 최지호)이 결성되고 제1회 팬암태권도대회가 열렸다. 멕시코태권도협회는 1973년 등록되었고 현재 후안 마누엘 로페즈 델가도씨가 회장이다.

This is a single stamp issued to commemorate the National University Games in Mexico in 2005. Although it is a little hard to discern whether the kicking scene is representing Taekwondo or Karate, I would like to include this as a Taekwondo stamp. In Mexico, Taekwondo was spread at an earlier stage of its development. Mexico is considered a powerful Taekwondo country, earning 2 gold medals in the Taekwondo championships at the Beijing Summer Olympics. Master Dae Won Moon, who moved to Mexico in 1968, and Master Sang Kwon Park, Young In Bang were well known Masters responsible for the development of Taekwondo in Mexico. Master Moon's Taekwondo kicking ability was revered worldwide, even influencing the kicking technique of movie star Bruce Lee. Master Moon and Bruce Lee were often invited to martial art tournaments in which they would share the same hotel room. There they would exchange their vast martial art knowledge and experiences with one another. Master Moon is regarded as a true Martial Artist that receives respect from many other people. The Pan-Am Taekwondo Federation was established in 1978 in Mexico City, which was also the host city for the very first Pan-Am Taekwondo Championships, made possible by the efforts of many Korean masters. The Mexico Taekwondo Association was enrolled in 1973 and Mr. Juan Manuel Lopez Delgado is the current president.

IV-21. 이집트 스포츠경기대회
The Sports Games in Egypt

2007년 이집트 카이로에서 열린 스포츠 대회를 기념한 소형시트에 태권도로 보이는 이미지가 나왔다. 대회 마스코트인 동물이 도복과 검정띠를 착용하고 동양식 경례를 하고 뛰어차기하는 모습이 표현되어 있다. 이집트는 아프리카 중에서 가장 태권도가 발전한 나라일 뿐 아니라 세계태권도연맹 아프리카태권도연합(AFTU) 회장국이다. 협회는 1979년에 세계태권도연맹에 공식 등록되었고 아메드 엘 파울리 씨가 회장이다. 아메드 회장은 이집트 태권도협회 회장일 뿐 아니라 아프리카대륙 태권도연맹 회장을 겸직하고 있다.

Taekwondo Stamp No. 050

In a small sheet of stamps to commemorate the 2007 Sports Games in Egypt, you can see images appearing to represent Taekwondo. In this stamp, the mascot wearing a Taekwondo uniform and a black belt is shown twice, doing a bow and a jump kick. Among African countries, Taekwondo has developed the most in Egypt, and its national association holds the presidency of the African Taekwondo Union. The Egyptian Taekwondo Federation was registered with the W.T.F. in 1979, and is led today by its president, General Ahmed El-Fouly, who is the president of both the Egyptian Taekwondo Federation and the African Taekwondo Union.

☞ 국가명 : 이집트 III. 2007
  Nation : Egypt III
☞ 자료 평가 Evaluation :
① 태권도가치성 Taekwondo Value ★★★★☆
② 도안성 Design ★★★★☆
③ 희귀성 Rarity ★★★☆☆
☞ 우표구성 : 소형시트 1종
  Stamp Composition : single souvenir sheet

기념 초일봉투
First Day of Cover

IV-22. 모로코 스포츠 창립 50주년
The 50th Anniversary of the Morocco Sports

Taekwondo Stamp No. 051

모로코 스포츠 창립 50주년 기념 우표가 2007년 발행되었다. 우표 속에 모로코 스포츠 참피온들이 종목별로 그림으로 표시되어 있다. 그 중 하나가 태권도 겨루기 경기를 표현한 그림자 도안이다. 모로코는 1974년 김명옥, 이용기, 윤창영 사범에 의해 태권도가 뿌리내렸다. 김명옥 사범은 어려운 여건을 극복하고 모로코 국왕 핫산 2세와 왕실 경호원들에게 태권도를 전수했다. 국가대표출신 김상천 사범은 1985년 대한태권도협회 추천으로 파견되어 본격적으로 태권도의 저변을 확대했고 선수들의 실력 수준도 높이는데 큰 기여를 했다. 모로코태권도협회는 1986년에 등록되었고 모하메드 사디 엘 만드쥬라 씨가 회장이다.

The 50th Anniversary stamp of Moroccan sports was issued in 2007. In the stamp, Moroccan sports champions are depicted according to their disciplines. We can see the shadow image of a Taekwondo sparring scene. Taekwondo in Morocco was spread thanks to Master Myung Ok Kim. Despite a difficult situation, he introduced Taekwondo to King Hassan the Second and his security guards. A Korean National Team Member, Master Sang Cheon Kim, was dispatched to Morocco through the recommendation of the Korean Taekwondo Association. He expanded the base of Taekwondo wholeheartedly and contributed to raising the athletes competition skill standard. The Morocco Taekwondo Federation was enrolled in 1986 and is led today by its president, Mr. Mohamed Saadi El Mandjra.

- 국가명 : 모로코. 2007
  Nation : Morocco
- 자료 평가 Evaluation :
  ① 태권도가치성 Taekwondo Value ★★★★☆
  ② 도안성 Design ★★★★☆
  ③ 희귀성 Rarity ★★★★☆
- 우표 구성 : 기념 우표 1종
  Stamp Composition : single stamp

IV-23. 호신술 개념의 도미니카공화국 우표
A Stamp Featuring Self-Defense from Dominican Republic

남미의 섬나라 도미니카공화국은 어린이들을 대상으로 한 성적(性的), 상업적 착취를 금지하는 특별우표를 발행했다. 어린이 보호단체인 '코나니 CONANI' 가 주도한 사회 계몽 운동의 일환이다. 우표에는 자기방어 호신술로서 동양 무술과 복싱이 상징적으로 도입되었다. 어린이들이 태권도를 포함한 동양무예의 발차기로 사회악에 당당하게 대항한다는 흥미로운 개념이 반영되었다. 동양무예의 호신술적 특성을 부각시킨 것은 이 우표가 처음이 아닐까 싶다.

The Dominican Republic issued a special stamp to advocate the prohibition of sexual and commercial exploitation of children. It is part of a social purification movement led by 'CONANI'(National Council for Children and Young People), which is a children advocacy and protection organization. In this stamp, the themes of East Asian martial arts and boxing are shown, to suggest these as means of self-defense. It is an interesting stamp that reflects the idea that social evil can be defeated by an East Asian, specifically Taekwondo, martial arts kick. This stamp may be the first that emphsizes the self defense concept of the Asian martial arts.

기념 초일봉투
First Day of Issue Cover

☞ 국가명 : 도미니카공화국 II. 2008
　Nation : Dominican Republic II
☞ 자료 평가 Evaluation :
① 태권도가치성 Taekwondo Value ★★★★☆
② 도안성 Design ★★★★☆
③ 희귀성 Rarity ★★★★☆
☞ 우표 구성 : 기념 우표 1종
　Stamp Composition : single stamp

우표로 보는 태권도 발자취 The Evolution of Taekwondo as Seen Through Postage Stamps

IV-24. 제18회 이스라엘 마카비아게임
The 18th Maccabiah Games in Israel

1921년에 창설된 유대인의 스포츠 기구인 세계마카비연맹이 주최하는 국제 스포츠대회가 마카비아경기이다. 전세계 여러 나라에 흩어져 살고 있는 유대인들이 국가를 대표하여 참가하며 4년마다 한 번씩 열린다. 태권도 경기도 종목에 포함되어 있는데 우표에 나온 태권도 이미지가 다소 어색하다. 2009년 마카비아 태권도 경기는 5개국 19명의 선수들이 참가하여 남자 3체급과 여자 4체급 등 총 7체급에 걸쳐 진행됐다. 종합우승은 주최국 이스라엘이 차지했다. 2005년에 한국대사배 이스라엘 청소년태권도대회가 열리기도 했다.

The Maccabiah Games is a sports event held by the Maccabiah Federation, associated with the Maccabi World Union established by Jewish sports leaders in 1921. The Games, initiated in 1932, are held every four years, and the worldwide Jewish diaspora represent the country in which they live. Taekwondo is included as a discipline, however the image depicted on the stamp is a little unorthodox. 19 competitors from 5 countries competed in three male divisions and four female divisions in the 2009 Maccabiah Taekwondo Championships. The winner of the overall total scores was Israel, the organizing country, which also hosted the Israel Youth Taekwondo Championships in 2005.

☞ 국가명 : 이스라엘 II. 2009
  Nation : Israel II

☞ 자료 평가 Evaluation :
① 태권도가치성 Taekwondo Value ★★★★☆
② 도안성 Design ★★★☆☆
③ 희귀성 Rarity ★★★☆☆

☞ 우표 구성 : 기념우표 1종
  Stamp Composition : single stamp

기념 초일봉투
First Day Cover

IV-25. 하계 스포츠 경기 종목
The Summer Sports Event in Nevis

2009년 남미 카리브해의 섬나라 네비스(정식국가명; 세인트 키츠 네비스)에서 태권도 우표가 발행되었다. 네 가지 하계 스포츠(올림픽) 종목중 태권도 그림이 포함되었고 발차기 동작을 픽토그램으로 표현했다. 아울러 두 가지 다른 크기와 색깔로 그려 넣고 햇살 무늬를 배경으로 깔아 역동성을 강조했다. 총인구 4만 명인 네비스의 태권도 역사와 현황은 잘 알려지지 않았다. 1998년에 세계태권도연맹 회원국으로 등록되었다.

This Taekwondo stamp was issued by Nevis (official name: Saint Kitts-Nevis), an island in the Caribbean, in 2009. Taekwondo was one of four sport disciplines included that are official summer Olympic events. The stamp depicts a pictogram figure doing a kicking movement with its shadow casting a different color. The history and current status of Taekwondo in Nevis, a country with a population of 40,000, is not well-known. Nevis was registered as a member country of the World Taekwondo Federation in 1998.

☞ 국가명 : 네비스. 2009
　 Nation : Nevis

☞ 자료 평가 Evaluation :
① 태권도가치성 Taekwondo Value ★★★★★
② 도안성 Design ★★★★★
③ 희귀성 Rarity ★★★☆☆

☞ 우표 구성 : 4종 중 1종
　 Stamp Composition : 1 of 4 stamps

소형쉬이트
a Souvenir Sheet

우표로 보는 태권도 발자취 The Evolution of Taekwondo as Seen Through Postage Stamps

IV-26. 제25회 세르비아 유니버시아드경기
The 25th University Games in Serbia

☞ 국가명 : 세르비아. 2009
   Nation : Serbia

☞ 자료 평가 Evaluation :
① 태권도가치성 Taekwondo Value ★★★★☆
② 도안성 Design ★★★★★
③ 희귀성 Rarity ★★★☆☆

☞ 우표 구성 : 2종 중 1종
   Stamp Composition : 1 of 2 stamps

2009년 세르비아에서 열린 제 25회 유니버시아드대회를 기념하는 우표에 태권도 이미지가 포함되었다. 대회 마스코트가 헤드기어와 몸통보호대를 착용하고 발차기하는 모습이 우표에 나온다. 이번 유니버시아드대회부터 태권도 품새 부문이 추가되어 5개 금메달이 추가 배정되는 성과를 올렸다. 국제스포츠 대회에 품새 부문이 정식 종목으로 채택된 최초의 사례가 되어 태권도 기술의 확장 보급에 큰 계기가 되었다. 1970년 박선재, 이경명 사범이 세르비아에 태권도 씨앗을 뿌렸다. 세르비아의 전신(前身) 공산국가 유고는 1975년 한국에서 개최된 제2회 세계태권도선수권대회에 참가했다. 세르비아태권도협회는 1975년에 세계태권도연맹으로 정식 등록되었고 에드먼드 슈람 씨가 회장이다.

A Taekwondo image is included among the stamps issued to commemorate the 25th Universiade held in Serbia in 2009. This stamp depicts the mascot of the event wearing a head and chest protector, and performing a kick. It also includes other images of the mascot participating in various other sports. Beginning with this event, the Taekwondo 'Poomsae'(form) division was included as an official sport, and as such, five additional gold medals were allocated. This was the first time that Taekwondo 'Poomsae' had been adopted as an official sport in an international sports event, and thusly marked an important occasion in the development and dissemination of Taekwondo techniques. In 1970, Masters Sun Jae Park and Kyung Myung Lee planted the seed of Taekwondo in Serbia. Yugoslavia, the former name for Serbia, participated in the 2nd World Taekwondo Championships held in South Korea in 1975. The Serbian Taekwondo Association became officially registered as a member of the World Taekwondo Federation in 1975, and is led today by President Edmund Schramm.

함께 나온 우표세트
accompanied stamp set

V

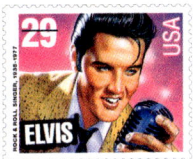

태권도와 동양무예를 사랑했던 엘비스 프레슬리

Elvis Presley, An Enthusiast of Taekwondo and Other Asian Martial Arts

미국인들로부터 가장 총애받는 엘비스 우표(1993년, 미국 발행)가 붙은 사제 초일봉투. 태권도 발차기 사진으로 만든 희귀한 우편자료다.

Here is the First Day Cover featuring the Elvis stamp most favored by Americans (Issued in the US, in 1993). This is a rare postal item created from a photo of a Taekwondo kick.

20세기를 살았던 가장 유명한 인물로 엘비스 프레슬리(1935~1977)가 꼽힌다. 엘비스는 세계적으로 널리 알려진 록큰롤의 황제이었기도 하지만 클린턴, 오바마 미국대통령과 더불어 태권도를 연마했던 태권도인이었다. 젊은 시절 가라테를 수련하여 일찍이 유단자가 되었고 그의 나이 38세에 한국의 이강희 대사범으로부터 태권도를 배워 고단자가 되었다. 엘비스 얼굴이 담긴 수 백장의 세계 각국 우표를 통해 그가 얼마나 많은 대중적인 인기를 누렸는지 알 수 있다. 그 중에 그가 태권도하는 모습이 담긴 3장의 우표가 있다. 아프리카 배냉 우표 2종과 아시아 타지키스탄 우표 1종에서 엘비스의 태권도 자세와 동작을 엿볼 수 있다.

Elvis Presley (1935~1977) is ranked as one of the most famous people of the 20th century. Elvis is known world-wide as the emperor of rock and roll, but like US Presidents Barack Obama and Bill Clinton, he was also a practitioner of Taekwondo. Training in Karate in his early days, he quickly earned a 1st degree black belt. At the age of 38, he learned Taekwondo from Grandmaster Kang Rhee and obtained the high rank of black belt in Taekwondo as well. With the several hundred stamps from various countries featuring Elvis' face, we can see the great popularity Elvis enjoyed. Out of all of these, there are three stamps that depict images of him doing Taekwondo. In two stamps from the African country of Benin and one type from Tajikistan, we can get a sense of Elvis's Taekwondo stances and movements.

우표로 보는 태권도 발자취　The Evolution of Taekwondo as Seen Through Postage Stamps

V-1. 엘비스 자신이 손수 디자인한 도복을 입고 태극기 앞에서 겨루기 자세를 취한 모습이 담긴 우표 2종

Taekwondo Stamp No. 056

엘비스가 자신이 손수 디자인한 특별도복을 입고 겨루기 자세를 취한 모습이 우표로 나왔다. 태극기 앞에서 이강희 대사범의 지도로 겨루기 자세를 잡은 엘비스가 멋진 모습을 연출하고 있다. 엘비스는 유명인사가 된 이후에 본인이나 외동딸 리사가 납치될지 모른다는 염려로 태권도를 시작했다고 한다. 수련 중에 이강희 대사범의 태권도 실력과 철학에 감명을 받아 항시 그에게 존경심을 표했다고 한다.

Shown on the stamp is an image of Elvis wearing his own custom-made Dobok(martial art uniform) readied in a sparring stance. Through the teachings of Grandmaster Kang Rhee, Elvis is stylishly performing while in a sparring stance in front of the Taegeukgi(The Korean Flag). After becoming a famous celebrity, Elvis began to learn Taekwondo from fears that either he or his only daughter Lisa would be kidnapped. During his training, Elvis was impressed by Grandmaster Kang Rhee's immense skill and philosophy and always expressed his utmost respect.

☞ 국가명 : 베냉 Ⅰ-1. 2003
　 Nation : Benin Ⅰ-1
☞ 자료 평가 Evaluation :
① 태권도가치성 Taekwondo Value ★★★★★
② 도안성 Design ★★★★★
③ 희귀성 Rarity ★★★☆☆
☞ 우표 구성 : 6종 중 1종
Stamp Composition :
1 of 6 stamps on a souvenir sheet

엘비스의 무예 수련 모습을 담은 소형시트
A Souvenir Sheet featuring Elvis's Sparring stance

2 Stamps of Elvis in a Sparring Stance in Front of the Taegeukgi(the Flag of Korea) While Wearing His Own Custom-made Uniform.

배냉에서 발행된 앞의 우표와 동일한 도안을 약간 변형하여 액면가가 높은 무공소형쉬이트로도 발행되었다. 원래 우표를 절단하는 구멍이 없는 무공쉬이트는 일반 우표나 구멍이 있는 소형시트보다 훨씬 희귀성이 높다. 엘비스의 동양 무예에 대한 열정은 대단했다. 이강희 대사범의 영향을 받아 특히 날쌔고 역동적인 태권도 발차기를 선호했던 엘비스였다. 가라테와 태권도, 권법(겜포) 등 여러 무예를 두루 배우면서 무술 영화를 제작하려는 계획도 있었다.

With a slight variation from the previously mentioned stamp issued in Benin, the same design was also issued as a single imperforated souvenir sheet and given a higher face value. Imperforated sheets with no holes in the stamps are much rarer than the stamps themselves or souvenir sheets that have no holes in them. Elvis had a huge passion for Asian martial arts. Through Grandmaster Kang Rhee's influence, Elvis preferred the particularly agile and dynamic kicks found in Taekwondo. During his martial arts training Karate, Taekwondo and Kempo, he had also planned to make a martial arts movie.

Taekwondo Stamp No. 057

☞ 국가명 : 베냉 Ⅰ-2, 2003
　Nation : Benin Ⅰ-2

☞ 자료 평가 Evaluation :
① 태권도가치성 Taekwondo Value ★★★★★
② 도안성 Design ★★★★★
③ 희귀성 Rarity ★★★★☆

☞ 우표 구성 : 무공 소형시트 1종
　Stamp Composition :
　Single imperforated souvenir sheet

엘비스가 겨루기 자세를 취한 모습이 담긴 무공 소형시트
An imperforated Souvenir Sheet depicting Elvis' sparring stance

우표로 보는 태권도 발자취　The Evolution of Taekwondo as Seen Through Postage Stamps

V-2. 태권도 발차기로 상대를 공격하는 엘비스
A Scene of Elvis Attacking an Opponent with a Taekwondo Kick

검정색 도복을 입고 연습 상대에게 발차기를 하는 엘비스의 무예 수련 모습이 다른 엘비스 추모 우표에 나와 있다. 우표의 원본 사진을 보면 앞 사진과는 다른 도안의 태극기 앞에서 돌려차기로 상대의 몸통을 공격하고 있다. 태권도, 가라테 등 동양무예를 지극히 사랑했던 엘비스는 빠듯한 일정 중에도 틈틈이 무예 수련을 즐겨했다. 엘비스는 정신적 집중과 심리적 평정을 취하기 위한 심신 수양을 추구했을 뿐 아니라 자신의 로큰롤 공연에도 무예 동작을 적극적으로 활용하기도 했다.

An image of Elvis training in martial arts while wearing a black uniform and performing a kick on a sparring partner appears in other memorial stamps. Looking at the original image we can see that he is attacking his opponent with a roundhouse kick to the body, in front of the Korean Flag. The image is a different design from that in the previous picture. A great lover of oriental arts such as Taekwondo and Karate, Elvis enjoyed training in them whenever he had a few moments to spare in his exceedingly busy schedule. In trying to achieve mental concentration and psychological serenity, Elvis not only pursued the cultivation of his body and mind, but he also enthusiastically made use of martial arts movements in his rock and roll performances.

☞ 국가명 : 타지키스탄 II. 2001
　Nation : Tajikistan II
☞ 자료 평가 Evaluation :
① 태권도가치성 Taekwondo Value ★★★★★
② 도안성 Design ★★★★★
③ 희귀성 Rarity ★★★★☆
☞ 우표 구성 : 9종 중 1종
Stamp Composition :
1 of 9 stamps on a souvenir sheet

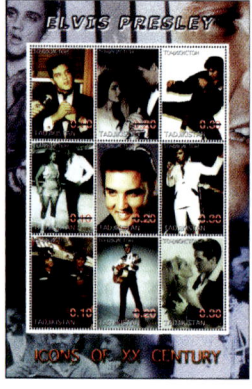

엘비스의 발차기 모습이 담긴 소형시트
A Souvenir Sheet featuring Elvis's Kicking scene

VI

태권도 발차기를 활용한 무술영화배우 부루스 리
Bruce Lee, The Famous Martial Arts Movie Star Used Taekwondo Kicks

부루스 리의 고향, 홍콩에서 발행된 기념 우표
A memorial stamp issued in Hong Kong, where Bruce Lee grew up

부루스와 수련중인 이준구 대사범
Bruce Lee & Grandmaster Jhoon Rhee

20세기 세계 저명인사 중에 부루스 리(1940~1973)도 빠지지 않는다. 부루스는 불과 단 4편의 무술 영화로 온 세계 젊은이들의 우상이 되어 동양무술 붐을 일으켰다. 부루스는 원래 손기술 위주의 영춘권 등 중국무술에 능숙했지만 후일 태권도, 복싱, 레슬링 등 여러 가지 무술을 취합하여 '절권도'를 창시했다. 그는 민첩하고 다양한 발차기가 장기인 태권도를 도입하여 그의 무술과 영화에 적극 활용했다. 부루스의 활약에 힘입어 태권도는 전 세계적으로 더욱 활발히 보급되는 성과를 올렸다. 이 장에서는 부루스 소재의 우표들 중 태권도와 관련된 발차기 테마 우표들을 소개한다.

When talking about the famous men in the 20th century, one simply cannot exclude the world-class actor Bruce Lee (1940-1973). Through his four famous martial arts movies, which were shown all over the world, Bruce Lee successfully created a boom in Asian martial arts, especially among those of the young generation. Although Bruce Lee was initially more proficient in the fist techniques of Wing Chun or Chinese martial arts, he later also developed his ability in other forms of martial arts such as Taekwondo, boxing, wrestling, and so forth. With combinations of techniques from all these martial arts and fighting art styles, Bruce Lee then created his own style, which is called Jeet Kune Do (or translated as 'The Way of the Intercepting Fist'). Consequently, in this chapter, I will introduce the postage stamps of Bruce Lee, those which are related to stamps with a theme of Taekwondo kicks.

VI-1. 날렵한 발차기는 부루스 리의 주특기
Bruce Lee's Signature Dynamic Kick

영화 맹룡과강 장면이 나온 우표. 경쾌한 발놀림과 훼인트 모션, 재빠른 연결 발차기 등 태권도 기술을 활용한 부르스의 영화마다 경이적 흥행 기록을 올렸다.

Stamps of "The Way of the Dragon". Bruce Lee's box office smash hit films all feature Taekwondo techniques such as dynamic footwork, feignt motions, and speedy combination kicks.

부루스는 여러 편의 영화에서 민첩한 발차기 연결 기술로 관객들을 사로잡았다. 그는 오랫동안 연마한 영춘권의 손기술보다 태권도식 발차기를 더 선호했다. 영화의 시각적 효과상 동작이 활발하고 화려한 발차기가 손기술에 비해 훨씬 멋있는 장면을 만들어 낼 수 있기 때문이었다. 실전에서도 빠르게 움직이는 상대방을 얼굴, 옆구리 등 급소를 차서 제압할 수 있는 강점도 있다. 태권도식 발차기는 신속하고 다양한 변화를 지닐 뿐 아니라 거리와 공방 타이밍을 적절히 조절하는 발놀림과 훼인트 모션을 보태어 더욱 위력을 발휘했다

In his movies, Bruce Lee was always able to fascinate the audience with his explosive and well-coordinated kicks. Although Bruce Lee had long-cultivated his Wing Chun-based fist techniques, he preferred doing scenes with Taekwondo kicks. This is because he considered kicking techniques to be more spectacular, and as a result, they made the movies more engaging to viewers. Kicking techniques also allow us to strike the enemy's vital spots, such as the face or trunk even while the opponent is moving quickly. Taekwondo kicking techniques are considered more powerful not only because they emphasize speed and a variety of footwork application but also because they enable one to control the timing of kicks as well as to create feignt motions.

부루스 리와 이준구 대사범 Bruce Lee & Grandmaster Jhoon Rhee

VI-2. 전광석화같은 부루스 리의 돌려차기
Bruce Lee's Roundhouse kick-like a Bolt of Lightning

영화 '용쟁호투'와 '사망유희'에서 부루스가 돌려차기를 연기하는 장면이 나온 우표. 부루스는 돌려차기를 응용한 갖가지 기술을 즐겨 구사했다. 돌려차기는 발차기 중 가장 빠르고 적중률이 높을 뿐 아니라 다양한 연결 기술을 구사할 수 있고 공격 후 수비 귀환이 빨라서 장점이 많은 기술이며 태권도의 장기로 꼽힌다. 발차기는 가라테, 우슈 등 다른 무술에서도 행해지지만 민첩하고 응용 기술이 다양한 태권도식 발차기가 더욱 많이 알려져 있다. 당시 미국에서는 지금의 이종격투기대회처럼 무술가끼리 겨루는 오픈 대회가 자주 열렸다. 실전 발차기에 능한 한국의 여러 태권도 사범들은 각종 실전 무술 대회에서 발군의 실력을 보였고 부루스는 이들과 친밀하게 교류했다. 부루스는 그의 절친한 친구가 된 이준구 대사범을 비롯하여 재미 사범 출신이자 멕시코 태권도계의 대부 문대원과 재미 유병용 대사범, 태권도 경기인 출신의 이규석 교수와도 교류하며 실전에 유용한 발차기 기술들을 습득했다.

The stamp below depicts a roundhouse kick which Bruce Lee used in movies such as 'Enter The Dragon (1973)' and 'The Game of Death (1978)'. Bruce Lee enjoyed and made full use of the roundhouse kick. Among all the kicking techniques in Taekwondo, the roundhouse kick is considered to be not only the fastest and most accurate kick, but also the most effective. This is bacause it can be combined with various other techniques and used as a defense technique to minimize the effect of an enemy's counterattack. This is one of Taekwondo's strong points. Even though other martial arts such as Karate and Wu-shu are also known for their distinctive kicks, Taekwondo kicks are more popular due to their quickness of application and variety of associated movements. During the time that Bruce Lee was living in the United States, open tournaments involving various martial arts were often held. Among the participants of these tournaments were also participants from Korea. They were mostly Taekwondo masters. Bruce Lee exchanged ideas and developed his kicking ability with them. Moreover, Bruce Lee then eventually became close friends with several Korean Taekwondo masters, such as Jhoon Rhee, David Moon(in Mexico), Byung Yoo and Professor Kyu-Seok Lee(who was initially a Taekwondo competitor). By interacting with these Taekwondo masters, Bruce was able to learn more about and further develop his kicking techniques.

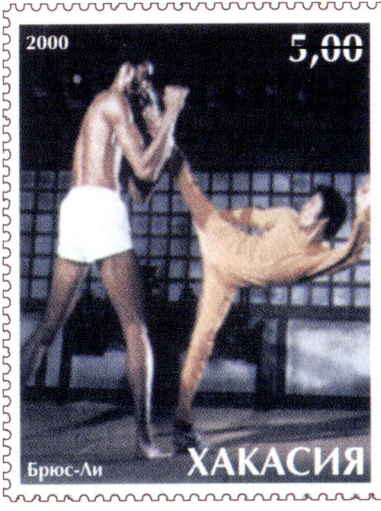

VI-3. 부루스 리의 옆차기와 후려차기
Bruce Lee's Side kick and Hook kick

기존의 형식에 치중한 고전 무술에서 벗어나서 실전성을 추구한 부루스에게 태권도의 실전적 발차기는 각별한 관심 대상이 되었다. 정작 부루스 본인은 공개적인 실전 겨루기 대회에 직접 참가하지는 않고 특별 시범만을 보였지만 실전 지향적인 무술가로서 진면목을 발휘했다. 부루스는 옆차기로 상대의 무릎이나 낭심, 명치 급소를 가격하는 호신술을 서적으로 펴내기도 했다

Aside from the classic martial arts that existed at his time, Bruce Lee was most strongly interested in Taekwondo's kicking techniques. Although Bruce Lee did not actually participate in open martial arts tournaments, he demonstrated various kinds of martial arts at them in order to display the true character of a fighter. In addition, Bruce Lee also published a book, which contains the invaluable art of self-defense by simply using Taekwondo's sidekick aimed at an opponent's knee, scrotum, solar plexus(the pit of the stomach), and other vital parts of the body.

우표에 나온 부루스의 옆차기는. 이준구 대사범으로 부터 전수 받은 발차기 기술로 알려져 있다.
The side kick, which is demonstrated by Bruce Lee in these stamps, was originally taught by Master Jhoon Rhee.

부루스의 영화에서 볼 수 있는 경쾌한 뒤후려차기 기술도 당시 그와 교류했던 한국의 여러 태권도 사범들의 영향을 받았다.
In Bruce Lee's movies, one can also see his nimble spinning hook kick. His technique was influenced by various Korean Taekwondo masters

부루스와 이규석 교수
Bruce Lee & Prof. Kyu-Seok Lee

VI-4. 부루스 리는 뛰어차기로 액션 효과를 높이다
Bruce Lee's Jumping Kicks were an Effective Aspect of His Movie Action Sequences.

부루스는 영화에서 뛰어차기 기술도 많이 사용했다. 뛰어앞차기, 뛰어옆차기, 뛰어돌려차기 등 박진감 있는 액션 기술로 적을 무찌르는 장면은 관객들을 열광시켰다. 뛰어차기는 실제 상대와 겨루는 상황에서는 적중력은 떨어지지만 영화에서는 박진감 있는 장면을 만들어낸다. 뛰어차기는 이준구 대사범의 특기였으며 태권도 주요 기술이었다. 이준구 대사범은 부루스에게 "아무리 무술 실력이 뛰어나도 정신수양이 따르지 않는다면 무도가 될 수 없다."고 부루스를 일깨우기도 했다.

In his movies, Bruce Lee performed a lot of jump kick techniques. With his front jump kick, side jump kick, roundhouse jump kick, and other dynamic techniques, Bruce Lee was able to capture the viewers' attentions. While in reality, jump kicks are less accurate than other types of kicks, a jump kick actually creates an eye-catching scene. As one of the main techniques in Taekwondo, the jump kick was originally the specialty of the great master Jhoon Rhee. Master Rhee once gave this piece of advice to Bruce Lee. "Even if one has developed various skills in martial arts, one cannot become anybody without developing his mental strength as well."

부루스의 뛰어차기가 나온 우표
Bruce Lee's jump kick within a stamp

부루스와 한국인 태권도 사범
Bruce Lee & A Taekwondo Master

VI-5. 무술 영화계의 전설이 된 부루스 리
Bruce Lee Becomes a Legend within Martial Arts Movies.

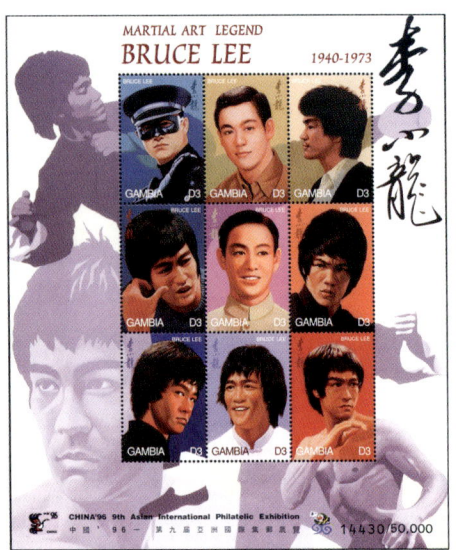

부루스와 태권도는 상호 발전적 관계였다. 부루스는 미국에서 활동했던 여러 한인 태권도 사범들의 발차기 기술들을 습득하여 영화 액션에 최대한 활용했다. 그의 무술 영화가 성공하기에는 태권도 발차기가 큰 몫을 담당했다. 한편 그의 영화는 성공적인 흥행과 비례하여 발차기가 중심 기술인 태권도를 널리 알리는데 막대한 기여를 했다. 부루스가 활동했던 1960-70년대 당시 미국 영화계에 등장하여 아시아인으로서 크게 성공한 사람은 오직 부루스 뿐이었다. 당시 그는 흑인과 아시아인들이 냉대받던 미국에서 뿐 아니라 전세계적으로 선풍적인 인기를 구가했던 유일한 동양계 영화인이자 무술가였다.

Both Bruce Lee and Taekwondo simultaneously developed together. In the United States, where he did the majority of his filming, Bruce Lee learned his kicking techniques from various Korean Taekwondo masters, and he performed these in his movies. On one hand, Taekwondo kicks greatly contributed to the success of Bruce's movies. On the other hand, with the success of his movies, Taekwondo also gained the opportunity to be spread all over the world. As a consequence, Taekwondo has been growing more and more popular ever since. During the 'Bruce Lee era' of the 1960s and 1970s, Bruce Lee was the only successful Asian actor in the American film industry. He was a martial artist as well as an actor and one who successfully gained popularity not only in the United States, where at the time, African-Americans and Asian-Americans were once discriminated against, but also all over the world.

1988년 제24회 서울 하계 올림픽 시범종목 거행
A Demonstration Sport at The 24th Olympiad – The 1988 Seoul Summer Olympic Games

1988년 서울 올림픽경기대회 개막식 광경
Opening ceremony of the 1988 Seoul Summer Olympic Games

대한민국 역사상 최대의 국제 행사인 서울올림픽은 160개국 13,304명의 임원, 선수가 참가하여 서구권과 공산권이 화합한 세계 평화 스포츠제전이었다. 주최국 한국의 제안 종목인 태권도는 야구, 배드민턴과 함께 시범종목으로 포함되었다. 한국의 서울올림픽 유치와 성공적인 대회 개최는 발전된 한국의 위상을 세계 만방에 떨치는 계기가 되었다. 아울러 태권도의 시범종목 거행은 태권도 종목이 올림픽 정식 종목으로 되는 중대한 발판이 되었다. 태권도가 올림픽에 등장하면서 태권도를 소재로 한 우표들이 계속해서 나타나기 시작했다. 이 단원에는 서울올림픽 기념으로 8개국에서 발행된 14종의 태권도 소재 및 관련 우취자료를 소개한다.

The Seoul Summer Olympic Games, the biggest international sports event in Korean history, was a peaceful world sports festival supported not only by western countries but also communist countries, and included 160 countries along with 13,304 officials and competitors. Taekwondo, the suggested discipline by the organizing country Korea, was included as a demonstration sport along with baseball and badminton. By successfully hosting the Seoul Summer Olympic Games, Korea took the opportunity to soar in national prestige throughout the world. At the same time, by being the host country's chosen demonstration sport, Taekwondo made an important step towards being accepted as an official sport in subsequent Olympics. With the appearance of Taekwondo in the Olympics, more stamps with a Taekwondo theme began to appear regularly. In this chapter, I will be introducing fourteen stamps and the related philatelic resources issued by eight different countries to commemorate the Seoul Summer Olympic Games.

VII-1. 마카오 태권도 우표
A Taekwondo Stamp from Macao

Taekwondo Stamp No. 059

☞ 마카오(포루투갈령) I . 1988
  (Portuguese) Macao I

☞ 자료 평가 Evaluation :
① 태권도가치성 Taekwondo Value ★★★★☆
② 도안성 Design ★★★★★
③ 희귀성 Rareness ★★★★☆

☞ 우표 구성 : 기념우표 5종 중 1종
  Stamp Composition : 1 of 5 stamps

1988년 서울올림픽 기념으로 마카오에서 멋진 태권도 우표를 발행했다. 마카오는 1999년까지 포르투갈의 행정적 통치를 받다가 1999년 중국의 특별 행정구(SAR)가 되었다. 서울올림픽 기념 마카오 우표 4종 중에는 태권도가 없었지만 별도의 소형시트에는 태권도가 추가되었다. 우표는 태권도 선수가 보호대를 착용하고 발차기하는 모습과 한문과 영어로 태권도 글자를 표기했다. 마카오의 이 우표는 완벽한 도안의 태권도 우표로 높이 평가할 수 있다. 마카오태권도협회(회장 와이퓨 웡씨)는 2000년에 창립되어 2002년도에 세계태권도연맹 회원국으로 등록되었다. 마카오 태권도 대부 이동섭 사범은 마카오 태권도 보급에 지대한 역할을 하여 2006년 태권도진흥재단(이사장 이대순)으로부터 자랑스런 태권도인상을 수상했다.

In 1988, Macao issued an appropriate Taekwondo stamp to commemorate the Seoul Summer Olympic Games. Macao had been ruled by Portugal administratively until 1999, wherafter it became a special administrative region of China. Macao issued four stamps to commemorate the Seoul Summer Olympics. Although it did not yet have an official national Taekwondo organization, Taekwondo was included in the release the small sheet. This stamp depicts a competitor wearing a chest protector throwing a kick. Taekwondo is written in Korean and English. This stamp issued by Macao is highly appreciated as a Taekwondo-themed stamp with a perfect design. The Macao Taekwondo Association (President, Mr. William Wai Pui Wong) was established in 2000 and became registered as a member country organization of the World Taekwondo Federation in 2002. The father of Macau Taekwondo, Grandmaster Dong Seob Lee, played an enormous role in promoting Taekwondo in Macao. For this reason, the Taekwondo Promotion Foundation (Chairman Dai Soon Lee) presented him with the merit award in 2006.

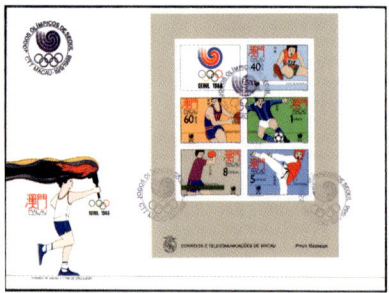

기념 초일봉투 The First Day Cover

VIII-2. 도미니카연방 태권도 우표 2종
Two Taekwondo Stamps from Dominica

도미니카연방은 중앙아메리카 카리브해에 위치한 섬나라로서 영국 자치령으로 있다가 1978년 독립한 신생국가이다. 서울올림픽을 기념하여 4종짜리 기념우표 중에 태권도가 포함되었다. 한 여성이 도복을 입고 옆차기를 하는 동작과 함께 태권도 영문 글씨가 선명히 표기되었다. 아래쪽 우표는 동일한 우표에다 글씨를 추가로 인쇄한 가쇄우표(假刷郵票)이다. 여자부 플라이급에서 우승을 차지한 한국의 추난률 선수 이름이 가쇄되어 재발매된 우표이다. 서울올림픽 시범 종목인 태권도 경기에서 남녀 각각 8체급씩 거행되었다. 여자부에서 미국이 금메달을 3개를 획득하여 금메달 두 개인 한국과 대만을 추월했다. 도미니카연방은 1999년에 등록되었고 현재 세드릭 펀블턴씨가 회장이다.

The Commonwealth of Dominica is an island country located in the Caribbean Sea. The country gained its independence in 1978 from the United Kingdom. Among the series of four stamps to commemorate the Seoul Summer Olympic Games, Taekwondo was included. Along with the figure of a woman performing a side kick, Taekwondo is written in English. The overprinted stamp below has printed letters in addition to the design mentioned above. The stamp depicting the female competitor who won the flyweight division, Nanryul Choo, was overprinted for reissuance. At the Seoul Olympic Games, Taekwondo was a demonstration sport that had 8 divisions each for both men and women. In the women's division, the US got three gold medals and surpassed Korea and Taiwan, who earned two gold medals each. The Commonwealth of Dominica was enrolled in 1999 and Mr. Cedric Pemberton is the current President.

Taekwondo Stamp No. 060-061

- 국가명 : 도미니카연방. 1988
  Nation : Dominica
- 자료 평가 Evaluation :
  ① 태권도가치성 Taekwondo Value ★★★★★
  ② 도안성 Design ★★★★★
  ③ 희귀성 Rareness ★★★★☆
- 우표 구성 : 4종 중 1종
  Stamp Composition : 1 of 4 stamps

우표로 보는 태권도 발자취 The Evolution of Taekwondo as Seen Through Postage Stamps

VII-3. 바레인 태권도 우표
A Taekwondo Stamp from Bahrain

Taekwondo Stamp No. 062

중동의 유일한 섬나라 바레인에서 발행된 태권도 우표는 서울올림픽 공식 엠블렘과 태권도 픽토그램을 도안했다. 바레인은 페르시아만에 위치한 인구 80만의 섬나라인데 1977년 중동태권도연맹 결성에 참여했다. 이후 중동태권도연맹 주최로 중동 지역 태권도 선수권대회가 열리는 등 태권도의 기틀이 잡히기 시작했다. 당시 중동 건설 붐을 타고 현지에 진출한 민간 기업체의 기술진에 태권도 유단자가 의외로 많아 태권도 열풍에 한 몫을 담당했다. 당시 바레인에는 한국인 사범이 진출하여 태권도 지도 활동을 전개했다. 1979년에는 한국의 태권도시범단이 바레인을 포함한 중동 지역에 파견되어 태권도 홍보 행사를 펼쳤다. 바레인태권도협회는 1977년 등록되었고 샤이크 모하메드 칼리파 씨가 회장이다.

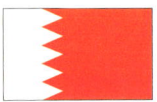

☞ 국가명 : 바레인 I. 1988
  Nation : Bahrain I
☞ 자료 평가 Evaluation :
① 태권도가치성 Taekwondo Value ★★★★★
② 도안성 Design ★★★★★
③ 희귀성 Rareness ★★★★☆
☞ 우표 구성 : 4종 중 1종
Stamp Composition : 1 of 4 stamps

The Taekwondo stamp issued by Bahrain, which is the only island country in the Middle East, contains a design that includes the official emblem of the Seoul Summer Olympic Games and a Taekwondo pictogram. Bahrain is an island nation with 800,000 people located in the Persian Gulf, and it took part in the formation of the Middle Eastern Taekwondo Federation in 1977. Thereafter, with the leadership of the Middle Eastern Taekwondo Federation, Taekwondo championships were held in the region and the Federation started to establish the foundation for a Taekwondo movement. At that time, quite a few South Korean workers who went to the Middle East during the construction boom were black belts in Taekwondo, and they contributed to the growth of Taekwondo there. During this period, Korean Taekwondo Masters arrived and developed Taekwondo education. In 1979, the Korean Taekwondo Demonstration Team was sent to Middle Eastern countries, including Bahrain. The Bahrain Taekwondo Association was enrolled in 1977 and Shaikh Mohamed bin Salman bin Abdulla Al Khalifa is currently President.

함께 나온 우표세트
accompanied stamp set

VII-4. 스와질랜드 태권도 우표
A Taekwondo Stamp from Swaziland

아프리카의 스위스라고 불리는 스와질랜드에서 서울올림픽 기념으로 태권도 우표를 발행했다. 우표에는 품새 태극8장에 나오는 외산틀막기과 태극5장의 옆차기를 담았다. 이 당시에는 태권도 품새든 겨루기 기술이든 태권도를 상징하는 이미지를 제대로만 도안해도 성공적인 태권도 우표가 된다. 그러나 2010년 현재에는 상황이 달라졌다. 1996년 제1회 세계품새선수권대회 개최 이래 품새가 겨루기 대회와는 별도로 국제대회 규모로 거행되고 있다. 앞으로는 올림픽처럼 겨루기 대회를 기념한다면 태권도 우표에도 겨루기 도안이 들어가야 한다. 1974년 김화일 사범이 수년 동안 머물면서 스와질랜드에 태권도를 보급했다. 1997년에는 한국 국가대표 시범단이 스와질랜드, 남아공화국 등을 방문하여 시범 행사를 가지기도 했다. 스와질랜드 태권도협회는 1985년에 등록되었다.

Taekwondo stamps were issued to commemorate the Seoul Summer Olympic Games by the Kingdom of Swaziland, which is called the Switzerland of Africa. The stamps depict the "Oisantul-makki ; Single Mountain Block" from Taegeuk Paljang (Forms # 8) and side kick from Taegeuk Ojang (Forms # 5). At the time, if an image symbolizing either a Taekwondo technique of kyeorugi (sparring) or poomsae (forms) was designed well, the stamp was considered a successful Taekwondo stamp. However, things changed in 2010. Since the 1st World Poomsae Championships, held in Seoul in 1996, Poomsae at the international level has established itself seperately from the kyeorugi event. Currently, if one wants to celebrate the kyeorugi event of Taekwondo, which is an official Olympic sport, a kyeorugi design must be included to differentiate it from the poomsae event. We know that Master Hwa Il Kim is the pioneer who initially promoted Taekwondo in Swaziland. In 1997, the Korean National Demonstration Team visited Swaziland and South Africa to perform Taekwondo demonstrations. The Swaziland Taekwondo Association was enrolled in 1985.

Taekwondo Stamp No. 063

☞ 국가명 : 스와질랜드. 1988
　Nation : Swaziland

☞ 자료 평가 Evaluation :
① 태권도가치성 Taekwondo Value ★★★★★
② 도안성 Design ★★★★★
③ 희귀성 Rareness ★★★★☆

☞ 우표 구성 : 4종 중 1종
　Stamp Composition : 1 of 4 stamps

기념 초일봉투
The First Day Cover

우표로 보는 태권도 발자취 The Evolution of Taekwondo as Seen Through Postage Stamps

VII-5. 터키 태권도 우표
A Taekwondo Stamp from Turkey

Taekwondo Stamp No. 064

☞ 국가명 : 터키 . 1988
   Nation : Turkey

☞ 자료 평가 Evaluation :
① 태권도가치성 Taekwondo Value ★★★★★
② 도안성 Design ★★★★★
③ 희귀성 Rareness ★★★★☆

☞ 우표 구성 : 4완 중 1완
   Stamp Composition : 1 of 4 stamps

서울올림픽을 기념하여 태권도 강국 터키에서 나온 태권도 우표이다. 사진이나 그림으로 표현된 다른 우표와는 달리 색상을 입힌 조그만 원으로 태권도 발차기를 도안한 것이 이채롭다. 터키는 오래 전부터 태권도가 보급되어 국제대회에서 상위권에 속한다. 유럽과 아시아를 이어주는 터키에는 조수세, 김두만, 박영철 사범 등이 진출하여 태권도 터전을 닦았다. 터키의 한 대학에서 태권도학과가 개설될 정도로 태권도 붐을 이룬 나라이다. 터키는 유럽태권도연맹 소속으로 1975년에 등록되었으며 메틴 사힌씨가 회장을 맡고 있다.

These are Taekwondo stamps issued by Turkey, a powerful Taekwondo nation, to commemorate the Seoul Summer Olympics. Different from the other stamps that depict a design or a photograph, this design depicting a Taekwondo kick with small colorful dots is quite unique. Taekwondo was introduced into Turkey a long time ago, and so Turkey places among the higher ranks in international tournaments. Turkey is a crossroads of the Eastern and Western worlds. Masters such as Soo Se Jo and Doo Man Kim arrived there and established the foundation for Taekwondo to be disseminated. Turkey is a country where Taekwondo has expanded to the extent that even a college now has a Taekwondo department. The Turkey Taekwondo Association was enrolled in 1975, and is a member of the European Taekwondo Union. It is led today by President Metin Sahin.

기념 초일봉투
The First Day Cover

VII-6. 잠비아 태권도 우표
A Taekwondo stamp from Zambia

서울올림픽을 기념하여 아프리카 잠비아에서 발행된 태권도를 소재로 한 우표로 보인다. 서울올림픽이 한국에서 열리고 한국 태권도가 시범종목으로 채택되자 잠비아에서 태권도 우표를 기획한 것 같다. 당시만 해도 태권도에 관한 정보가 부족해서인지 태권도와 유도가 혼합된 어색한 그림의 소형시트가 되었다. 공신력 있는 우표 발행을 위해 도안 소재에 대한 정확한 정보가 중요하다. 세계태권도연맹은 2006년 베트남에서 열린 총회에서 잠비아를 새 회원국으로 승인했다. 아울러 매년 9월4일을 '태권도의 날'로 정했다. 이 날은 1994년 파리에서 열린 국제올림픽위원회 총회에서 태권도가 올림픽 정식종목으로 채택된 날이다. 첸타 칠루파 씨가 잠비아태권도협회 회장을 맡고 있다.

This is a Taekwondo stamp issued by Zambia commemorating the Seoul Summer Olympic Games. The release of the stamp in Zambia coincided with Taekwondo's adoption as a demonstration sport at the 1988 Seoul Olympics. This small sheet depicts a figure awkwardly performing a mixture of Taekwondo and Judo movements, which is probably due to the nation's lack of proper knowledge regarding Taekwondo at the time. It is important to have accurate information on the subject of a design in order to have public confidence in the depiction. Zambia registered as a member country in the African Taekwondo Union in 2006 and is represented today by President Chenta Chilupa.

Taekwondo Stamp No. 065

☞ 국가명 : 잠비아. 1988
　Nation : Zambia

☞ 자료 평가 Evaluation :
① 태권도가치성 Taekwondo Value ★★★★★
② 도안성 Design ★★★★☆
③ 희귀성 Rareness ★★★★☆

☞ 우표 구성 : 소형시트 1종
　Stamp Composition : single souvenir sheet

함께 나온 우표세트
accompanied stamp set

VII-7. 제24회 서울하계올림픽 경기대회 기념 에콰도르 태권도 우표 1종

1982년 제5회 세계태권도선수권대회를 개최했던 남미 태권도 강국 에콰도르가 서울올림픽이 끝난 이듬 해에 무려 7종의 서울올림픽 기념 우표를 발행했다. 서울올림픽에 대한 에콰도르 정부의 각별한 관심을 엿볼 수 있다. 서울올림픽 공식 마스코트인 호돌이가 7종목 우표로 도안되었는데 태권도 우표에 태권도 대신 유도 호돌이로 바뀌는 큰 오류가 발생했다. 우표의 위쪽 오른편 서울올림픽 엠블렘 바로 아래에 영문으로 'Taekwondo'란 글자가 분명히 씌어져 있음에도 불구하고 태권도 도안 대신 유도가 들어간 보기 드문 사례이다.

Taekwondo savvy country Ecuador, where the 5th World Taekwondo Championships were held in 1982, issued seven stamps to commemorate the upcoming Seoul Olympic Games a year after Seoul was awarded the Games. We can see the special interest that the Ecuador government had for the Seoul Summer Olympic Games. Figurines of the mascot of the event, 'Hodori' (design of a tiger), were designed depicting seven sports, but the stamp designers made a glaring mistake by placing the Judo Hodori instead of the Taekwondo Hodori on the Taekwondo stamp. Switching the Judo design for that of the Taekwondo design was an unfortunate mistake, even though the word Taekwondo is seen clearly written in English in the upper right corner.

☞ 국가명 : 에콰도르 I. 1989
  Nation : Ecuador I

☞ 자료 평가 Evaluation :
① 태권도가치성 Taekwondo Value ★★★★★
② 도안성 Design ★★☆☆☆
③ 희귀성 Rarity ★★★★☆

☞ 우표 구성 : 7종 중 1종
  Stamp Composition : 1 of 7 stamps

함께 나온 우표세트 accompanied stamp set

Two Taekwondo Stamps from Ecuador for the 24th Seoul Summer Olympic Games

우표와 함께 발행된 1장짜리 소형시트에는 태권도를 포함한 7가지 올림픽 종목들이 중앙의 서울올림픽 엠블렘 테두리로 배치되었다. 이 소형시트에도 앞쪽과 같이 도안 착오가 그대로 옮겨졌다. 사실 20년 전만 해도 한국, 일본, 중국 이외의 다른 나라사람들이 맨손 동양무술인 태권도, 유도, 가라테, 우슈를 제대로 구별하는 사람이 그리 많지 않았으리라 판단된다. 태권도는 서울올림픽을 계기로 '날쌔고 다양한 발차기를 특징으로 한국에서 나온 맨손 타격무예이자 올림픽에서도 거행되는 세계적 스포츠 경기'로 널리 인식되었다. 초창기 에콰도르 태권도하면 이범재와 안대섭 사범이 잘 알려져 있다. 안대섭 사범은 1972년 에콰도르에 건너가 대통령 경호실과 육군사관학교에 태권도를 전수하는 등 유능한 지도자로 이름을 떨쳤다. 에콰도르는 1980년 제2회 팬암태권도선수권 대회를 개최했다.

In the souvenir sheet issued along with the stamp, seven Olympic disciplines including Taekwondo are displayed along the border of the center emblem of the Seoul Olympic Games. In this small sheet, the same design mistake is again made. In actuality, about 20 years ago, not many people outside of Korea, China and Japan could differentiate the unarmed disciplines such as Taekwondo, Judo, Karate, and Wushu from each other. Thanks to the Seoul Summer Olympic Games, Taekwondo is known worldwide as an unarmed martial art originating in Korea with signature agile and various kicking techniques and the status of an international sport contest performed even in the Olympics. Masters Bum Jae Kim and Dae Sup An are well-known as the initiators of the promotion of Taekwondo in Ecuador. Master Dae Sup An introduced Taekwondo to the President's security guards and the military academy in 1972, and earned distinction as an proficient leader of Taekwondo. Ecuador held the 2nd Pan Am Taekwondo Championships in 1980.

서울올림픽 공식 태권도 포스터
An Official Poster of Taekwondo
for the 1988 Seoul Summer Olympics

우표로 보는 태권도 발자취 The Evolution of Taekwondo as Seen Through Postage Stamps

VII-8. 다른 방식의 태권도를 추구하는 북한 태권도 관련 우표 9종

1992년 북한에서 열린 제8차 태권도 세계선수권대회 기념 소형시트 1종 및 우표 5종
Single Souvenir Sheet and 5 stamps for the 8th Taekwondo World Championship held in North Korea in 1992

여기 나온 우표들은 북한에서 나온 태권도 우표들이다. 남한과 북한은 같은 민족이면서 불행히도 1945년 이래 수십년 동안 분단되어 군사적, 정치적, 외교적 대결 상황이 작용하여 태권도계에도 큰 영향을 주었다. 1970년대 남한의 태권도 행정단체인 세계태권도연맹이 세계적 위상을 확립하고 태권도가 유수한 스포츠 종목 반열에 올라서자 이전에 활동했던 국제태권도연맹이 극구 반발하는 과정에서 첨예한 갈등도 생겨나기도 했다. 특히 1980년에 접어들어 서울에서 올림픽 개최가 확정되자 스포츠 외교적 열세를 인식한 북한은 태권도를 정치적으로 활용하기 시작했다. 이름은 같은 태권도이지만 경기 방식과 태권도 기술 내용, 행정 관리 조직 면에서 차이를 보인다.

These are the stamps from North Korea. Those of South and North Korea are of the same people, but unfortunately they have been separated since 1945 and have confronted each other militarily, politically and diplomatically since then. This has deeply affected the development of Taekwondo. In the 1970's, the World Taekwondo Federation, the international administrative organization of Taekwondo in South Korea, consolidated its international prestige and rose to the level of many of the leading world sports organizations. The prior existing International Taekwondo Federation protested the development of the World Taekwondo Federation. Sharp conflicts arose between the two organizations. Especially in the 1980's, once South Korea was chosen to host the Summer Olympic Games, North Korea perceived this as an acknowledgement of its inferiority in international sports diplomacy and began to use Taekwondo politically in the international arena. Even though North Korean Taekwondo shares the same name, Taekwondo, it differs in terms of competition style, techniques, administration and organization.

Nine items of Taekwondo Stamps from North Korea (D.P.R.K) where a different style of Taekwondo is persued.

태권도 종목 세계 참피온 (1993)
The I.T.F World Champion

민족 고유 무예 태권도(1995)
The Traditional Korean Martial Art, Taekwondo

예술영화, 평양 날파람 (2008)
An Art Movie, The Pyongyang Martial Art

1980년경 남한의 태권도가 국제적 스포츠로 부상하게 되자 북한은 당시 남한 정부와 반목하고 있던 전(前) 대한태권도협회장이자 국제태권도연맹 총재 최홍희씨를 초청하여 북한에 태권도를 적극 보급했다. 대규모 태권도 전용 체육관을 짓고 태권도 교본을 편찬하고 태권도 소재 우표, 동전 등을 발행하는 등 북한이 태권도의 주도권을 갖기 위해 다방면으로 노력을 기울였다. 북한의 방해에도 불구하고 남한이 주도한 태권도는 올림픽 정식종목으로 채택되었다.

In the 1980's, when South Korean Taekwondo soared as an international sport, North Korea invited Hong Hee Choi, a former President of the Korean Taekwondo Association and President of the International Taekwondo Federation, to North Korea to promote and disseminate Taekwondo within North Korea. North Korea put a lot of effort into devising various ways to take the initiative in promoting the worldwide image of Taekwondo, such as building a grand Taekwondo gymnasium exclusively for its promotion, publishing Taekwondo textbooks, and issuing Taekwondo-themed stamps and coins. South Korean Taekwondo, as opposed to North Korean Taekwondo, was adopted as an official Olympic sport despite opposition from North Korea.

우표로 보는 태권도 발자취   The Evolution of Taekwondo as Seen Through Postage Stamps

 쉼터 · Break Time

서울올림픽 기념 한국우표 5종

Five South Korean Stamps relating to the Seoul Olympic Games

서울올림픽 유치 기념 (1981)
Postage Stamp in Commemoration of
The IOC Decision to hold
The 1988 Olympic Games in Seoul

제5차 세계올림픽연합회 총회기념 (1986)
Postage Stamp Commemorative of
the 5th ANOC General Assembly held
in Seoul

제 109차 I.O.C총회 기념
The 109th IOC Congress

서울올림픽 유치 5주년 기념 (1986) 사마란치 I.O.C 위원장이 실렸다.
5th Anniversary of the IOC Decision to hold
1988 Olympic Games in Seoul (Mr. Juan Autonio Samaranch,
the former International Olympic Committee President)

제29차 국제경기연맹 총연합회 총회 기념
The 29th G.A.I.S.F. Congress & General Assembly

 # 올림픽 정식종목을 향한 힘찬 발걸음
The Critical Steps Toward Becoming An Official Olympic Sport

태권도는 1988년 서울올림픽 시범종목으로 거행된 후 올림픽 정식 종목 승격을 위한 활동을 전개했다. 당시 태권도의 지상 과제는 올림픽 정식종목 채택이었다. 굿윌게임스, 아시안게임 등 메이저 스포츠대회는 물론 각 대륙별, 국가별 스포츠 경기에 태권도가 정식 종목으로 추가되었다. 1992년 제25회 스페인 바르셀로나 올림픽에서 또 다시 시범종목으로 실시되는 성과를 올렸다.

이후 세계태권도연맹은 태권도 홍보와 활동에 더욱 박차를 가해 세계올림픽위원회(I.O.C)가 요구하는 까다로운 심사와 절차를 모두 통과하는 쾌거를 올리게 된다. 이 항목에서 올림픽 채택 과정과 관련하여 12개 나라에서 선보인 태권도 우표들을 소개한다.

After being performed as a demonstration sport in the 1988 Seoul Summer Olympic Games, Taekwondo developed a movement to be accepted as an official sport in the Olympics. After the Seoul Olympics, the next step and ultimate goal for Taekwondo was to be adopted as an official sport. Taekwondo was already included as an official sport in continental and national sports games, as well as in the Goodwill Games and the Asian Games. In 1992, Taekwondo got good news; it was once again being adopted as a demonstration sport in the Olympics. Since then, the World Taekwondo Federation had begun to hasten the promotion and name-recognition of Taekwondo and succeeded in passing all the difficult tests and procedures that the International Olympic Committee demanded. In this chapter, I will be introducing Taekwondo stamps that have been issued from twelve different countries.

우표로 보는 태권도 발자취 The Evolution of Taekwondo as Seen Through Postage Stamps

VIII-1. 태권도, 올림픽 종목 채택 기원 우표
Taekwondo to be Adopted as an Olympic Sport

Taekwondo Stamp No. 076

☞ 북사이프러스(터키계) II. 1984
  Northern Cyprus (Turkey) II

☞ 자료 평가 Evaluation :
① 태권도가치성
  Taekwondo Value ★★★★☆
② 도안성 Design ★★★★★
③ 희귀성 Rarity ★★★☆☆

☞ 우표 구성 : 3종 중 1종
  Stamp Composition : 1 of 3 stamps

지중해의 섬에 위치한 터키계 북사이프러스가 L.A.올림픽을 기념하여 발행한 3종짜리 우표에 태권도 도안이 포함되었다. 태권도 우표에는 L.A. 올림픽 엠블렘을 배경으로 무릎을 접어 앞차는 동작과 뛰어옆차기 등 3종의 태권도 이미지가 나와 있다. 1984년 L.A.올림픽 기념 우표에 태권도 도안이 삽입되었다는 것은 특별한 의미가 있다. 1981년에 차기 올림픽은 한국 서울에서 열리기로 확정되었고 세계태권도연맹은 태권도를 시범종목으로 올리기 위해 다방면의 활동을 전개하던 시기였다. 마침내 1985년 베를린에서 열린 제 90차 I.O.C. 총회와 이사회에서 태권도를 서울올림픽 시범종목으로 결정하게 되었다

This Taekwondo-themed stamp is among the three stamps issued in Northern Cyprus, mainly Turkish descendants in the Mediterranean Sea, that commemorate the 1984 Los Angeles Summer Olympic Games. In these Taekwondo stamps, three Taekwondo figures are performing a front snap and a jumping side kick, with the L.A. Olympic emblem in the background. Having a Taekwondo design on stamps commemorating the 1984 L.A. Olympics has a special meaning. It is that, in 1981, the next Olympic Games site was chosen as Seoul, Korea, and at that time the World Taekwondo Federation was engaged in various activities to have Taekwondo accepted as a demonstration sport. Finally, at the 90th I.O.C. General Assembly Session and Executive Board Meeting held in Berlin in 1995, Taekwondo was chosen as a demonstration sport for the Seoul Summer Olympic Games.

기념 초일봉투
First Day Cover

VIII-2. 제25회 바르셀로나 올림픽 시범종목 거행 기념 바레인 우표
A Bahrain Taekwondo Stamp for the Barcelona Olympics

태권도는 서울올림픽에 이어 바르셀로나 올림픽에서도 시범 종목으로 경기가 치루어졌다. 1992년 제25회 스페인 바르셀로나 올림픽 대회를 기념하여 중동의 섬나라 바레인이 태권도 경기를 도안한 우표를 발행했다. 4년 전 서울올림픽에 이어 바레인에서 나온 두 번째 태권도 우표이다. 우표에는 보호대를 착용한 겨루기 경기를 벌이는 두 선수가 그림으로 도안되었다. 바르셀로나 올림픽 태권도 경기는 남녀 각 8체급씩 배정 받았고 남자부는 27개국 64명, 여자부는 25개국 64명의 선수가 참가했다. 남자부는 한국이 금메달 3개를 획득하여 종주국의 명예를 지켰고 여자부는 대만이 금메달 3개를 따내 한국을 누르고 최고의 성과를 거두었다.

After the Seoul Olympic Games, Taekwondo was a demonstration sport in the Barcelona Olympic Games. In 1992, the Kingdom of Bahrain, an island country in the Middle East, issued a stamp depicting a Taekwondo match to commemorate the Barcelona Olympic Games. This is the second Taekwondo stamp in a row by Bahrain, the first celebrating the Seoul Olympic Games from four years prior. On the stamp is a portrait of two competitors sparring while wearing protective gear. Taekwondo has been allocated 8 weight divisions for both men and women. In the men's division, 64 competitors from 27 countries participated, while 64 competitors from 25 countries participated in the women's division. In the men's division, Korea showed its pride as Taekwondo's country of origin by earning 3 gold medals, yet in the women's division, Taiwan surpassed Korea and achieved the best result by earning 3 gold medals.

Taekwondo Stamp No. 077

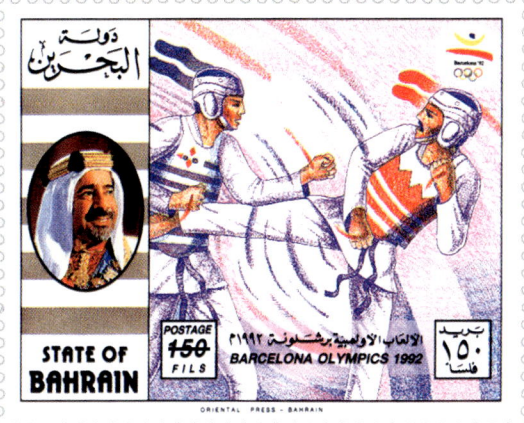

☞ 국가명 : 바레인 II. 1992
　Nation : BahrainI II

☞ 자료 평가 Evaluation :
① 태권도가치성 Taekwondo Value ★★★★★
② 도안성 Design ★★★★★
③ 희귀성 Rarity ★★★★☆

☞ 우표 구성 : 4종 중 1종
　Stamp Composition : 1 of 4 stamps

함께 나온 우표세트
accompanied stamp set

VIII-3. 1992년 바르셀로나 올림픽 시험종목 거행 기념 이집트 우표
An Egyptian Taekwondo Stamp for the Barcelona Olympics

Taekwondo Stamp No. 078

바르셀로나 올림픽을 기념하여 이집트가 발행한 우표 속에 조그만 크기의 발차기 모습이 들어 있다. 이집트 정부가 3번이나 태권도 우표를 발행하는 등 태권도 종목에 관심을 쏟는 이유가 있다. 올림픽을 비롯한 주요한 국제 태권도 경기에서 자국 선수들이 메달을 가져오기 때문이다. 이집트 선수들은 서울올림픽 태권도경기 미들급 은메달, 바르셀로나 올림픽 동메달 2개, 9회 세계태권도대회 헤비급 금메달 등 괄목할만한 성적을 올렸다. 이집트의 정기영 사범은 1984년부터 이집트에 태권도를 보급했고 2006년 국기원으로부터 '자랑스런 태권도인상' 을 받았다. 이집트는 아프리카태권도연맹 회장국으로 아메드 엘 파울리 장군이 회장을 맡고 있다.

In this stamp issued by Egypt to commemorate the Barcelona Olympic Games, you can see a small figure kicking. There is a reason why the Egyptian government has been showing its interest in Taekwondo by issuing Taekwondo stamps three times. It is because its competitors bring medals home from major international Taekwondo championships, including the Olympic Games. Egyptian competitors have made such notable achievements as: winning a silver medal in the middleweight division at the Seoul Olympic Games; winning 2 bronze medals in the Barcelona Olympic Games; and winning a gold medal in the heavyweight division at the 9th World Taekwondo Championships. Master Ki Young Jeong has promoted Taekwondo in Egypt since 1984, and received the 'Proud Taekwondo Master Award' in 2006 from the Kukkiwon.

☞ 국가명 : 이집트 II. 1992
　　Nation : Egyp II

☞ 자료 평가 Evaluation :
① 태권도가치성 Taekwondo Value ★★★★☆
② 도안성 Design ★★★★★
③ 희귀성 Rarity ★★★☆☆

☞ 우표 구성 : 기념우표 1종
　　Stamp Composition : single stamp

기념 초일봉투
First Day Cover

VIII-4. 바르셀로나 올림픽기념 나이지리아 우표
A Nigerian Taekwondo Stamp for the Barcelona Olympics

1992년 바르셀로나 올림픽을 기념하는 나이지리아 우표에 태권도가 포함되었다. 나이지리아 우표에 태권도가 나오는 연유는 당연하다. 바르셀로나 올림픽 태권도경기에서 나이지리아 선수가 은메달을 따냈기 때문이다. 남자 헤비급의 임마뉴엘 오젠요보 선수는 유럽, 아랍 등의 강호를 물리치고 결승에 진출하는 파란을 일으켰다. 나이지리아 선수의 은메달 획득은 아프리카 국가들도 태권도 강국으로 성장할 수 있는 가능성을 심어 주었다. 나이지리아의 성공 사례는 우수한 사범진의 역할로부터 기인한다. 1983년 김무천과 박정래 사범이 파견되어 태권도 경기 기술을 본격적으로 전수했다. 두 사범은 나이지리아 태권도협회 창립에도 큰 힘을 쏟았다. 뒤이어 김영석, 이병호 사범이 가세하여 태권도를 널리 확장시켰다.

Taekwondo Stamp No. 079

Taekwondo was included in Nigerian stamps to commemorate the Barcelona Olympic Games in 1992. It is not surprising to see Taekwondo stamps issued by Nigeria because, in the Barcelona Olympic Games, a Nigerian competitor earned a silver medal. Mr. Emmanuel Oghenejobo, in the heavyweight division, caused a stir in the tournament by entering the final match by defeating powerful competitors from Europe and Arabic countries. This Nigerian competitor's earning of a silver medal in the Olympics gave hope to athletes of other African countries that they may be able to develop into a powerful Taekwondo force. Master Byung Ho Lee put a lot of effort into promoting Taekwondo in Nigeria.

- 국가명 : 나이지리아 I. 1992
  Nation : Nigeria I
- 자료 평가 Evaluation :
  ① 태권도가치성 Taekwondo Value ★★★★★
  ② 도안성 Design ★★★★★
  ③ 희귀성 Rarity ★★★☆☆
- 우표 구성 : 4종 중 1종
  Stamp Composition : 1 of 4 stamps

에러판 소형쉬이트
A Souvenir Sheet with error

우표로 보는 태권도 발자취   The Evolution of Taekwondo as Seen Through Postage Stamps

VIII-5. 1996년 제26회 아틀란타 올림픽 기념 부탄 우표
A Bhutanese Taekwondo Stamp for the 26th Atlanta Olympic Games

Taekwondo Stamp No. 080

☞ 국가명 : 부탄. 1996
   Nation : Bhutan

☞ 자료 평가 Evaluation :
① 태권도가치성 Taekwondo Value ★★★★★
② 도안성 Design ★★★★★
③ 희귀성 Rarity ★★★☆☆

☞ 우표 구성 : 3종 중 1종
   Stamp Composition : 1 of 3 stamps

아시아의 산악 왕국 부탄이 아틀란타 올림픽 기념으로 근사한 태권도 우표를 선사했다. 태권도 우표는 금으로 된 동전 속에 태권도 옆차기가 도안되었다. 세트로 함께 발행된 축구, 농구 종목은 은화로 도안되어 상대적으로 태권도의 가치가 더욱 돋보인다. 인구 56만명의 부탄에 태권도 인구가 1만 6,000명에 달해 인구의 약 3%가 태권도를 하는 열성국이다. 아틀란타 올림픽은 근대올림픽 경기가 시작된 지 100주년이 되는 뜻깊은 올림픽이었지만 태권도가 채택되지 못했다. '부탄 태권도의 아버지'로 불리는 신재균 사범이 한국과 국교 수교도 맺지 않은 상황에서 부탄에서 태권도 기합소리가 울려 퍼지게 했고 부탄태권도 협회 창립에도 큰 기여를 했다.

Bhutan, a mountainous kingdom in Asia, offered an appropriate stamp to commemorate the Atlanta Olympic Games. This Taekwondo stamp has the design of a golden coin with a figure performing a Taekwondo side kick. Because the soccer and basketball stamps of the series only have the silver coin design, the value of the Taekwondo stamp is raised. Bhutan is an enthusiastic Taekwondo country, with 3 percent of the population practicing Taekwondo (16,000 Taekwondoists among a total population of 560,000). The Atlanta Olympic Games has the special significance of being held on the centennial Olympic year, but Taekwondo was unfortunately not included. Master Jae Gyun Shin, who is respected as the "Father of Bhutanese Taekwondo," helped to spread the "kihap" in Bhutan when there were no diplomatic exchanges or agreements with Korea. He also tremendously contributed to the formation of the Bhutan Taekwondo Association.

맥시멈카드   A Maximum Card

VIII-6. 아틀란타 올림픽 기념 요르단 우표
A Jordanian Taekwondo Stamp for the Atlanta Olympic

중동의 요르단이 1996년 미국 아틀란타 올림픽 기념우표에 태권도 픽토그램을 넣었다. 실제로 아틀란타 올림픽에서 태권도 경기가 열리지 않았지만 요르단의 기념우표에 태권도를 삽입했다. 요르단은 길거리에서 태권도복을 입은 아이들을 쉽게 볼 수 있을 정도로 태권도가 보편화되어 있다. 모든 군과 경찰의 기본 무술이 태권도일 정도로 그 애착이 대단하다. 유영한 사범이 요르단 태권도 대부로 알려져 있다. 요르단은 1979년 아시아태권도연맹에 등록되었고 현재 라시드 엘 핫산 왕자가 회장이다.

Taekwondo Stamp No. 081

Jordan, a country in the Middle East, stamp with a issued a Taekwondo pictogram to commemorate the 1996 Atlanta Olympic Games. In actuality, Taekwondo matches were not held in the Atlanta Olympic Games, however a Taekwondo theme is included on this Jordanian stamp. In Jordan, Taekwondo is so popular that you can see children in Taekwondo uniforms everywhere on the street. Their interest in Taekwondo is so great that the basic martial arts discipline for the army and the police is Taekwondo. Master Young Han Yoo is known as the "Godfather of Taekwondo" there. Jordan registered as a member country in the Asian Taekwondo Federation in 1979, and today Prince Rashed bin El-Hassan is the President.

☞ 국가명 : 요르단 I. 1996
　Nation : Jordan I

☞ 자료 평가 Evaluation :
① 태권도가치성 Taekwondo Value ★★★★☆
② 도안성 Design ★★★★☆
③ 희귀성 Rarity ★★★☆☆

☞ 우표 구성 : 4종 중 1종
　Stamp Composition : 1 of 4 stamps

함께 나온 우표세트
accompanied stamp set

VIII-7. 국제올림픽위원회(I.O.C) 창립 100주년
The 100th Anniversary of the Establishment of the I.O.C.

Taekwondo Stamp No. 082

1994년은 국제올림픽위원회(I.O.C)가 창립된지 정확히 100주년이 되는 뜻깊은 해이다. 베트남에서 발행된 올림픽 100주년 기념 우표에 조그만 크기의 태권도 발차기 그림이 실려있다. 베트남 정부가 올림픽 정식 종목인 태권도를 배려한 조치이다. 1994년 I.O.C 창립 100주년을 축하하는 태권도 행사가 한국에서 열렸다. 한국, 호주, 스페인, 미국 등 4개국 32명의 남녀 선수들이 참가한 서울국제태권도선수권대회로서 6명의 IOC 위원들이 참가한 대규모 행사였다

1994 was a meaningful year, because in that year it had been 100 years since the establishment of the I.O.C. In the stamp that was issued by Vietnam to commemorate the centennial of the modern Olympic Games, you can see a depiction of a Taekwondo kick. It appears that the Vietnamese government actively chose to be attentive to Taekwondo, which is an official sport in the Olympics. In 1994, a Taekwondo event was held in Korea to celebrate the centennial of the foundation of the I.O.C. It was the I.O.C. Centenary Seoul International Taekwondo Championships, which hosted 32 competitors from 4 countries including Korea, Australia, Spain, and the United States of America, as well as 6 I.O.C. members.

☞ 국가명 : 베트남 III. 1994
　Nation : Vietnam III

☞ 자료 평가 Evaluation :
① 태권도가치성 Taekwondo Value ★★★★☆
② 도안성 Design ★★★★★
③ 희귀성 Rarity ★★★☆☆

☞ 우표 구성 : 2종 중 1종
　Stamp Composition : 1 of 2 stamps

함께 나온 우표세트
accompanied stamp set

VIII-8. 국가 스포츠 권장 종목인 태권도
Taekwondo as a Sport for Encouragement

유럽 발칸반도에 위치한 보스니아헤르체고비나가 자국 올림픽위원회 스포츠 경기 종목으로 태권도가 포함된 기념우표를 발행했다. 태권도는 이미 1994년 파리 I.O.C 총회에서 시드니올림픽 정식종목으로 확정된 이후이므로 태권도에 대한 세계적 인지도가 높아진 것 같다. 과거 보스니아헤르체고비나가 속했던 유고슬라비아 연방 시기인 1970년대 초반에 동유럽의 공산권 국가 최초로 태권도를 받아들였다. 당시 박선재 이탈리아 주재사범 및 이경명 오스트리아 주재사범의 노력으로 태권도가 전파되었다. 보스니아헤르체고비나는 1993년에 유럽태권도연맹에 공식 가입되었고 현재 미오드락 디레틱 씨가 회장이다.

Bosnia and Herzegovina, located on the Balkan Peninsula in Europe, issued a Taekwondo commemorative stamp celebrate Taekwondo's inclusion as a sport discipline by its national Olympic Committee. The worldwide public awareness of Taekwondo seemed to have increased due to the decision made in Paris in 1994 at the I.O.C. General Assembly meeting to adopt it as an official sport in the Sydney Olympics. Among communist countries in the 1970s, Taekwondo was accepted for the first time by the Yugoslavian Taekwondo Federation in Yugoslavia, a country which Bosnia and Herzegovina belonged to in the past. Thanks to the efforts of Master Sun Jae Park name residing in Italy, and Master Kyung Myung Lee, residing in Austria, Taekwondo grew in Eastern Europe. The Taekwondo Federation of Bosnia and Herzegovina officially joined the European Taekwondo Federation in 1993, and Mr. Miodrag Deretic is currently the President.

Taekwondo Stamp No. 083

함께 나온 우표세트
accompanied stamp set

☞ 국가명 : 보스니아헤르체고비나, 1997
　 Nation : Bosnia and Herzegovina

☞ 자료 평가 Evaluation :
① 태권도가치성 Taekwondo Value ★★★★☆
② 도안성 Design ★★★★☆
③ 희귀성 Rarity ★★★★☆

☞ 우표 구성 : 3종 중 1종
　 Stamp Composition : 1 of 3 stamps

VIII-9. 새로운 올림픽 정식 종목, 태권도
Taekwondo as a New Olympic Sport

Taekwondo Stamp No. 084

유럽 남동부에 위치한 루마니아는 올림픽 정식종목으로 처음으로 등장한 태권도를 멋진 우표로 표현했다. 시드니올림픽 1년 전인 1999년에 나온 이 우표는 태권도 겨루기 경기를 도안한 그림을 싣고 태권도를 영문으로 표기했다. 과거 동구 공산권에 속했던 루마니아는 한때 태권도 전파에 많은 장애가 있기도 했다. 1997년에 제1회 한국대사배 태권도대회가 루마니아에서 거행되었다. 2010년은 루마니아와 한국이 수교 20주년을 맞는 해이다. 양국 정상 간의 축하 서한 교환이 이루어졌고 태권도 시범경기, 무용단 상호파견 등 행사가 양국에서 개최되었다. 루마니아는 1991년에 유럽태권도연맹에 공식 등록되었고 콘스따땡 아포스톨 씨가 회장을 맡고있다.

Romania, located in the southeastern part of Europe, supported Taekwondo with an appropriate stamp when Taekwondo became an official sport in the Olympics. This stamp issued in 1999, a year before the Sydney Olympic Games, depicts a Taekwondo sparring match with the inscription of Taekwondo in English. Romania, which belonged to the eastern European communist bloc, experienced several difficulties in the dissemination of Taekwondo. In 1997, the 1st Korean Ambassador's Cup Taekwondo Championship was held in Romania. The year 2010 is the 20th anniversary of the establishment of diplomatic ties between Korea and Romania. The presidents of both countries exchanged congratulatory notes, and Taekwondo exhibition games and mutual exchanges of dance performances were held in both countries. Romania registered as a member country of the European Taekwondo Federation in 1991, and the Romanian Taekwondo Federation is led today by President Constatin C. Apostol.

☞ 국가명 : 루마니아, 1999
　Nation : Romania

☞ 자료 평가 Evaluation :
① 태권도가치성 Taekwondo Value ★★★★★
② 도안성 Design ★★★★★
③ 희귀성 Rarity ★★★☆☆

☞ 우표 구성 : 3종 중 1종
　Stamp Composition : 1 of 3 stamps

기념 초일봉투
First Day Cover

VIII-10. 불가리아 올림픽위원회 창립 기념
The Bulgarian Olympic Committee's Anniversary

동부 유럽의 불가리아가 자국 올림픽위원회 창립 기념으로 2003년에 태권도 우표를 선보였다. 한 여자선수가 겨루기 경기를 하는 장면을 도입했고 불가리아 글자로 태권도를 표기했다. 불가리아의 이 우표는 시드니올림픽 이후 태권도가 정식 종목으로 자리를 굳히고 있는 분위기를 전하고 있다. 2010년은 불가리아와 한국이 수교 20주년이 되는 해로 태권도가 문화 행사에 주요한 프로그램이 되어 국가대표 시범단이 불가리아를 방문하여 태권도 시범을 보였다. 불가리아 태권도협회는 1990년에 공식 등록되었고 안드레이 키오지에프 씨가 회장이다.

Bulgaria, in Eastern Europe, issued a Taekwondo stamp in 2003 to commemorate the establishment of its National Olympic Committee. This stamp depicts a sparring scene of a female competitor with the inscription Taekwondo in Bulgarian. This Bulgarian stamp transmits the atmosphere of Taekwondo competition, as it has been an official sport since the Sydney Olympic Games. The year 2010 is the 20th anniversary of establishment of diplomatic ties between Korea and Bulgaria, and Taekwondo has become an important program among their cultural events. The Korean National Demonstration Team visited Bulgaria to perform demonstrations. The Bulgarian Taekwondo Federation joined the European Taekwondo Federation in 1991, and is led today by President Andrey Georgiev.

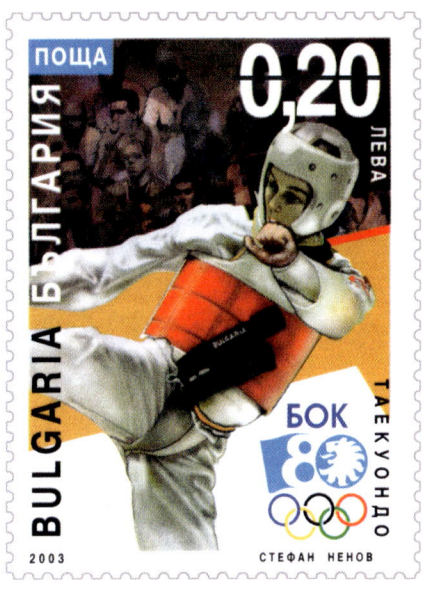

Taekwondo Stamp No. 085

- 국가명 : 불가리아, 2003
  Nation : Bulgaria
- 자료 평가 Evaluation :
  ① 태권도가치성 Taekwondo Value ★★★★★
  ② 도안성 Design ★★★★★
  ③ 희귀성 Rarity ★★★☆☆
- 우표 구성 : 4종 중 1종
  Stamp Composition : 1 of 4 stamps

맥시멈카드
A Maximum Card

우표로 보는 태권도 발자취 The Evolution of Taekwondo as Seen Through Postage Stamps

VIII-11. 에콰도르 인기 스포츠, 태권도
Taekwondo as a Popular Sport in Ecuador

Taekwondo Stamp No. 086

☞ 국가명 : 에콰도르 IV. 2006
   Nation : Ecuador IV

☞ 자료 평가 Evaluation :
① 태권도가치성 Taekwondo Value ★★★★☆
② 도안성 Design ★★★★★
③ 희귀성 Rarity ★★★★☆

☞ 우표 구성 : 기념우표 1종
   Stamp Composition : single stamp

5회 세계태권도대회를 주최한 남미의 태권도 강국 에콰도르가 올림픽위원회 기념 우표에 태권도 종목을 포함시켰다. 이로써 에콰도르는 4종의 태권도 우표를 찍는 손꼽히는 태권도 열성국이 되었다. 우표를 발행하는 권한을 가진 정부 부처 에콰도르 우정성이 태권도를 국민적 관심을 받는 주요 스포츠 종목으로 인식한다고 볼 수 있다. 시드니에 이어 아테네올림픽에서 정식 종목으로 거행된 이후 태권도는 올림픽 종목으로서 탄탄한 기반을 확보해가고 있다. 1983년 에콰도르로 건너가 국가대표 태권도 감독을 역임했던 공명규 사범이 알려져 있고 최근에는 황창기 사범이 활동하고 있다.

The Taekwondo power country of Ecuador, in South America, hosted the 5th W.T.F. World Taekwondo Championships, and has included Taekwondo-themed stamps among the commemorative stamps of the Olympic Committee. These stamps assert that Ecuador is a country that is enthusiastic about Taekwondo, as it has issued four Taekwondo stamps. We can see that the post office department, which has authority to issue stamps, perceives Taekwondo as an important sport with strong national support. Master Myung Kyu Gong, who arrived in Ecuador in 1983, has led the national team and is well-known there. Currently, Master Chang Ki Hwang is spreading Taekwondo there.

Ⅷ-12. 2010년 세계청소년올림픽, 태권도 경기
Taekwondo in the 2010 Youth Olympic Games

아프리카 튀니지가 베이징올림픽 기념우표에 이어 두 번째 태권도 우표를 제공했다. 2010년 제1회 세계청소년올림픽 기념 우표로서 대회는 싱가포르에서 열렸지만 우표는 튀니지에서 나왔다. 뛰어 발차기로 태권도를 표현한 조그만 그림이 세련되어 보인다. 세계청소년올림픽은 자크 로게 국제올림픽위원회(IOC) 위원장의 주창에 의해 14~18세 청소년을 대상으로 2010년에 제1회 대회가 열리게 되었다. 경기 종목은 하계올림픽과 똑같은 26개 종목이었지만 금메달은 100개가 적은 201개 세부 종목이 시행되어 중국, 러시아, 한국이 종합 순위를 기록했다. 제2회 대회는 4년 뒤 중국 난징에서 개최될 예정이다. 튀니지는 태권도 협회 등록 인원이 2만명을 넘어섬으로써 무한한 발전이 예견된다. 현재 정부에서도 태권도의 사회·국민적 가치를 인식하고 적극적인 지원을 펴고 있다. 1994년에 임봉덕 사범이 튀니지에 건너가 십오 년이 넘도록 태권도 보급에 전력한 결실로 태권도 붐이 가능했다. 튀니지태권도협회는 1978년에 등록되었고 아르캄 즈리비 씨가 회장이다.

The African country Tunisia sponsored the second commemorative Taekwondo stamp for the Beijing Olympics. Although the stamp commemorates the Youth Olympic Games in 2010 in Singapore, the stamp came out in Tunisia. We can see a jumping Taekwondo kick depicted in this small, elegant picture. Committee member Jacques Rogge of the International Olympic Committee (IOC) advocated that the Youth Olympic Games should have their own competition for Youth between the ages of 14-18 in the year 2010. These games include the same 26 sports categories as the Summer Olympics, with 201 sub-categories, 100 less than the normal Olympics. In total, they were recorded in the following rank: 1st place China, 2nd place Russia, 3rd place Korea. Since the Tunisian Taekwondo Association has over 20,000 registered members, it has unlimited potential for future development. Also, the current Tunisian government actively supports and recognizes the societal and civic values of Taekwondo. The Taekwondo boom in Tunisia was made possible by Taekwondo Master Bong-Deok Lim's hard effort when he first arrived in Tunisia in 1994 and spent over 15 years exerting himself. The Tunisian Taekwondo Association was registered in 1978 and is chaired by Mr. Akram Zribi.

☞ 국가명 : 튀니지 Ⅱ. 2010
　Nation : Tunisia Ⅱ

☞ 자료 평가 Evaluation :
① 태권도가치성 Taekwondo Value ★★★★☆
② 도안성 Design ★★★★★
③ 희귀성 Rarity ★★★★☆

☞ 우표 구성 : 기념우표 1종
　Stamp Composition : single stamp

우표로 보는 태권도 발자취   The Evolution of Taekwondo as Seen Through Postage Stamps

 쉼터 · Break Time

1994년 9월 4일 프랑스 파리에서 개최된 제103차 IOC 총회에서 태권도가 올림픽 정식종목으로 채택된 날을 기념하기 위해 2006년에 '태권도의 날'이 지정되었다. 세계태권도연맹(총재 조정원)은 나만의 우표를 담은 4쪽짜리 기념 우표첩을 제작했다.

On September 4th, 1994 at the 103rd I.O.C General Assembly in Paris, France, Taekwondo officially became recognized as an Olympic event. In 2006, this date was appointed as 'Taekwondo Day' to commemorate its introduction. The World Taekwondo Federation, headed by President Chungwon Choue, manufactured 4 pages of the commemorative customized stamps for this occasion.

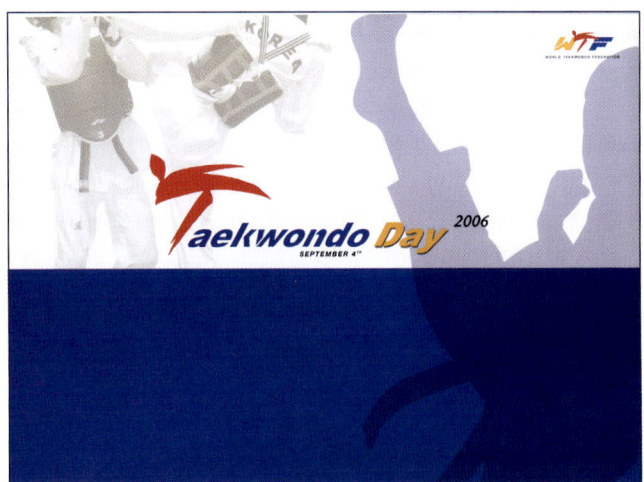

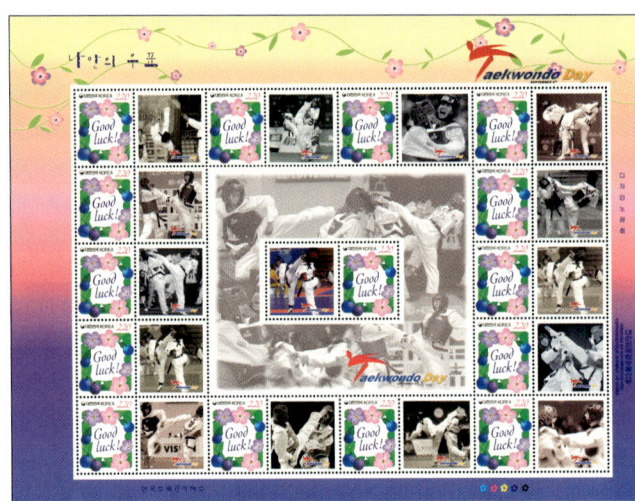

마침내 2000년 제27회 시드니 하계 올림픽에 정식종목으로 채택

At Long Last, the Adoption of Taekwondo as an Official Sport at The 27th Olympiad
– The 2000 Sydney Summer Olympic Games

태권도는 1994년 파리에서 열린 제103차 I.O.C 총회에서 2000년 시드니올림픽 정식종목으로 확정되었다. 태권도는 심신 수양의 이상향이 담긴 새로운 무예 스포츠로서 올림픽 공식 무대에 서게 되었다. 남녀 각각 네 개의 메달이 배정되어 아시아 스포츠 종목으로는 일본의 유도에 이어 태권도가 두 번째로 올림픽 종목이 되는 영광을 안았다. 대부분의 스포츠가 올림픽에 진입하기까지 최소한 50년 이상 소요되는데 비해 태권도는 불과 20년 만에 정식종목이 되었다. 태권도는 시드니올림픽 정식종목을 계기로 이전의 호신 무예적 성격에서 대중스포츠 영역으로 그 가치와 유용성을 확대하게 되었다. 아울러 시드니올림픽을 계기로 세계 각국에서 수많은 태권도 소재 우표들이 등장하기 시작했다.

In 1994, the 103rd Paris Olympic Assembly decided to include Taekwondo as an official sport in the 2000 Sydney Olympic Games. Taekwondo, a new martial art-sport practiced to discipline both body and mind, debuted on the official stage of the Olympics as the second official Olympic event, behind Judo, to come from an Asian country offering 8 gold medals, 4 for male events and 4 for female events. It usually takes at least 50 years for sports to become official Olympic events, but Taekwondo took only 20 years. The adoption of Taekwondo as an official event in the Sydney Olympics expanded Taekwondo's previous characteristics of simply being a martial art to becoming a worldwide disciplinary sport. This in turn lead to Taekwondo becoming much more of a mass recognized sport as well. Out of the Sydney Olympics, many postage stamps based on Taekwondo were published by governments of various countries.

우표로 보는 태권도 발자취   The Evolution of Taekwondo as Seen Through Postage Stamps

IX-1. 시드니올림픽 주최국인 오스트레일리아에서 발행된 태권도 우표

Taekwondo Stamp No. 088

시드니올림픽 주최국인 호주는 정식종목으로 처음 채택된 태권도 종목에 대한 기념우표를 발행하지 않았다. 다행히 시드니올림픽에서 입상한 자국 선수들을 축하하는 특별우표에 태권도가 포함되었다. 태권도 종목 여자부 -49kg 체급에서 우승을 차지한 로렌 번즈 선수가 대회가 끝난 후 발행된 특별 우표에 나오는 영광을 누렸다.

The host country for the Sydney Olympics, Australia, did not publish Taekwondo, a new official event, as a stamp. Fortunately, however, special commemoration stamps of Australian gold medalists were published with Taekwondo athletes. In the female -49kg weight division, gold medalist Lauren Burns had the priviledge of being placed on a stamp issued by the Australian government.

☞ 국가명 : 오스트레일리아. 2000
　Nation : Austrailia

☞ 자료 평가 Evaluation :
① 태권도가치성 Taekwondo Value ★★★★☆
② 도안성 Design ★★★★★
③ 희귀성 Rarity ★★★☆☆

☞ 우표 구성 : 기념우표 17종 중 1종
　Stamp Composition : 1 of 17 stamps

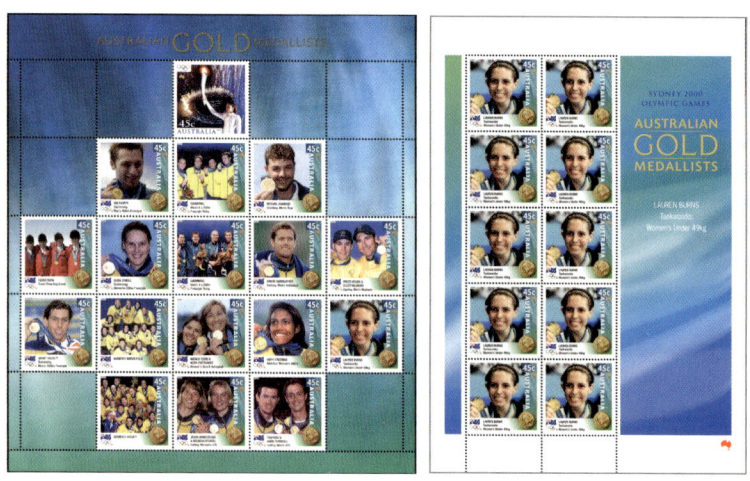

시드니올림픽에서 우승한 오스트레일리아 선수들이 담긴 특별기념우표 전지 2종
2 full stamp sheets for the Sydney Olympics by Australia

A Taekwondo Stamp and Other Postal Materials for the Sydney Summer Olympic Games in Australia, the Host Country

호주는 제2회(1976년), 제7회(1986년), 제12회(1996년) 등 3회에 걸쳐 아시아태권도선수권대회를 주최했다. 조용대, 노계형, 이종철, 노의준, 이종원 등 여러 사범들이 활약하여 호주 태권도를 발전시켰다. 호주는 11개 회원국을 가진 오스트레일리아 대륙 협회 회장국이며 필립 콜레스씨가 회장을 맡고 있다.

Australia sponsored the 2nd (1976), the 7th (1986) and the 12th (1996) Asian Taekwondo championships. Many Taekwondo masters such as Yongdae Cho, Kyaehyeong Roe, Jongchul Lee, Euijune Roe and Jongwon Lee proliferated and promoted Taekwondo in Australia. 11 country members belong to the Australian Continental Taekwondo Federation. The federation based in Australia has Mr. Phillip Walter Coles as the current president.

호주가 발행한 시드니올림픽 태권도종목 기념 주화
An Australian Taekwondo coin commemorating the Sydney Olympics.

시드니올림픽에서 태권도 종목에서 우승한 선수들 모습이 나온 초일봉투
The First Day Covers for the winners of the Taekwondo events in the Sydney Olympics

초일봉투　The First Day Covers

우표로 보는 태권도 발자취 The Evolution of Taekwondo as Seen Through Postage Stamps

IX-2. 시드니올림픽대회 벨기에 태권도 우표
A Belgian Stamp and Postal Materials for the Sydney Olympic Games

유럽의 선진국 벨기에가 멋진 태권도 우표를 발행했다. 태권도 가치성과 도안성 면에서 시드니올림픽 정식종목을 기념한 최고의 태권도 우표로 꼽힌다. 우표에는 내려차기 기술을 펼치는 태권도 선수의 모습과 영문 태권도 글씨가 함께 나온다. 벨기에는 시드니 올림픽 기념 태권도 우표를 낼 정도로 일찍이 태권도가 뿌리내렸다. 시드니 올림픽 태권도 경기에 남녀 각 4체급씩 금메달 8개가 배정되었다. 한국이 금메달 3개를 따냈고 호주, 쿠바, 미국, 그리스, 중국 등 5개국이 금메달 1개씩을 획득했다.

Belgium, a developed country in Europe, issued an excellent Taekwondo stamp. This is one of the best designed and highly valued examples among Taekwondo stamps. An athlete performing an axe kick is shown and Taekwondo is written using English characters on the stamp. This stamp shows that Taekwondo rooted and developed early in Belgium. 8 gold medals in total are presented to both male and female winners for the Taekwondo event in Sydney Olympics. South Korea won 3 divisions, while the remaining 5 gold medals were won by Australia, Cuba, USA, Greece, and China.

☞ 국가명 : 벨기에. 2000
　　Nation : Belgium
☞ 자료 평가 Evaluation :
　① 태권도가치성 Taekwondo Value ★★★★★
　② 도안성 Design ★★★★★
　③ 희귀성 Rarity ★★★☆☆
☞ 우표 구성 : 3종 중 1종
　　Stamp Composition : 1 of 3 stamps

발행 수량이 적어 희귀한 증정용 쉬트
A very rare presentational sheet

세계태권도연맹 전 부총재인 박수남 사범이 벨기에협회 기술위원장을 지냈고 이범주, 진윤섭, 김명만 등 수많은 사범들이 숱한 역경을 이겨내며 벨기에 태권도 발전에 기여했다. 벨기에태권도협회는 1975년에 등록되었고 현재 스티브 그로먼 씨가 회장이며 필립 피네루씨가 국가대표팀 코치를 맡고 있다. 현 국제올림픽위원회 위원장이자 유능한 스포츠맨이었던 자크 로게씨도 벨기에 출신이다.

Vice President of the World Taekwondo Federation, Master Soonam Park, was the technical chairman of the Belgium Taekwondo Association. Several Korean masters such as Bumju Lee, Yoonsup Jin, and Myungman Kim played important roles in developing Belgium Taekwondo while also overcoming many difficulties. The Belgium Taekwondo Association was enrolled in 1975 as a member of the W.T.F. Mr. Steve Grommen is the current president and Mr. Phillip Pinneru is the national team coach. Mr. Jacques Rogge, the president of the International Olympic Committee (I.O.C.) and also a prominent sportsman, is from Belgium.

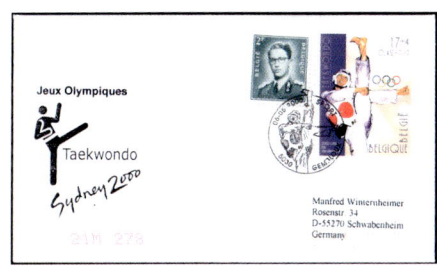

3가지 기념 초일봉투
3 First Day Covers

맥시멈카드
A Maximum Card

IX-3. 브라질 태권도 우표
A Taekwondo Stamp from Brazil

Taekwondo Stamp No. 090

- 국가명 : 브라질. 2000
  Nation : Brazil
- 자료 평가 Evaluation :
  ① 태권도가치성
     Taekwondo Value ★★★★★
  ② 도안성 Design ★★★★★
  ③ 희귀성 Rarity ★★★☆☆
- 우표 구성 : 40종 1종
  Stamp Composition : 1 of 40 stamps

만화 캐릭터로 도안된 깜찍한 태권도 우표가 브라질에서 나왔다. 시드니올림픽 기념으로 브라질이 발행한 올림픽 종목 우표 속에 태권도가 당당히 자리잡았다. 어린이들에게 친숙한 만화 타입의 이미지는 태권도가 남녀노소 누구나 즐길 수 있는 무예 스포츠임을 나타낸다. 브라질은 1996년 제7회 월드컵 태권도대회를 개최했다. 1970년 조상민 사범이 첫 발을 디뎠고 이희섭, 김남웅, 오주열, 정재규 사범의 노고로 태권도가 공식 체육종목으로 인정되었다. 권금순, 방건모, 이계준, 이백수 등 수 많은 한국인 사범들이 브라질에서 활약했다. 브라질태권도협회는 1975년에 등록되었고 김용민씨가 회장을 맡고 있다.

A cute Taekwondo stamp featuring a cartoon character was issued in Brazil. Taekwondo was adopted with glory to Brazil's stamp set for the Sydney Olympics. The stamp, featuring a child friendly image, signifies that Taekwondo had become a martial arts sport for all ages and genders. Brazil sponsored the 7th World Cup Taekwondo Championships in 1996. Master Sangmin Cho was the first to bring Taekwondo to Brazil in 1970. Korean Masters such as Heesup Lee, Namung Kim, Juyul Oh and Jaekyu Chung played great roles in obtaining official approval for Taekwondo to become a subject of physical education in Brazil. Because of Brazil's wide territory, many Taekwondo masters such as Kum Soon Kwon, Keun Mo Bang, Kye Joon Lee, Baek Soo Lee took an active part in spreading Taekwondo throughout Brazil. The Brazil Taekwondo Association was enrolled in 1975 and Master Yong Min Kim is the current president.

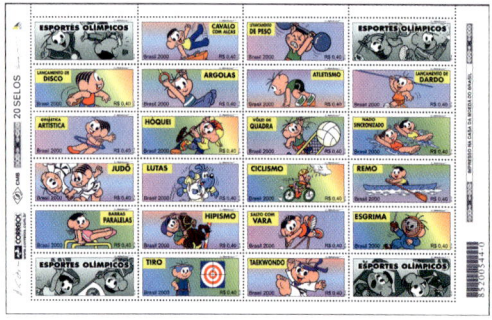

함께 나온 우표세트
accompanied stamp set

IX-4. 카자흐스탄 태권도 우표
A Taekwondo Stamp from Kazakhstan

카자흐스탄이 선수들의 경기 장면을 도안한 멋진 태권도 우표를 선사했다. 두 선수가 돌려차기와 뒤후리기를 구사하는 순간을 박진감 있게 표현했다. 구 소비에트연방에서 독립한 카자흐스탄은 태권도 진출이 비교적 늦은 편이었지만 곧 인기 스포츠 종목으로 부상되었다. 오선택 사범은 카자흐스탄 국가대표팀 감독을 맡아 2010년 제19회 아시아태권도대회에서 금 1, 은 1, 동 3개를 획득하여 역대 최고의 성과를 거두었다. 아시아태권도연맹 회원국인 카자흐스탄 태권도협회는 1993년에 정식 회원이 되었으며 현재 이사베코프 차실노코비치 씨가 회장이다.

Taekwondo Stamp No. 091

Kazakhstan presented a nice Taekwondo stamp featuring a Taekwondo sparring competition. The stamp shows a dynamic atmosphere where two athletes are exchanging a roundhouse kick and a back spinning kick. Taekwondo in Kazakhstan has become quite a popular sport even though it was introduced a little later compared to other countries. Master Suntaek Oh contributed Taekwondo promotions for the national team in the 19th Asian Taekwondo Championships in 2010. They won 1 gold, 1 silver, and 3 bronze medals, which resulted in the best achievement in Kazakhstan's Taekwondo history. Kazakhstan's Taekwondo Association enrolled as a member of the Asian Taekwondo Union in 1993 and Mr. Isabekov Shamsa Zhaksylikovich is the current president.

☞ 국가명 : 카자흐스탄. 2000
　Nation : Kazakhstan

☞ 자료 평가 Evaluation :
① 태권도가치성 Taekwondo Value ★★★★★
② 도안성 Design ★★★★★
③ 희귀성 Rarity ★★★☆☆

☞ 우표 구성 : 4종 중 1종
　Stamp Composition : 1 of 4 stamps

함께 나온 우표세트
accompanied stamp set

IX-5. 카보베르데 태권도 우표
A Taekwondo Stamp from Cape Verde

아프리카 대서양 연안의 섬나라 카보베르데가 시드니올림픽 기념 태권도 우표를 선보였다. 태권도 옆차기 그림과 함께 시드니 올림픽 상징인 성화와 태권도 영문 글자를 우표에 담았다. 카보베르데는 4년에 한 번씩 거행되는 루소포니아 경기대회 회원국이다. 루소포니아 경기대회는 포르투갈어권 10여 개국이 참가하는 국제 종합 스포츠 경기대회이다. 태권도는 2006년 제1회 대회 때부터 정식종목으로 채택되었고 유도는 2009년 제2회 대회에서 정식종목으로 추가되었다. 카보베르데 태권도협회는 2000년에 등록되었고 오스카 산토스씨가 회장이다.

The African Atlantic Ocean island country Cape Verde introduced a Taekwondo stamp for the Sydney Olympics. This stamp features Taekwondo written in English characters and a Taekwondo side kick together with the Olympic flame. Cape Verde is a member of the Lusophony Games which is an international complex sports games where 10 countries participate using Portuguese. Taekwondo was adopted as an official event for the first games in 2006. Judo was later added for the second games in 2009. The Cape Verde Taekwondo Association was enrolled in 2000 and Mr. Oscar Santos is the current president.

Taekwondo Stamp No. 092

☞ 국가명 : 카보베르데 I. 2000
   Nation : Cape Verde I
☞ 자료 평가 Evaluation :
① 태권도가치성 Taekwondo Value ★★★★★
② 도안성 Design ★★★★★
③ 희귀성 Rarity ★★★☆☆
☞ 우표 구성 : 3종 중 1종
   Stamp Composition : 1 of 3 stamps

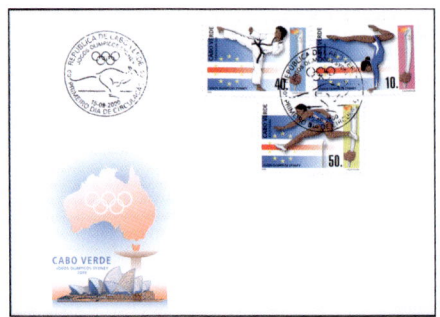

기념 초일봉투
First Day Cover

IX-6. 필리핀 태권도 우표
A Taekwondo Stamp from the Philippines

시드니올림픽 태권도 경기를 표현한 멋진 우표가 필리핀에서 나왔다. 정사각형 태권도 경기장에서 벌어지는 두 선수의 겨루기 경기 장면이 산뜻한 색상의 그림자로 도안되었다. 필리핀은 동남아시아 국가 중 태권도를 가장 열성적으로 받아들인 나라이다. 필리핀은 1984년 제6회 아시아태권도대회를 열었고 1995년에는 제12회 세계태권도대회를 마닐라에서 개최했다. 1970년 최초로 태권도를 전한 김복만 사범을 필두로 박용만, 이성수, 홍성천 사범이 뒤를 이어 필리핀에 태권도를 심었다. 홍성천 사범은 육군사관학교 생도를 가르치면서 성공적인 태권도 보급 활동을 폈다. 필리핀태권도협회는 1973년 등록되었고 로베르토 아벤타자도씨가 회장이다.

In the Philippines, a stylish stamp commemorating Taekwondo at the Sydney Olympic Games was released. The simple yet elegant design features two sparring atheletes colorfully silhouetted above a square Taekwondo arena. Among all the Southeast Asian countries, the Phillipine nation is by far the most enthusiastic about Taekwondo. The Phillipines hosted the 6th Asian Taekwondo Championship in 1984, and in 1995 the 12th World Taekwondo Championship was held in Manila. Taekwondo was first introduced to the Philippines in 1970 by Master Bokman Kim. He paved the way for Masters such as Yongman Park, Sungsoo Lee, and Sungchun Hong to continue teaching and spreading Taekwondo throughout the country. Master Sungchun Hong was able to successfully spread his knowledge of Taekwondo by teaching students in the military academy. The Philippine Taekwondo Association was enrolled in 1973 and Mr. Robert N. Aventajado is the current president.

기념 초일봉투 First Day Cover

☞ 국가명 : 필리핀 I. 2000
　Nation : Philippines I

☞ 자료 평가 Evaluation :
① 태권도가치성 Taekwondo Value ★★★★★
② 도안성 Design ★★★★★
③ 희귀성 Rarity ★★★★☆

☞ 우표 구성 : 4종 중 1종
　Stamp Composition : 1 of 4 stamps

IX-7. 코스타리카 태권도 우표
A Taekwondo Stamp from Costa Rica

Taekwondo Stamp No. 094

- 국가명 : 코스타리카 I, 2000
  Nation : Costa Rica I
- 자료 평가 Evaluation :
  ① 태권도가치성 Taekwondo Value ★★★★★
  ② 도안성 Design ★★★★★
  ③ 희귀성 Rarity ★★★★☆
- 우표 구성 : 8종 중 1종
  Stamp Composition : 1 of 8 stamps

남미 코스타리카가 시드니올림픽 기념으로 멋진 태권도 우표를 제공했다. 호주 대륙을 배경으로 태권도 경기 장면이 실렸다. 1994년 제9회 팬암 태권도대회가 코스타리카에서 열렸다. 코스타리카는 2010년 제3회 코스타리카 오픈대회에서 겨루기와 품새 종목을 거행했다. 이 대회는 세계태권도연맹과 팬암태권도연맹으로부터 승인을 받은 공식 국제 대회이다. 양원근 사범이 1970년대부터 코스타리카에 태권도를 보급했다. 코스타리카 태권도협회는 1984년에 등록되었고 현재 윌리엄 알바라도 카스틸로가 회장이다.

The South American country of Costa Rica presented a beautifully designed Taekwondo stamp for the Sydney Olympic Games. The stamp features a sparring scene with a background in the shape of the continent of Australia. In 1994, the 9th PanAm Taekwondo Championship was held in Costa Rica. The 3rd Costa Rica Open Tournament, consisting of Poomsae (Forms) and Kyeorugi (Sparring), was also held in 2010. The tournament was approved by the World Taekwondo Federation as well as the PanAm Taekwondo Federation. Master Won-Geun Yang popularized Taekwondo in Costa Rica in the 1970s. The Costa Rica Taekwondo Association was enrolled in 1984 and Mr. Wilmar Alvarado Castillo is the current president.

함께 나온 우표세트   accompanied stamp set

IX-8. 베트남 태권도 우표
A Taekwondo Stamp from Vietnam

태권도 열정의 나라 베트남이 시드니올림픽 기념으로 겨루기 경기 장면을 도안한 세번째 태권도 우표를 발행했다. 베트남에서 사상 최초의 올림픽 메달리스트가 배출되어 온 국민이 열광했다. 태권도 여자부 57kg급 경기에서 쩐히에우응환 선수가 준결승에서 유럽챔피언 버지니아 로린스를 꺾고 은메달을 목에 걸어 일약 베트남의 영웅이 되었다. 베트남은 특히 태권도가 세계무대에 내놓을 수 있는 유일한 종목인데 천히에우응안 선수의 은메달 획득은 전국적인 태권도 붐을 일으켰다. 2001년부터 한국의 대우자동차의 후원으로 전국에서 30개팀 400여 명의 선수들이 참가하는 베트남 최고 권위의 클럽컵 태권도대회가 개최되고 있다.

The country of Vietnam is remarkably passionate for Taekwondo. Shown is the 4th stamp designed for the Sydney Olympic games displaying a sparring scene. During the games, Vietnam received their first ever Olympic medal. Naturally, the whole nation was overwhelmed with joy. In the female under 57kg division Jeon Hiaeoong Hwan became a national heroine by defeating the European champion Virginia Laurens and receiving the silver medal. For Vietnam, Taekwondo just may be their best chance for medaling at the Olympics. Her silver Olympic medal brought a nationwide Taekwondo fever. Since 2001, an elite level Club Cup Taekwondo Championship, sponsored by the Daewoo Motor Company of Korea, has been held yearly consisting of 30 teams and 400 athletes.

Taekwondo Stamp No. 095

함께 나온 우표세트
accompanied stamp set

☞ 국가명 : 베트남 IV. 2000
   Nation : Vietnam IV

☞ 자료 평가 Evaluation :
① 태권도가치성 Taekwondo Value ★★★★★
② 도안성 Design ★★★★★
③ 희귀성 Rarity ★★★☆☆

☞ 우표 구성 : 3종 중 1종
   Stamp Composition : 1 of 3 stamps

IX-9. 쿠웨이트 태권도 우표 및 소형쉬이트
A Taekwondo Stamp and Souvenir Sheet from Kuwait

쿠웨이트에서 시드니올림픽 기념으로 2종의 태권도 우표를 선사했다. 몸통보호대를 착용하고 발차기를 하는 픽토그램이 기념우표와 소형시트에 함께 실려 있다. 1992년 바르셀로나올림픽 태권도 경기에서 라이트급의 모하메드자셈 알 카이미 선수가 동메달을 따내 쿠웨이트 태권도계의 영웅이 되기도 했다. 1976년 이해운 사범이 쿠웨이트에 진출해 태권도를 전파했다. 주상헌, 이효주 등 경기인 출신의 지도자들이 쿠웨이트의 경기력을 향상시켰다.

Kuwait issued two types of Taekwondo stamps to commemorate the Sydney 2000 Games. One features a pictogram of an athlete wearing a protective vest and executing a kick. The same pictogram is included alongside others on the souvenir sheet. During the 1992 Barcelona Olympic Games Mohammad Jassem Al Qaimi won the bronze medal in the men's Taekwondo lightweight division. A new Kuwaiti hero was born. In 1976 Master Hae-Yoon Lee introduced and proliferated Taekwondo throughout Kuwait. Thereafter, Masters specializing in sparring competition such as Sang-Heon Choo and Hyo-Joo Lee further helped to elevate Taekwondo competitions in Kuwait to the next level.

☞ 국가명 : 쿠웨이트. 2000
　Nation : Kuwait

☞ 자료 평가 Evaluation :
① 태권도가치성 Taekwondo Value ★★★★★
② 도안성 Design ★★★★★
③ 희귀성 Rarity ★★★☆☆

☞ 우표 구성 : 6종 중 1종
　Stamp Composition : 1 of 6 stamps

☞ 자료 평가 Evaluation :
① 태권도가치성 Taekwondo Value ★★★★☆
② 도안성 Design ★★★★★
③ 희귀성 Rarity ★★★★★

☞ 우표 구성 : 소형시트 1종
　Stamp Composition : single souvenir sheet

소형쉬이트　A Souvenir Sheet

IX-10. 타지키스탄 태권도 우표
A Taekwondo Stamp from Tadzhikistan

타지키스탄이 시드니올림픽 기념주화를 담은 특이한 태권도 우표를 선보였다. 보호대를 착용한 여자선수가 뛰어뒤후려차기를 하는 모습이 새겨진 호주달러 5불짜리 주화가 태권도 우표 속에 담겼다. 중앙아시아 5개국이 참가하는 종합 스포츠 대회인 중앙아시안게임에서 태권도는 2003년 타지키스탄 제4회 대회에서 정식종목으로 거행되었다. 타지키스탄인 국가대표 태권도 코치는 "우리나라에서는 신체적인 태권도 수련 뿐 아니라 태권도의 역사와 가치 등 지식과 한국의 문화 예절까지도 배우고 있다"며 타지키스탄인들의 태권도에 대한 각별한 열정을 대변했다. 타지키스탄 태권도협회는 1995년 등록 되었으며 마리크소 네마토프씨가 회장이다.

Tadzhikistan's Sydney 2000 commemorative Taekwondo stamp incorporated a uniquely distinct design. The stamp features a female athlete wearing a protective vest executing a fierce jumping back spinning kick engraved on an Australian 5 dollar coin. In 2003 Tadzhikistan held the 4th Central Asian Games in which 5 Central Asian countries participated in complex sports games, including Taekwondo. Beginning with the 4th Central Asian Games, Taekwondo became an official event. The Tadzhikistan National Team coach has said that "we are studying Taekwondo, not only physically, but also mentally, gaining knowledge such as history and values. And by doing so we are also learning about Korean culture and manners." This signifies the nation's endearing enthusiasm for Taekwondo.

The Tadjikistan Taekwondo Association was enrolled in 1995. The current president is Mr. Maliksho Nematov.

우표전지 Full Sheet

Taekwondo Stamp No. 098

☞ 국가명 : 타지키스탄 I, 2000
  Nation : Tadzhikistan I

☞ 자료 평가 Evaluation :
① 태권도가치성 Taekwondo Value ★★★★★
② 도안성 Design ★★★★★
③ 희귀성 Rarity ★★★☆☆

☞ 우표 구성 : 9종 중 1종
  Stamp Composition : 1 of 9 stamps

우표로 보는 태권도 발자취   The Evolution of Taekwondo as Seen Through Postage Stamps

IX-11. 라오스 태권도 우표
A Taekwondo Stamp from Laos

시드니올림픽 대회 기념으로 라오스에서 멋진 태권도 우표가 나왔다. 올림픽을 상징하는 오륜기 색깔을 역동성 있게 도안하고 겨루기 경기를 펼치는 두 선수의 모습을 담았다. 라오스는 공산국가였던 관계로 태권도 보급이 늦었지만 그 열기는 높은 편이다. 라오스에서는 2008년부터 해마다 라오스수상배 태권도대회가 열리고 있다. 수상으로부터 하사 받은 순은제 우승컵이 걸린 이 대회는 한국국제협력단에서 2000년부터 태권도 봉사요원을 파견한 성과이다. 대전태권도협회(회장 오노균)는 라오스와 자매결연을 맺고 선수 교류와 태권도 용품을 지원하고 있다. 라오스태권도협회는 1996년에 등록되었고 웰라이 두왕마니씨가 회장이다.

☞ 국가명 : 라오스. 2000
　Nation : Laos

☞ 자료 평가 Evaluation :
① 태권도가치성 Taekwondo Value ★★★★★
② 도안성 Design ★★★★★
③ 희귀성 Rarity ★★★☆☆

☞ 우표 구성 : 4종 중 1종
　Stamp Composition : 1 of 4 stamps

Commemorating the Sydney Olympic Games, Laos released a wonderfully designed Taekwondo stamp. Colorful stripes representing the Olympic rings are placed behind an intense scene of two sparring athletes. The spread of Taekwondo in Laos was hindered by the former communist government, but the people's passion for the martial art was undeniable. Since 2008 Laos has annually held the "Prime Minister's Taekwondo Tournament" in which the winner is honored by receiving a silver championship trophy presented by the prime minister. The creation of the tournament was a result of the KOICA President Noh-Gyoon Oh sending volunteers to Laos in order to teach and spread the knowledge of Taekwondo, starting in 2000. The Daejeon Taekwondo Association has formed a sister relationship with Laos, supplying the country with Taekwondo supplies and also participating in an athlete exchange program. The Laos Taekwondo Association was enrolled in 1996 and Mr. Pol. Col. Vilay Douangmany is the current president.

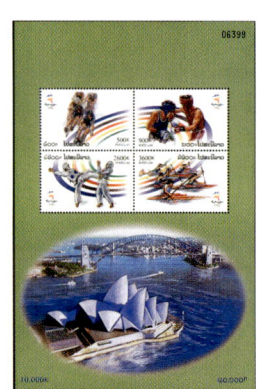

소형쉬이트
A Souvenir Sheet

IX-12. 예멘 태권도 우표
A Taekwondo Stamp from Yemen

날렵한 발차기를 구사하는 픽토그램이 도안된 태권도우표로서 시드니올림픽을 기념하여 예멘에서 발행되었다. 중동에 위치한 사막의 나라 예멘에서 태권도는 신체 발달은 물론 정서함양에도 큰 도움을 주기 때문에 생활체육으로 자리잡고 있다. 예멘은 학교 대항전과 클럽 중심 대항전을 하기 때문에 태권도 인구가 해마다 크게 늘고 있다. 현재 협회 등록 선수가 1만명에 육박하고 있다. 김병훈 사범이 예멘에서 태권도 보급을 담당했다. 예멘 태권도협회는 서울올림픽이 거행된 해인 1988년에 등록되었고 모아파크 모나세르씨가 회장을 맡고 있다.

A pictogram displaying a swift kicking strike can be seen on the Taekwondo stamp Yemen released commemorating the Sydney Olympics. Taekwondo is not simply a means to strengthen the physical body, but it also aids in the development of the mind and spirit. The Middle-Eastern desert country of Yemen utilized these benefits in creating an active and robust sports conscious community. Interscholastic college teams and clubs often participate in Taekwondo competitions, and as a result, the popularity of Taekwondo in Yemen has grown year by year. Taekwondo was widely spread throughout Yemen by Master Byung Hoon Kim and presently the number of registered members of Taekwondo associations is close to approaching ten thousand. The Yemen Taekwondo Association was registered the same year as the Seoul Olympic Games, 1988. The current president is Mr. Moafak Monasser.

함께 나온 우표세트
accompanied stamp set

☞ 국가명 : 예멘. 2000
　Nation : Yemen

☞ 자료 평가 Evaluation :
① 태권도가치성 Taekwondo Value ★★★★★
② 도안성 Design ★★★★★
③ 희귀성 Rarity ★★★☆☆

☞ 우표 구성 : 4종 중 1종
　Stamp Composition : 1 of 4 stamps

IX-13. 세네갈 태권도 우표
A Taekwondo Stamp from Senegal

Taekwondo Stamp No. 101

일반적인 '유공 우표' / a perforated stamp

☞ 국가명 : 세네갈. 2000
　　Nation : Senegal

☞ 자료 평가 Evaluation :
① 태권도가치성　Taekwondo Value　★★★★★
② 도안성　Design　★★★★★
③ 희귀성　Rarity　★★★☆☆

☞ 우표 구성 : 4종 중 1종
　　Stamp Composition : 1 of 4 stamps

시드니올림픽 기념으로 세네갈이 발행한 태권도 우표이다. 태권도 경기 장면과 함께 '태권도' 영문 글자와 세계태권도연맹마크가 선명히 인쇄되어 있다. 우표를 뜯어내는 구멍이 없고 발행량이 적어 희귀성이 높은 무공 우표도 함께 나왔다. 1970년대 초반 프랑스에서 활동했던 이관영 사범은 1974년 세네갈 박람회 행사장에서 태권도 시범을 성공리에 수행하며 태권도를 널리 알렸다. 박익수, 박순근 사범이 세네갈에 태권도를 심었다.

희귀성이 높은 '무공우표'
a imperforated stamp

Shown here is a Taekwondo stamp issued by Senegal to commemorate the Sydney Olympics. The word "Taekwondo" in English and the World Taekwondo Federation logo are distinctly placed beneath a sparring scene. This stamp was released in a perforated and much rarer non-perforated version. Masters living in France would often visit and were responsible for the spreading popularity of Taekwondo in Senegal. In the early 1970s, France released their colonial hold over Senegal and in 1974, a Taekwondo demonstration was held at a festival that catapulted the martial art to the mainstream. The popularity of Taekwondo in Senegal has been strong ever since. Master Ik Soo Park and Soon Geun Park played great roles in popularizing Taekwondo in Senegal.

IX-14. 러시아령 타타르스탄 태권도 우표
A Taekwondo Stamp from Russian Tatarstan

러시아 내 최대의 자치공화국 타타르스탄이 시드니올림픽 기념으로 태권도 우표를 발행했다. 태권도 겨루기 경기에서 두 선수가 공방하는 장면이 우표에 담겼다. 타타르스탄이 속한 러시아는 시드니올림픽 태권도 경기 여자부 나탈리아 이바노바 선수(+67kg급)가 은메달을 획득하는 성과를 올렸다. 시드니올림픽 본선에 진출한 나라는 모두 44개국인데 한국, 필리핀, 타이완, 쿠바, 미국, 스페인 등 6개국만이 남녀 두 체급 모두 출전했다. 타타르스탄은 근래에 한국기업이 많이 진출해 있는 관계로 한국관광공사와 한국문화원과 공동으로 태권도 시범 등 각종 한국 문화 공연이 펼쳐지고 있다.

Russian Tatarstan also released a Taekwondo stamp commemorating the 2000 Sydney Olympics. The stamp design features two athletes battling in full sparring gear. The scene is an actual photograph taken of the silver medal winner in the Women's Taekwondo over 67kg division, Russia's Natalia Ivanova. There were a total of 44 countries that advanced to the finals in Taekwondo, but only 6 countries, South Korea, the Philippines, Taiwan, Cuba, USA, and Spain, had both two men and women participating in the four weight divisions. Recently, many Korean companies have begun to operate in Russian Tatarstan. As a result, various Korean cultural events have been held, including Taekwondo demonstrations, sponsored by both the Korean Tourism Agency and the Korean Cultural Center.

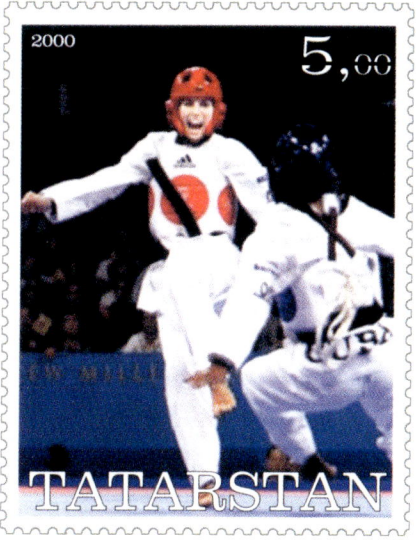

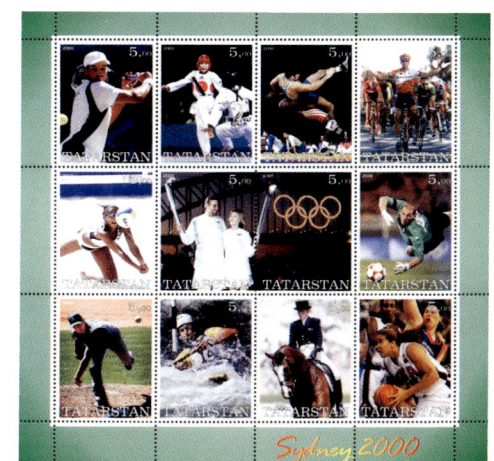

소형쉬이트
A Souvenir Sheet

☞ 러시아령 타타르스탄, 2000
　Russian Tatarstan

☞ 자료 평가 Evaluation :
① 태권도가치성 Taekwondo Value ★★★★☆
② 도안성 Design ★★★★★
③ 희귀성 Rarity ★★★☆☆

☞ 우표 구성 : 12종 중 1종
　Stamp Composition : 1 of 12 stamps

우표로 보는 태권도 발자취 The Evolution of Taekwondo as Seen Through Postage Stamps

 쉼터 · Break Time

시드니올림픽 기념 우취자료
Philatelic Items for Sydney Olympic Games

시드니올림픽을 기념하여 중국에서 발행된 태권도 기념 엽서 2종. 오른쪽 엽서는 태권도 여자부 경기에서 중국의 천종 선수(+67kg)가 금메달을 획득한 기념 엽서이다.

China published 2 postcards to celebrate the Sydney Olympic Games. The right one commemorates Chen Zhong, the female gold medalist of the women's division (+67kg).

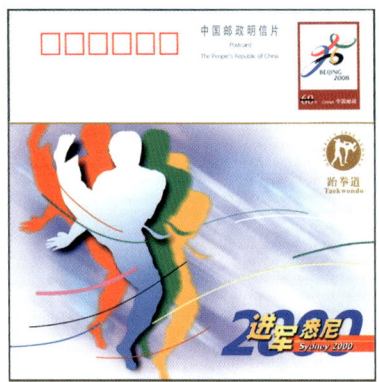 

시드니올림픽을 기념하여 독일에서 발행된 미터스탬프 1종.
시드니올림픽에서 첫 정식종목이 된 태권도와 시범종목인 철인삼종경기가 함께 도안되었다. 머지않아 독일에서 태권도 정식우표가 발행되길 기대해 본다.

A Taekwondo meterstamp published in Germany for the Sydney Olympics. Taekwondo, first appearing as an official event in Sydney, is placed alongside the Triathlon, an exhibitional event. We hope the German government will issue a Taekwondo stamp in the near future.

2004년 제28회 아테네 하계올림픽 정식종목 거행

Taekwondo As an Official Sport at The 28th Olympiad – The 2004 Athens Summer Olympic Games

아테네올림픽 기념 공식 우편 엽서
Official Postcard for the Athens Olympics

시드니올림픽에 이어 2004년 아테네올림픽에서도 태권도는 정식종목으로 거행되었다. 1896년 프랑스 쿠베르탱 남작(1863~1937)은 고대올림픽을 근거로 스포츠를 통해 인류 공존과 평화 증진을 구현한다는 기치 아래 아테네에서 근대 올림픽을 처음으로 개최했다. 태권도 경기 정신은 "목표를 이루기 위해 고통스런 훈련 과정을 견디며 경기에서 최선을 다하고 승리하더라도 자만하지 않고 패배하더라도 비굴하지 않는다."는 스포츠맨십과도 일치한다. 경기에서 정정당당한 대결이 이루어지도록 공명정대한 판정을 뒷받침하는 것이 심판진과 운영진의 책무이다. 선수, 코치, 심판, 운영진 등 태권도 경기 참여자들은 '태권도 경기를 통해 올림픽 이상의 실천'이란 사명감으로 바람직한 태권도 경기 문화를 형성하는 데 앞장서야 한다. 아테네올림픽 태권도 경기는 시드니와 동일하게 남녀 각각 4체급으로 총 8개의 금메달이 배정되었다.

In the same fashion as the Sydney Games, Taekwondo was included as an official event at the 2004 Summer Olympic Games in Athens, Greece. French Baron Pierre de Coubertin (1863-1937) is considered to be the father of the modern Olympic Games for reviving the Games from the ancient Greek Olympics. It was his belief that sports could be used as a catalyst to promote peaceful coexistence between people of all nations, and so in 1896 the first modern Olympic Games were held in Athens, Greece. The spirit of Taekwondo states that "in the enduring of painful and difficult training, one is able to perform at their highest capacity. One must be humble in victory and accept defeat without bitterness." This code of sportsmanship is taught to all practitioners of Taekwondo. It is also the duty and obligation of the management staff and referee officials to always conduct Taekwondo matches in a fair, just, and equal manner. Taekwondo athletes, coaches, management staff, referees, and all participants are responsible for upholding the ideals of Taekwondo on the world stage of the Olympic Games. Identical to the Sydney Games, Taekwondo at the Athens Games consisted of 4 weight divisions for both men and women. 8 gold medals in total were offered for Taekwondo events.

우표로 보는 태권도 발자취 The Evolution of Taekwondo as Seen Through Postage Stamps

X-1. 아테네올림픽 주최국 그리스가 발행한 태권도 우표 1종

올림픽 주최국인 그리스가 최초의 올림픽 주최국 태권도 종목 우표를 발행했다. 그리스 우정국은 아테네올림픽을 기념하여 태권도를 포함한 22개 종목을 담은 우표첩을 발행했다. 아테네 올림픽 공식 마스코트인 그리스 고대 인형인 페보스가 몸통보호대를 착용하고 익살스런 표정으로 발차기를 하는 모습이 이채롭다. 올림픽이 열리는 해에 세계 각국에서 올림픽 기념우표를 발행하는데 특히 올림픽 주최국에서 발행하는 기념우표에 태권도가 포함된 것이 큰 의미가 있다.

The host nation of Greece was the first to release a Taekwondo stamp for the 2004 Olympic Games. The Greek postal service issued 22 stamps commemorating Olympic events including Taekwondo stamps. The stamp displayed here shows the Athens Olympic mascot, an ancient greek doll named "Phevos", wearing a chest protector and playfully performing a kick. The year the Olympics were held, many participating nations released their own versions of stamps commemorating the Olympic Games, but the Taekwondo stamps issued by the host nation hold much more significance than those issued by other countries.

☞ 국가명 : 그리스 I, 2004
　Nation : Greece I

☞ 자료 평가 Evaluation :
① 태권도가치성 Taekwondo Value ★★★★★
② 도안성 Design ★★★★★
③ 희귀성 Rareness ★★★★☆

☞ 우표 구성 : 우표 20종 중 1종
　Stamp Composition : 1 of 25 stamps

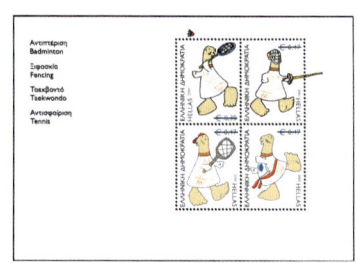

아테네올림픽을 기념하여 주최국인 그리이스가 발행한 특별 우표첩.
설명문을 포함하여 총 14쪽에는 태권도를 포함한 22개 올림픽 종목 우표가 담겨있다.
A postal booklet issued by the host nation Greece celebrating the Athens Olympic Games. The booklet contains 22 Olympic events including Taekwondo detailed within 14 pages.

For the 2004 Athens Summer Olympic Games
A Taekwondo Stamp from Greece, the Host Country

2004년 아테네 올림픽 태권도 +80Kg급 남자부 결승전에서 한국의 문대성은 그리스의 강호 니콜라이디스 선수에게 뛰어뒤 후리기로 K.O승을 거둠으로서

태권도의 묘미를 북돋웠다. 문대성이 쓰러진 니콜라이디스 선수를 일으켜 세워 포옹하며 그의 손을 들어주는 아름다운 행동은 관중들에게 감동의 순간을 선사했다. 태권도 종목에서 남녀 합쳐서 총 8개의 금메달이 배정되었고 한국은 여자부 -57Kg급에서 우승한 장지원 선수를 포함하여 2개의 금메달을 땄다. 중국과 타이완이 각각 금메달 두 개로 한국과 동일하며 이란과 미국이 각각 금메달 1개를 획득했다.

In the Men's Taekwondo over 80kg division finals, Korea's Dae Sung Moon knocked out Greece's top athlete Alexandros Nikolaidis with a beautifully executed jumping back spinning kick. In a truly heart-warming gesture, Dae Sung Moon offered his hand to his defeated opponent. The two hugged and Moon raised Nikolaidis' hand drawing emotional applause from the audience. Combining both male and female events, a total of 8 Taekwondo gold medals were available at the Games. South Korean athletes took 2 gold medals, including Chang Ji Won in the Women's under 57kg division. China and Taiwan won 2 gold medals respectively, while Iran and the USA each acquired one gold medal each.

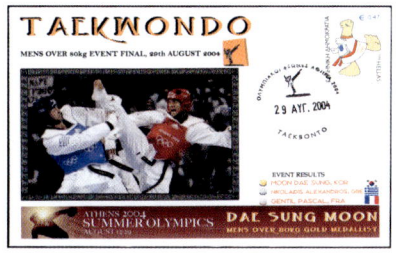
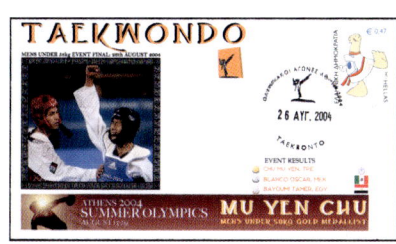
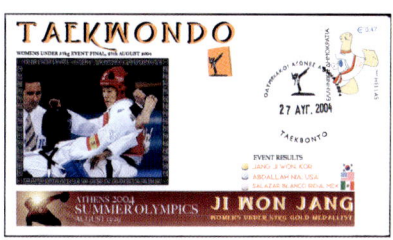

아테네올림픽 태권도 종목에서 우승한
선수들 모습이 나온 초일봉투
The First Day Covers for the winners of
the Taekwondo event in the Athens
Olympics

우표로 보는 태권도 발자취 The Evolution of Taekwondo as Seen Through Postage Stamps

X-2. 아테네올림픽에서 주최국 그리스의 명예를 높인 태권도 메달리스트 우표 2종

☞ 국가명 : 그리스 II-1. 2004
　 Nation : Greece II-1

☞ 자료 평가 Evaluation :
① 태권도가치성 Taekwondo Value ★★★★☆
② 도안성 Design ★★★★★
③ 희귀성 Rareness ★★★☆☆

☞ 우표 구성 : 16종 중 1종
　 Stamp Composition : 1 of 16 stamps

그리스 우정국은 주최국의 명예와 긍지를 높인 16명의 아테네올림픽 자국 메달리스트들을 기념우표로 발행했다. 태권도 종목에서는 남녀 각각 은메달의 딴 2명의 선수가 인물 우표에 나오는 영광을 얻었다. 남자부 +80Kg급에서 그리스의 선수인 니콜라이디스는 은메달을 획득하여 주최국의 체면을 살렸다. 그는 절치부심하여 4년 후 베이징 올림픽에서 결승전에 진출했지만 한국 선수 차동민에게 얼굴 득점을 허용하여 5:4로 분패했다. 그리스는 1991년 제10회 세계태권도 선수권대회와 2002년에는 제4회 세계주니어 선수권대회 등 적극적으로 태권도 경기를 개최하며 태권도 발전에 기여했다

The Greek postal service honored all medal winners from Greece by commemorating their achievements on postage stamps. Of the 16 medals awarded to Greece, 2 were silver medals won in male and female Taekwondo events. Greece's Alexandros Nikolaidis won the silver medal in the Men's over 80 kg division. The medal was not simply a great personal achievement, but also an honor to his country. 4 years later at the Beijing Olympics, Nikolaidis was narrowly defeated 5 to 4 by Korea's Dong Min Cha by an unfortunate blow to the face. In 1991, Greece held the 10th World Taekwondo Championships and the 4th World Junior Taekwondo Championships in 1992. Greece has continually contributed to the expansion and development of Taekwondo worldwide.

기념 우표 전지   A full sheet of the stamp

2 Taekwondo Stamps and First Day Covers From Greece the Host Country for the Athens Olympic Games

주최국 그리스는 아테네올림픽 태권도 경기에서 은메달 하나를 추가했다. 여자부 -67Kg급에서 엘리사벳 미스타키도우는 결승전에서 중국 웨이루 선수에 패해 준우승했지만 그리스 국민들의 열렬한 환영을 받았다. 그리스가 태권도 강국이 되기까지는 안헌기, 강찬진, 김정흠, 오영주 사범진들의 노고가 컸다. 그리스는 유럽 지역 49개국이 가입되어 있는 유럽태권도연맹 회장국이다. 그리스태권도 협회는 1985년 정식 등록되었으며 아타나시오스 프라갈로스씨가 회장이다.

The host nation of Greece released this stamp to commemorate Elisavet Mystakidou's silver medal performance in the Woman's under 67kg Taekwondo event. Although she lost before the finals to China's Wei Luo, she had a strong second-place performance and was well received by her fellow Greeks. Before Greece became so fervent for Taekwondo, Masters such as Hun Gi Ahn, Chan Jin Kang, Jung Hum Kim, and Young Ju Oh helped to spread Taekwondo throughout the country. Greece is the head of the European Taekwondo Union which consists of 49 countries in the European region. The Greek Taekwondo Federation was enrolled in 1985 and Mr. Athanasios Pragalos is the current president.

Taekwondo Stamp No. 105

- 국가명 : 그리스 II.-2 2004
  Nation : Greece II-2
- 자료 평가 Evaluation :
  ① 태권도가치성 Taekwondo Value ★★★★☆
  ② 도안성 Design ★★★★★
  ③ 희귀성 Rareness ★★★☆☆
- 우표 구성 : 16종 중 1종
  Stamp Composition : 1 of 16 stamps

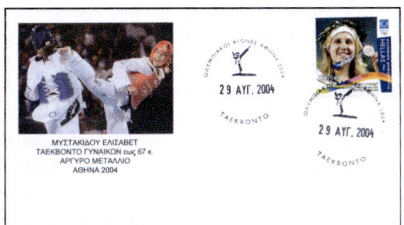

기념 초일봉투 2종 2 kinds of First Day Cover   기념 우표 전지 A full sheet of the stamp

우표로 보는 태권도 발자취 The Evolution of Taekwondo as Seen Through Postage Stamps

X-3. 콩고 태권도 우표
A Taekwondo Stamp from Congo

Taekwondo Stamp No. 106

☞ 국가명 : 콩고, 2004
  Nation : Congo

☞ 자료 평가 Evaluation :
① 태권도가치성 Taekwondo Value ★★★★★
② 도안성 Design ★★★★★
③ 희귀성 Rareness ★★★☆☆

☞ 우표 구성 : 4종 중 1종
  Stamp Composition : 1 of 4 stamps

아프리카 중부 내륙에 위치한 콩고 민주공화국에서 태권도 우표를 선보였다. 우표에는 여자부 +67Kg에 출전한 중국의 첸종 선수가 우승이 확정되자 중국 국기를 휘날리며 기쁨을 만끽하는 장면이다. 이 우표는 올림픽에서 금메달을 딴 선수들을 소재로 한 기념우표로서 해외 우표 수집가를 위해 발행되었다. 콩코민주공화국 태권도협회는 2005년도에 등록되었고 아레인 바댜실레 카얕시 씨가 회장이다. 2010년에 100명 규모의 세계태권도평화봉사단 (재단 총재 이휴원, 이사장 조정원)이 콩코민주공화국에 파견되어 활동할 예정이다.

The Democratic Republic of Congo, located inland in central Africa, released a Taekwondo stamp for the Athens Olympic Games. The stamp features China's Cheng Jong, an athlete in the Woman's over 67kg division. She is joyously waiving her nation's flag after receiving news that she had won the gold medal. This stamp was released to commemorate gold medal winners and was specially issued for collectors of foreign stamps. The Federation Congolaise de Tae Kwon Do was enrolled in 2005 and Mr. Alain Badiashile Kayatshi is currently president. In 2010, one hundred volunteers from the World Taekwondo Peace Corps (founded by Director Hyu Won Lee and President Chungwon Choue of the World Taekwondo Federation), are scheduled to be dispatched to the Democratic Repulic of Congo.

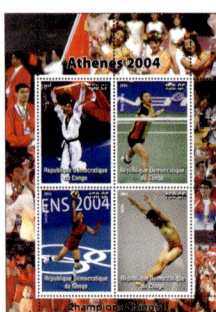  

소형쉬이트와 시쇄용 색도 프루프   A Souvenir Sheet & Color Proofs

X-4. 이란 태권도 우표
A Taekwondo Stamp from Iran

아테네 올림픽 기념으로 이란 태권도의 영웅 사에이 하디 보네코할 선수가 펼치는 겨루기 경기 모습이 도안되었다. 하디 선수는 2000년 시드니올림픽 동메달에 이어 2004년 아테네올림픽에서 금메달을 따냈다. 1998년 세계태권도 선수권대회 우승을 차지하면서 일약 세계적인 선수로 떠올랐다. 당시 부친상을 당하는 어려움을 딛고 이후 올림픽 메달을 휩쓸었다. 2008년 베이징 올림픽까지 석권하면서 10년 동안 세계 최정상의 자리를 지켰다. 2003년 이란 대지진이 났을 때 하디는 자신의 모든 메달과 트로피를 경매에 부쳐 이재민을 도우며 이란 국민들에게 희망을 선사했다.

Hadi Bonehkohal, a national Taekwondo icon and hero in Iran, was placed on this commemorative stamp displaying a sparring match issued by the Iranian postal service during the 2004 Athens Games. Hadi won bronze at the 2000 Sydney Games and gold at the 2004 Athens Olympics. With his victory at the 1998 World Taekwondo Championships, Hadi garnered instant worldwide recognition. He had been mourning the death of his father at the time, but he then would go on to completely dominate every Taekwondo competition. Up until the 2008 Beijing Olympic Games, Hadi continually proved his dominance for 10 years as one of the world's best Taekwondo athletes. In 2003, Iran experienced a disastrous earthquake. In a truly noble and selfless gesture, Hadi auctioned all of the medals and trophies he accumulated over the years and donated the proceeds to victims of the earthquake. A true hero of his people, Hadi helped bring hope back to the suffering in Iran.

Taekwondo Stamp No. 107

- 국가명 : 이란 II. 2004
  Nation : Iran II

- 자료 평가 Evaluation :
  ① 태권도가치성 Taekwondo Value ★★★★★
  ② 도안성 Design ★★★★★
  ③ 희귀성 Rareness ★★★☆☆

- 우표 구성 : 4종 중 1종
  Stamp Composition : 1 of 4 stamps

맥시멈 카드 a Maximun Card

기념 초일봉투 First Day Cover

우표로 보는 태권도 발자취　The Evolution of Taekwondo as Seen Through Postage Stamps

X-5. 키리바시 태권도 우표
A Taekwondo Stamp from Kiribati

☞ 국가명 : 키리바시, 2004
　 Nation : Kiribati
☞ 자료 평가 Evaluation :
① 태권도가치성 Taekwondo Value ★★★★★
② 도안성 Design ★★★★★
③ 희귀성 Rareness ★★★☆☆
☞ 우표 구성 : 우표 구성 : 4종 중 1종
　 Stamp Composition : 1 of 4 stamps

호주의 동북방 남태평양의 섬나라 키리바시가 아테네 올림픽을 기념하여 산뜻한 태권도 우표를 발행했다. 키리바시는 올림픽 사상 최초로 참가한 기념으로 발행한 우표 4종 중 1장을 태권도 겨루기 경기 장면으로 도안했다. 키리바시는 바다 멀리 고립된 위치적 조건과 11만명 남짓한 적은 인구수 때문에 태권도 보급이 다른 나라에 비해 상당히 늦어졌다. 키리바시는 2006년도 베트남에서 열린 제 18차 세계태권도연맹 정기총회에서 새 회원국으로 승인되었다. 같은 해에 태국에서 열린 제1회 월드컵 단체대항 태권도겨루기 선수권대회에 키리바시 선수단도 참가했다. 에디 카로우아 씨가 키리바시 태권도협회를 이끌고 있다.

The small island nation of Kiribati, located in the Southern Pacific northeast of Australia, released this elegant Taekwondo stamp commemorating the Athens Olympics. Four stamp sets were released, one of which contained stamps featuring a Taekwondo sparring match. Because Kiribati is such a small isolated island nation, having a population of just slightly over one hundred ten thousand, proportionately the spread of Taekwondo was less great compared to other nations. At the 2006 18th World Cup Taekwondo Federation Conference in Vietnam Kiribati was officially approved as a new nation member. That same year Kiribati particapated in the very first World Cup Taekwondo Team Championships. Currently, Mr. Eddie N. Karoua is head of the Kiribati Taekwondo Association.

함께 나온 우표세트
accompanied stamp set

X-6. 베트남 태권도 우표
A Taekwondo Stamp from Vietnam

베트남은 시드니올림픽에 이어 아테네올림픽 기념으로 태권도 우표를 발행했다. 우표에는 태권도 겨루기 장면과 영문으로 태권도란 글자가 새겨졌다. 베트남은 아테네올림픽에서는 메달을 따내지 못했지만 아시아권에서는 두각을 나타내고 있다. 2004년 아테네올림픽 한 달 전에 열린 'LG배 국제 태권도 대회'에서 베트남은 금메달 6개로 종합 우승을 차지했다. 이 대회에는 한국, 베트남, 대만, 말레이지아, 태국 등 5개국의 200여 선수단이 참여했다. 베트남 태권도협회는 1989년 등록되었고 당 쿠오 티엔 씨가 회장이다.

As they had done for the Sydney Games, Vietnam again released a commemorative Taekwondo stamp for the Athens 2004 Games. The stamp design features a sparring scene with Taekwondo written across in English. Although Vietnam did not medal in any Taekwondo events during the Athens Games, they are still among the elite Asian nations practicing Taekwondo. One month before Athens, Vietnam won a total of 6 gold medals in a dominating performance at the LG International Taekwondo Championships. Over 200 athletes from South Korea, Vietnam, Taiwan, Malaysia, and Thailand competed in the tournament. The Vietnam Taekwondo Association was enrolled in 1989 and Mr. Dang Quoc Tien is currently president.

Taekwondo Stamp No. 109

- 국가명 : 베트남 V. 2004
  Nation : Vietnam V
- 자료 평가 Evaluation :
  ① 태권도가치성 Taekwondo Value ★★★★★
  ② 도안성 Design ★★★★★
  ③ 희귀성 Rareness ★★★☆☆
- 우표 구성 : 4종 중 1종
  Stamp Composition : 1 of 4 stamps

함께 나온 우표세트
accompanied stamp set

실체 봉투
a used Cover

X-7. 트리니다드 토바고 태권도 우표
A Taekwondo Stamp from Trinidad and Tobago

남미 카리브해에 위치한 섬나라인 트리니다드토바고가 아테네 올림픽을 기념한 태권도 우표를 발행했다. 태권도 수련자가 발차기하는 모습을 세련된 그래픽으로 처리하고 영문 글자로 태권도를 새겼다. 세계태권도연맹은 2013년 창설 40주년을 맞아 'WTF 창설40주년 준비위원회'를 발족했다. 준비위원회 인사로 팬암 지역은 트리니다드토바고태권도협회 회장인 안토니 퍼거슨씨가 맡았다. 트리니다드토바고 태권도 보급은 정진영 사범에 의해 활성화되었다. 트리니다드 토바고 태권도협회는 1983년에 세계태권도연맹에 등록되었다.

The Caribbean island nation of Trinidad and Tobago issued a commemorative Taekwondo stamp for the Athens Olympic games. The stamp includes the figure of an athlete practicing a kick with "Taekwondo" inscribed in English. In 2013, the World Taekwondo Federation will celebrate its 40th anniversary. To prepare for this special occasion, the W.T.F.'s 40th Anniversary Ad-Hoc Committee was established. Mr. Anthony Ferguson, president of the Republic of Trinidad and Tobago Taekwondo Association, will head the Pan-American region. The spread of Taekwondo in Trinidad & Tobago can be attributed to the diligent efforts of many Masters in the region. The Republic of Trinidad and Tobago Taekwondo Association was enrolled in 1983.

☞ 국가명 : 트리니다드앤토바고. 2004
　 Nation : Trinidad and Tobago
☞ 자료 평가 Evaluation :
① 태권도가치성 Taekwondo Value ★★★★★
② 도안성 Design ★★★★★
③ 희귀성 Rareness ★★★★☆
☞ 우표 구성 : 4종 중 1종
　 Stamp Composition : 1 of 4 stampsa

함께 나온 우표세트
accompanied stamp set

X-8. 필리핀 태권도 우표
A Taekwondo Stamp from the Philipines

필리핀이 시드니올림픽에 이어 아테네올림픽 기념으로 태권도 우표를 발행했다. 우표에는 태권도란 영문 글씨와 함께 태권도 겨루기 장면이 세련된 도안의 그림자로 처리되어 역동적으로 표현되었다. 필리핀은 아테네 올림픽 태권도 경기에서 메달을 따지 못했지만 아시아권에서는 강호에 속한다. 2006년 도하아시안게임에서 필리핀은 은메달 2개, 동메달 3개를 획득했다. 필리핀은 고유 무술인 아르니스가 있는 데다 일찍이 가라테가 보급되어 있었다. 1970년 김복만 사범이 혈혈단신으로 진출해 태권도 보급에 앞장섰다. 1971년에 박용만, 1973년에 이성수, 1975년에 홍성천 사범이 진출했다. 홍성천 사범은 태권도를 필리핀 제2의 국기로 격상시켰다. 근래에는 김홍식 사범이 필리핀 경기 태권도를 활성화시켰다. 필리핀 태권도협회는 1973년에 세계태권도 연맹에 등록되었고 회장은 로버트 아벤타자도 씨가 맡고 있다.

In line with the commemorative Taekwondo stamps released for the Sydney Games, the Philippines issued Taekwondo stamps for the Athens 2004 Games. The Athens' stamp consists of a stylized silhouette of a sparring scene along with the English spelling of Taekwondo. The Philippines did not medal in any Taekwondo events at the Athens Olympics, but are still regarded as a dominant force among Asian countries. At the 2006 Asian Games the Philippines won 2 silver and 3 bronze medals. Before the arrival of Taekwondo, the traditional martial art Arnis and Karate were both well practiced in the Philippines. In 1970, Master Bok Man Kim was the first to introduce and spread Taekwondo throughout the country. Later, other masters would follow, including Master Yong Man Park (1971), Master Seong Soo Lee (1973), and Master Seong Cheon Hong (1975). Master Seong Cheon Hong helped to elevate Taekwondo to the nations second largest sport. Recently, Master Hong Sik Kim has been actively supporting Taekwondo events in the Philippines. The Philippines were enrolled in 1973 and the active president is Mr Robert N. Aventajado.

- 국가명 : 필리핀 II. 2004
  Nation : Philippines II
- 자료 평가 Evaluation :
  ① 태권도가치성 Taekwondo Value ★★★★★
  ② 도안성 Design ★★★★★
  ③ 희귀성 Rareness ★★★☆☆
- 우표 구성 : 4종 중 1종
  Stamp Composition : 1 of 4 stamps

기념 초일봉투
First Day Cover

X-9. 코스타리카 태권도 우표
A Taekwondo Stamp from Costa Rica

남미의 코스타리카는 시드니올림픽에 이어 아테네올림픽에서 연속 태권도 우표를 발행했다. 이번에는 다른 종목과 함께 부분적인 도안이어서 태권도 가치성이 한 단계 떨어졌다. 우표는 태권도 발차기를 그림자로 처리하고 빨간 색을 입혀 돋보이게 했다. 1971년에 양원건 사범이 코스타리카에서 태권도 보급을 위해 첫 발을 디뎠다. 코스타리카는 1975년 한국에서 열린 제2회 세계태권도선수권대회에 참가했다. 1997년에 박현서 사범이 코스타리카에 건너가 태권도 겨루기 경기 기술을 향상시켰다. 2010년에 서울에서 열린 '밝은사회(GCS)클럽 국제본부-의장. 조정원' 회의가 'UN 세계평화의 날'을 기념해 열린 행사이고 그 시초는 코스타리카와 관련된다. 1981년 코스타리카에서 개최된 제6차 세계대학총장회의(IAUP)에서 "UN 세계평화의 날"이 제안되었다. 이 행사는 우리 고유의 태권도 정신이 GCS운동과 접목되어 GCS태권도평화봉사단을 발족하는데 산파 역할을 했다.

☞ 국가명 : 코스타리카 II. 2004
　Nation : Costa Rica II

☞ 자료 평가 Evaluation :
① 태권도가치성　Taekwondo Value　★★★★☆
② 도안성　Design　★★★★★
③ 희귀성　Rareness　★★★☆☆

☞ 우표 구성 : 4종 중 1종
　Stamp Composition : 1 of 4 stamps

The Central American nation of Costa Rica released a commemorative Taekwondo stamp for the Athens Olympics, just as they had done for the 2000 Sydney Games. For the new stamp, Taekwondo was placed alongside another event resulting in a slight loss in overall Taekwondo value. On the stamp, the figure of a kicking strike can be seen accented in the color red. In 1971, Master Won Geon Yang introduced and laid the foundation for Taekwondo in Costa Rica. Soon thereafter, Costa Rica participated in the 2nd World Taekwondo Championships in South Korea. The nation's excitement for the sport was evident. In 1997, Master Hyeon Seo Park went to Costa Rica to share his knowledge of Taekwondo to the people. The GCS Club UN World Peace Day celebration in 2010 in Seoul, South Korea has a connection with Costa Rica. The Peace Day festival was first proposed at the 6th IAUP conference, held in Costa Rica in 1981. At the festival the spirit of Taekwondo was fused with GCS sports helping to bridge the two together.

실체봉투
a Used Cover

X-10. 기니 태권도 우표 2종
2 Taekwondo Stamps from Guinea

서아프리카 대서양 연안의 기니공화국이 아테네올림픽 기념으로 2종의 우표를 발행했다. 도안은 동일하지만 우표에 새겨진 액면가(판매가)가 다르게 매겨져 있으므로 내용이 다른 2종의 우표가 된다. 우표에는 태권도 발차기를 하는 모습이 담겨 있다. 태권도 영문 글자가 오류로 표기되어 다소 어색한 우표가 되었다. 아프리카태권도연맹 부회장인 권택일 씨는 기니를 포함한 아프리카 여러 나라에서 태권도 보급과 무역 사업을 병행하며 왕성한 활동을 하고 있다. 여러 나라 대통령에게 태권도를 가르치고 명예 단증과 도복을 수여하는 등 스포츠를 통한 협력 관계 증진에 나서고 있다.

The Republic of Guinea, located on the western shores of Africa, released 2 Taekwondo stamps in commemoration of the Athens Olympic Games. The 2 stamps both include the same design of a kicking strike but are priced differently technically qualifying them as 2 separate stamps. Also, a unique feature of these stamps is the mispelling of the word "Taekwando." The African Taekwondo Federation Vice-President Taek Il Kwon is currently hard at work spreading Taekwondo throughout the continent, to countries such as the Republic of Guinea, as well as promoting trade and commerce between those nations. He also teaches Taekwondo to leaders of various African countries using sports as a catalyst for peace and cooperation.

Taekwondo Stamp No. 113-114

☞ 국가명 : 기니. 2004
　Nation : Guinea

☞ 자료 평가 Evaluation :
　① 태권도가치성 Taekwondo Value ★★★★★
　② 도안성 Design ★★★★☆
　③ 희귀성 Rareness ★★★★☆

☞ 우표 구성 : 4종 중 1종 및 소형시이트 1종
　Stamp Composition :
　　1 of 4 stamps & 1 souvenir Sheets

2종의 소형쉬이트
2 kinds of Souvenir Sheets

우표로 보는 태권도 발자취   The Evolution of Taekwondo as Seen Through Postage Stamps

X-11. 카보 베르데 태권도 우표
A Taekwondo Stamp from Cape Verde

Taekwondo Stamp No. 115

☞ 국가명 : 카보베르데 II. 2004
  Nation : Cape Verde II

☞ 자료 평가 Evaluation :
① 태권도가치성 Taekwondo Value ★★★★★
② 도안성 Design ★★★★★
③ 희귀성 Rareness ★★★☆☆

☞ 우표 구성 : 3종 중 1종
  Stamp Composition : 1 of 3 stamps

아프리카 대륙의 서쪽 대서양에 있는 섬나라 카보베르데가 시드니올림픽에 이어 아테네올림픽 기념 태권도 우표를 발행했다. 우표에는 영문 태권도 글자와 함께 두 사람의 수련자가 마주 서서 태권도 발차기를 하는 모습이 도안되었다. 카보베르데는 18개의 섬으로 구성되어 인구는 55만명이다. 태권도 인구는 많은 편이 아니지만 시드니올림픽 정식종목 채택 이래 꾸준히 늘고 있다. 태권도 우표가 두 장이나 발행된 것을 보면 그 인기를 짐작할 수 있다. 세계태권도대회 등 큰 규모의 태권도 대회에 꾸준히 참가하고 있다.

In the Atlantic Ocean west of the continent of Africa lies the island nation of Cape Verde. Following their commemorative Taekwondo stamps issued for the Sydney Olympics, Taekwondo stamps were again released for the Athens Olympic Games. The stamp displayed features the word "Taekwondo" written in English along with two kicking athletes training with one another. Cape Verde actually consists of 18 islands and has a total population of 550,000 people. Taekwondo in Cape Verde still has a relatively small following, but after Taekwondo's inclusion as an official Olympic event at the Sydney Games, its popularity has steadily risen. With the nation's release of these Taekwondo stamps, it can be assumed that there is indeed a growing interest in the sport. Cape Verde's participation in Taekwondo tournaments and other Taekwondo related events has also steadily increased.

함께 나온 우표세트   accompanied stamp set

X-12. 타이완 태권도 우표 3종
3 Taekwondo Stamps from Chinese Taipei

중국 타이완이 아테네 올림픽 기념으로 무려 3종의 태권도 우표를 발행했다. 이 우표는 통상적인 올림픽 기념 우표가 아닌 아테네올림픽에서 금메달을 딴 자국 선수들을 축하하기 위해 발행된 특별한 기념 우표이다. 태권도 소재 우표가 한 번에 3종이나 나온 사례는 보기 드물다. 중국 타이완은 태권도 경기에서 최강의 실력으로 정평이 나 있다. 아테네올림픽 태권도 경기에서도 첫 날 남녀 경량급에 걸린 두 개의 금메달을 독차지했다. 추무옌은 남자부 58kg급에서, 천쉬신은 여자부 49kg급에서 각각 우승하여 타이완에 올림픽 금메달을 한꺼번에 2개나 선사했다.

Taekwondo Stamp No. 116-118

To commemorate the Athens Olympic Games Taiwan issued three distinct Taekwondo stamps. These stamps were released not only to commemorate the Olympics, but also to congratulate the gold medal winners at the Games. Releasing 3 Taekwondo stamps, as Taiwan did, is an uncommon but welcome sight. Taiwan has established itself as a serious contender at Taekwondo events. In the lightweight division for both men and women, Taiwan seized both gold medals from all competing nations. Mu Yen Chu won gold in the Men's 58 kg division and Shih Hsin Chen took gold in the Woman's 49 kg division. In one quick stroke Taiwan had received two Olympic gold medals.

기념 초일봉투
First Day Cover

☞ 국가명 : 타이완, 중국 Ⅳ. 2004
　Nation : Chinese Taipei Ⅳ

☞ 자료 평가 Evaluation :
① 태권도가치성 Taekwondo Value ★★★★★
② 도안성 Design ★★★★★
③ 희귀성 Rareness ★★★☆☆

☞ 우표 구성 : 4종 중 3종
　Stamp Composition : 3 of 4 stamps

우표로 보는 태권도 발자취 The Evolution of Taekwondo as Seen Through Postage Stamps

쉼터 · Break Time

아테네올림픽 기념 중국 우취자료
Chinese Philatelic Items for Athens Olympic Games

중국에서 공식 태권도 테마 우표는 발행되지 않지만 태권도 소재의 우편엽서나 중국국가올림픽위원회에서 발행하는 주문형 우표류와 태권도 일부인이 찍힌 우표봉투들이 선보였다.

Official Taekwondo-themed stamps were not published in China for the Beijing Olympics, but a governmental postcard was released. The Chinese Olympic Committee also issued customized stamps and Taekwondo-themed envelopes with dated stamps.

중국은 아테네올림픽에서 타이완과 함께 금메달 두 개를 획득하는 괄목할만한 성과를 올렸다. 중국의 두 개의 금메달은 모두 여자부 몫이었다. -67Kg에서 루오 웨이선수, +67kg에서 첸종 선수가 우승의 영광을 안았다.

China accomplished a successful feat in the Taekwondo Tournament at the Athens Olympic Games, taking 2 gold medals, the same number as Chinese Taipei. Both medals were won by female athletes, -67kg Wei Luo, and +67kg Zhong Chen.

2008년 제29회 베이징 하계올림픽 정식종목 거행
Taekwondo As an Official Sport at The 29th Olympiad – The 2008 Beijing Summer Olympic Games

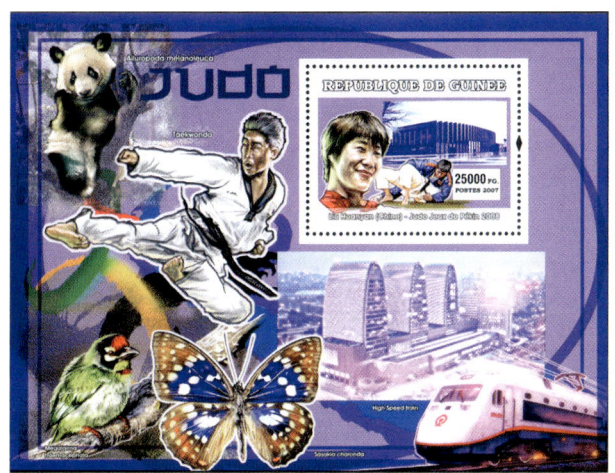

베이징올림픽 기념 기니 소형시트. 태권도 발차기 도안이 액면이 있는 테두리 바깥의 변지에 위치하고 있어 태권도 테마우표에서 제외되었다.
A souvenir sheet from Guinea for the Beijing Olympic Games. This is unfortunately excluded from being an official Taekwondo-Themed stamp because the Taekwondo kicking design is placed outside of the face-valued area.

2008년 베이징 하계 올림픽에서 태권도 경기는 8월 20일부터 나흘간 베이징 과학기술대 체육관에서 열렸다. 태권도 경기에서 남녀 모두 8체급이 배정되어 64명의 남자와 64명의 여자 총 128명이 출전하였다. 남녀 각각 2명씩 총 4명의 한국 선수와 남녀 각각 1명씩 2명의 멕시코 선수가 금메달을 따냈다. 주최국 중국은 금1, 동1을 기록했다. 이란의 하디 선수는 아테네에 이어 베이징에서도 금메달을 따내는 영광을 차지했다. 미국은 은1, 동2, 터키는 은1, 동1을 얻어냈다. 도미니카공화국과 태국이 자국 올림픽 사상 첫 은메달을 따내 큰 수확을 올렸다. 베네수엘라, 아프가니스탄 선수가 조국에 올림픽 사상 첫 번째 메달을 안겼다.

At the 2008 Beijing Summer Olympic Games, the Taekwondo championships was held at the Beijing Science and Technology University Gymnasium for 4 days. 8 weight divisions for both men and women were allocated. 64 male and 64 female competitors, for a total of 128, participated in the championships. Two male and two female competitors from Korea won gold medals along with 1 male and 1 female from Mexico. The host country, China, won one gold and one silver medal. Mr. Hadi from Iran had the honor of earning his second Olympic gold medal, his other one being at the Athens Summer Olympic Games. The USA earned one silver and two bronze medals, while Turkey earned one silver and one bronze medal. The Dominican Republic and Thailand each had a bumper crop, with both earning their first silver medal in the Olympics. Competitors from Venezuela and Afghanistan also took home their first medals in the Olympics.

우표로 보는 태권도 발자취 The Evolution of Taekwondo as Seen Through Postage Stamps

XI-1. 베냉 태권도 우표 1종
A Taekwondo Stamp from Benin

☞ 국가명 : 베냉 II. 2007
  Nation : Benin II

☞ 자료 평가 Evaluation :
① 태권도가치성 Taekwondo Value ★★★★★
② 도안성 Design ★★★★★
③ 희귀성 Rarity ★★★★☆

☞ 우표 구성 : 20종 중 1종
  Stamp Composition : 1 of 20 stamps

아프리카 베냉은 베이징올림픽 1년 전 2종의 태권도 우표를 포함한 올림픽 기념 우표를 미리 발행했다. 태권도 겨루기 경기 장면과 디즈니 캐릭터가 조화를 이루어 어린이들에게 친근한 분위기를 주는 태권도 우표이다. 어린이 우표 수집가들을 위해 인기 높은 만화 그림과 스포츠를 소재로 개발된 특이한 우표이다.

The Republic of Benin, in Africa, issued 2 Taekwondo stamps to commemorate the Olympics one year prior to the Beijing Summer Olympics. These Taekwondo stamps are promoting a friendly atmosphere among children by depicting a harmonious scene involving Taekwondo sparring and a Disney character. These are examples of special stamps designed with cartoons and sports themes popular among children philatelists.

소형쉬이트   A Souvenir Sheet   함께 나온 소형쉬이트 세트 accompanied Souvenir Sheets

희귀 우취 자료인 실용판 색분해 시쇄 Rare items of the progressive main plate proofs

XI-2. 베냉 태권도 우표 2종
Two Taekwondo Stamps from Benin

아프리카 서부 대서양 연안국 베냉이 베이징올림픽 기념으로 태권도 우표 2종을 발행했다. 우표에는 태권도 수련자의 다양한 발차기와 품새 동작을 담고 있다. 베냉은 모두 3회에 걸쳐 6종의 태권도 우표를 선사한 태권도 열성국이다. 베냉은 베이징 올림픽 참가를 위해 태권도 선수를 포함한 15명의 대표단을 파견했다. 베이징 올림픽 선수촌은 베냉을 위해 처음으로 국기게양식을 거행하는 특별 대우를 했다. 베냉이 속한 아프리카대륙 태권도 연맹 회원국은 현재 44개국에 달한다. 베냉 태권도협회는 1978년에 등록되었고 자케 노타이스 씨가 회장이다.

The Republic of Benin, located along the west coast of Africa, issued two Taekwondo stamps to commemorate the Beijing Summer Olympics. The stamps depict various kicks and Poomsae movements of a Taekwondoist. Benin is an enthusiastic Taekwondo country, and has issued a total of 6 stamps on 3 different occasions. Benin dispatched 15 Taekwondo team members, including competitors, to participate in the Olympics. At the Beijing Summer Olympics Athlete's Village, the organizing committee offered a special treat to Benin by holding a ceremony to raise its national flag. The number of member countries of the African Taekwondo Union, including Benin, has now reached 44. The Benin Taekwondo Federation was registered in 1978, and is led today by its current President, Mr. Jacques Emmanuel Enagnon Noutais.

소형쉬이트
A Souvenir Sheet

☞ 국가명 : 베냉 III. 2008
   Nation : Benin III

☞ 자료 평가 Evaluation :
① 태권도가치성 Taekwondo Value ★★★★★
② 도안성 Design ★★★★★
③ 희귀성 Rarity ★★★☆☆

☞ 우표 구성 : 4종 중 2종
   Stamp Composition : 2 of 4 stamps

우표로 보는 태권도 발자취   The Evolution of Taekwondo as Seen Through Postage Stamps

XI-3. 베트남 태권도 우표 1종
A Taekwondo Stamps from Vietnam

Taekwondo Stamp No.122

동남아시아의 베트남이 베이징올림픽 기념으로 태권도 우표를 선보였다. 베트남은 무려 6번째 태권도 우표를 발행함으로써 한국(9종)에 이어 두 번째로 많은 태권도 우표를 발행한 나라이다. 베트남은 시드니올림픽 때부터 3회 연속해서 올림픽 기념 태권도 우표를 발행했다.

Vietnam, in Southeastern Asia, issued a Taekwondo stamp to commemorate the Beijing Summer Olympics. Vietnam has issued Taekwondo stamps six times, and thus is second only to Korea (9 times) in issuing stamps. Vietnam has issued Taekwondo stamps to commemorate 3 consecutive Olympics, starting from the Sydney Summer Olympics.

☞ 국가명 : 베트남 VI. 2008
   Nation : Vietnam VI
☞ 자료 평가 Evaluation :
① 태권도가치성 Taekwondo Value ★★★★★
② 도안성 Design ★★★★★
③ 희귀성 Rarity ★★★☆☆
☞ 우표 구성 : 4종 중 1종
   Stamp Composition : 1 of 4 stamps

희귀성이 높은 '무공우표' an imperforated stamp

기념 초일봉투   First Day Cover

국제실체봉투   An International Used Cover

XI-4. 필리핀 태권도 우표
A Taekwondo Stamp from The Philippines

동남아시아의 필리핀이 베이징올림픽 기념으로 태권도 우표를 발행했다. 필리핀은 태권도가 시드니올림픽 정식종목이 되면서 치러진 3회의 올림픽 대회 기념으로 매번 태권도 우표를 발행함으로써 태권도에 대한 국가적 관심을 보이고 있다. 필리핀은 베이징올림픽 태권도 경기에서 두 명의 기대주에 희망을 걸었지만 아쉽게도 입상하지 못했다. 남자부 58kg급 촘리 고와 여자부 67kg급 마리 리베르토 등이 김홍식 한국인 코치로부터 쌓은 실력을 발휘했지만 유효타가 적어 입상하지 못했다.

The Philippines, in Southeastern Asia, issued a Taekwondo stamp to commemorate the Beijing Summer Olympics. The Philippines has issued Taekwondo stamps for 3 consecutive Olympics after Taekwondo was adopted as an official event at the Sydney Summer Olympics, thus expressing its national interest in Taekwondo. At the Beijing Summer Olympics Taekwondo event, the Philippines had hoped to earn medals in two categories, but unfortunately did not earn any medals. Tshomlee Go in the 58kg male division and Mary Antoinette Rivero in the 67kg female division, who trained with Korean coach Hong Sik Kim, performed excellent skills yet could not earn a medal due to the lack of valid scores.

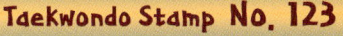

Taekwondo Stamp No. 123

☞ 국가명 : 필리핀 Ⅲ. 2008
  Nation : Philippines Ⅲ

☞ 자료 평가 Evaluation :
① 태권도가치성 Taekwondo Value ★★★★★
② 도안성 Design ★★★★★
③ 희귀성 Rarity ★★★☆☆

☞ 우표 구성 : 4종 중 1종
  Stamp Composition : 1 of 4 stamps

기념 초일봉투
First Day Cover

우표로 보는 태권도 발자취　The Evolution of Taekwondo as Seen Through Postage Stamps

XI-5. 터키 태권도 우표
A Taekwondo Stamp from Turkey

Taekwondo Stamp No. 124

유럽의 태권도 강국 터키가 베이징올림픽 기념 태권도 우표를 발행했다. 터키에서 두 번째로 나온 태권도 우표는 태권도 경기 장면을 그래픽으로 역동성 있게 처리했다. 터키는 올림픽 태권도 경기에서 매번 입상하는 좋은 성적을 올렸다. 베이징올림픽 태권도 경기에서 여자부 -48kg급에서 아지지 탄리쿨루가 은메달을 땄고 남자부 68kg급에서 서베트 타제굴이 동메달을 추가했다. 2004년 아테네 올림픽에서는 남자부 -80kg급에서 바흐리 탄리쿨루가 은메달을 획득했다. 2000년 시드니올림픽에서도 여자부 57kg급에서 하미드 비킨 토선 선수가 동메달을 수상했다.

Turkey, a Taekwondo power in Europe, issued a Taekwondo stamp to commemorate the Beijing Summer Olympics. This Taekwondo stamp, the second one issued by Turkey, depicts a Taekwondo sparring scene with dynamic graphics. Turkey has achieved excellent results in the Taekwondo event at each Olympics. In the Beijing Summer Olympics, Azize Tanrikulu earned a silver medal in the -48kg female division and Servet Tazegul added a bronze medal in the -68kg male division. In the 2004 Athens Summer Olympics, Bahri Tanrikulu earned a silver medal in the -80kg male division. In the 2000 Sydney Summer Olympics, Hamide Bikcin Tosun received a bronze medal in the 57kg female division.

☞ 국가명 : 터키 II. 2008
　Nation : Turkey II

☞ 자료 평가 Evaluation :
① 태권도가치성 Taekwondo Value ★★★★★
② 도안성 Design ★★★★★
③ 희귀성 Rarity ★★★☆☆

☞ 우표 구성 : 4종 중 1종
　Stamp Composition : 1 of 4 stamps

기념 초일봉투
First Day Cover

XI-6. 도미니카공화국 태권도 우표
A Taekwondo Stamp from the Dominican Republic

아름다운 카리브해의 섬나라 도미니카공화국이 세 번째 태권도 우표를 발행했다. 베이징올림픽 기념으로 태권도 경기 장면이 그래픽으로 도안되어 우표에 담겼다. 선수들이 펼치는 박진감 있는 태권도 경기 동작과 영문 글자 태권도가 함께 표현되었다. 베이징올림픽 태권도 경기에서 도미니카공화국 사상 처음으로 올림픽 메달을 따내는 성과를 올렸다. 율리스 가브리엘 메르세데스 선수가 남자부 58kg급에서 당당히 은메달을 따냄으로서 도미니카공화국의 저력을 세상에 떨쳤다. 도미니카공화국이 세 번이나 태권도를 도안한 우표를 펴낸 것도 전국적으로 활성화된 태권도 분위기를 대변한다.

A beautiful country in the Caribbean Sea, the Dominican Republic issued its third Taekwondo stamp, which depicts a Taekwondo sparring scene, to commemorate the Beijing Summer Olympics. This stamp shows a dynamic Taekwondo competition scene performed by athletes, and the inscription, 'Taekwondo', in English. The Dominican Republic achieved an excellent result by earning its very first medal in the Olympics at the Beijing Summer Olympics. Gabriel Mercedes proudly earned his medal in the 58kg male division, thus demonstrating the strength of the Dominican Republic to the world. The fact that the Dominican Republic has issued Taekwondo stamps three times represents the dynamism of the nations Taekwondo.

Taekwondo Stamp No. 125

☞ 국가명 : 도미니카공화국 Ⅲ. 2008
　Nation : Dominican Republic Ⅲ

☞ 자료 평가 Evaluation :
① 태권도가치성 Taekwondo Value ★★★★★
② 도안성 Design ★★★★★
③ 희귀성 Rarity ★★★☆☆

☞ 우표구성 : 4종 중 1종
　Stamp Composition : 1 of 4 stamps

기념 초일봉투
First Day Cover

우표로 보는 태권도 발자취 The Evolution of Taekwondo as Seen Through Postage Stamps

XI-7. 아르헨티나 태권도 우표
A Taekwondo Stamp from Argentina

Taekwondo Stamp No. 126

☞ 국가명 : 아르헨티나. 2008
  Nation : Argentina

☞ 자료 평가 Evaluation :
① 태권도가치성 Taekwondo Value ★★★★★
② 도안성 Design ★★★★★
③ 희귀성 Rarity ★★★☆☆

☞ 우표 구성 : 4종 중 1종
  Stamp Composition : 1 of 4 stamps

남미의 아르헨티나가 첫 태권도 우표를 선보였다. 베이징올림픽 태권도 경기 장면을 우표로 도안하고 영문 태권도 글자를 붙였다. 우표에는 태권도 경기에서 아르헨티나 선수가 내려차기로 상대의 얼굴을 가격하는 모습이 실감나게 표현되었다. 1970년대 이소룡 영화로 인해 날렵한 발차기를 특기로 하는 태권도가 아르헨티나에서 큰 인기를 끌었다. 최남성, 김한창, 정문종, 이석원, 구영채, 원용상 사범이 아르헨티나 태권도 보급에 이바지했다. 구영채 사범은 1977년에 아르헨티나로 이주하여 협회를 창립하고 태권도를 체계적으로 보급했다. 당시 아르헨티나올림픽위원회 위원장이었던 안토니오 로드리게스씨의 적극적 협조로 태권도 경기가 활성화되었다. 뻬레스 꼴만 씨가 아르헨티나 태권도 협회를 이끌고 있다.

The Argentine Republic, in South America, has issued its first Taekwondo stamp. This stamp depicts a Taekwondo competition scene; a dynamic drop kick by an Argentine athlete on his opponent's face, and the inscription, "Taekwondo," in English. Thanks to Bruce Lee's movies in the 1970's, Taekwondo gained national attention in Argentina. Masters such as Nam Sung Choi, Han Chang Kim, Moon Jong Jung, Suk Won Lee, Young Chae Ku, and Yong Sang Won contributed to the development of Taekwondo in Argentina. Master Young Chae Ku emigrated to Argentina in 1977, established the Argentine Taekwondo Confederation and promoted Taekwondo in a systematic way. The President at that time, Mr. Antonio Rodriguez, proactively supported Taekwondo, and competitions were initiated. The Argentine Taekwondo Confederation is currently led by its President, Mr. Edgar Enrique Perez Colmando.

기념 초일봉투 First Day Cover

XI-8. 뉴칼레도니아 태권도 우표
A Taekwondo Stamp from New Caledonia

호주 동쪽에 있는 섬나라 뉴칼레도니아가 베이징올림픽 기념으로 태권도 우표를 발행했다. 이 우표는 도안 면에서 두 가지 흥미로운 특성을 갖고 있다. 우표에는 태권도 경기에서 두 선수가 접전하는 장면 뿐 아니라 배심과 기록원을 함께 넣어 경기장 분위기를 전달한 것이 이채롭다. 두 번째는 우표의 배경화면으로 발행 당사국인 뉴칼레도니아 지도와 함께 태권도 종주국 한국의 지도도 표시되어 태권도가 섬세하게 표현되었다. 2010년 10월 우즈베키스탄 타시켄트에서 열린 세계태권도연맹 임시 총회에서 뉴칼레도니아가 192번째 회원국으로 승인되었다. 1984년 윤승로 사범에 의해 뉴칼레도니아에 태권도가 보급되었다. 앙리 모리니씨가 뉴칼레도니아 태권도 협회 회장이고 앞으로 국제 태권도 행사에 적극 참여할 예정이다.

Taekwondo Stamp No. 127

An island country located east of Australia, New Caledonia, issued a Taekwondo stamp to commemorate the Beijing Summer Olympics. This stamp has two interesting characteristics in terms of its design. The first unique feature is that it includes not only two competing athletes but also the judges and referee, to transmit the entire atmosphere of the arena. The second feature is that it shows the maps of New Caledonia and Korea, the country Taekwondo originated in, as the background, in order to portray Taekwondo in more detail. New Caledonia was approved as the 192nd member country at the extraordinary General Assembly meeting of the World Taekwondo Federation held at Tashkent, Uzbekistan in October 2010. Taekwondo was introduced in New Caledonia in 1984 by Master Seung Ro Yoon. The New Caledonian Taekwondo Association is led by its current President, Mr. Jouanno Henri, and plans to more actively participate in international Taekwondo competitions.

☞ 뉴칼레도니아. 2008
   New Caledonia
☞ 자료 평가 Evaluation :
   ① 태권도가치성 Taekwondo Value ★★★★☆
   ② 도안성 Design ★★★★★
   ③ 희귀성 Rarity ★★★☆☆
☞ 우표 구성 : 3종 중 1종
   Stamp Composition : 1 of 3 stamps

기념 초일봉투
First Day Cover

우표로 보는 태권도 발자취   The Evolution of Taekwondo as Seen Through Postage Stamps

XI-9. 네팔 태권도 우표
A Taekwondo Stamp from Nepal

☞ 국가명 : 네팔 II. 2008
　Nation : Nepal II

☞ 자료 평가 Evaluation :
① 태권도가치성 Taekwondo Value ★★★★★
② 도안성 Design ★★★★★
③ 희귀성 Rarity ★★★☆☆

☞ 우표 구성 : 1종
　Stamp Composition : Single stamp

기념 초일봉투   First Day Cover

네팔이 베이징 올림픽을 기념한 태권도 우표를 발행했다. 올림픽 엠블렘 아래에 두 선수가 겨루기하는 모습이 세련되게 도안되었다. 단 1장의 베이징올림픽 기념우표에 태권도 종목만 선정된 것은 네팔 내의 태권도 위상을 알 수 있다. 태권도 선수 디팍 비스타는 아시안게임에서 동메달 2회, 서남아시아대회에서 금메달 3회를 수상했고 전문직 모델이기도 해 네팔 젊은이들의 우상이 되었다. 2009년에는 국기원과 협력하여 '제2회 한국대사배(홍승목) 전국태권도대회'가 개최되었다. 이 대회에서 람 바란 야다프 대통령과 수상, 그리고 국회(제헌의회) 의장이 직접 참가하여 국기원 명예단증을 증정받기도 했다. 태권도를 네팔의 국기로 추진하려는 네팔 정부의 체육 정책이 태권도 발전에 큰 기여를 했기 때문이다. 네팔에는 신재균 사범이 태권도를 최초로 심고 협회를 이끌었고 권영달, 권혁중 사범이 활성화에 기여했다.

Nepal issued a Taekwondo stamp to commemorate the Beijing Summer Olympics. A scene of two competitors sparring under the Beijing Olympic Emblem is clearly depicted. The fact that a Taekwondo theme was adopted as the country's only commemorative Beijing Olympic stamp indicates the prestige of Taekwondo in Nepal. Nepalese Taekwondo competitor, Mr. Deepak Bista, earned a bronze medals in two Asian Games, and gold medals in three South Asian Games. He is a professional model, and is considered a hero by many Nepalese youngsters. The second National Taekwondo Championships for the Korean Ambassador's Cup was held in Nepal in 2009, with the cooperation of the Kukkiwon. The President of Nepal, Dr. Ram Baran Yadav, the Prime Minister, and the Chairman of the National Assembly attended this event, and each received an honorary dan certificate from Kukkiwon. This was done to recognize and celebrate the huge contribution to the development of Taekwondo by the Nepalese government, as it instituted a national sports policy to adopt Taekwondo as its national sport. Master Jae Gyun Shin introduced Taekwondo to Nepal, and led the Nepal Taekwondo Association. Masters Young Dal Kwon and Hyuk Joon Kwon have contributed to the growth of Taekwondo in the country.

XI-10. 상투메프린시페 태권도 우표
A Taekwondo Stamp from São Tomé and Principe

아프리카 서부의 섬나라 상투메 프린시페가 베이징올림픽 기념으로 특별한 태권도 우표를 선보였다. '우표 속의 우표' 형태로서 태권도 발차기가 나온 다른 나라 우표를 도안했다. 특히 흥미로운 점은 인근 다른 아프리카 나라인 카보 베르데에서 발행된 아테네올림픽 기념 우표가 모습 그대로 옮겨져 상투메프린시페 베이징올림픽 기념 우표로 둔갑되었다는 데 있다. 상투메프린시페 태권도협회는 아테네올림픽이 열리던 2004년에 세계태권도연맹에 등록되었다. 루이 마누엘 두아테씨가 회장이다.

The Democratic Republic of Sao Tome and Principe, in the western part of Africa, issued a special Taekwondo stamp to commemorate the 2008 Beijing Summer Olympics. It looks like a stamp within a stamp, and depicts two figures doing Taekwondo kicks above the name of a different country. The interesting thing is that the copy of the stamp within it had been issued by a neighboring country, Cape Verde, to commemorate the 2004 Athens Summer Olympics. They copied and then put that Cape Verde stamp within their own stamp, and then issued it to commemorate the Beijing Summer Olympics. The Sao Tome and Principe Taekwondo Federation was registered with the WTF in 2004, when the Athens Summer Olympics was held. Mr. Rui Manuel Gomes Duarte is currently serving as the Federation President.

☞ 국가명 : 상투메프린시페 I, 2008
  Nation : Sao Tome and Principe I

☞ 자료 평가 Evaluation :
① 태권도가치성 Taekwondo Value ★★★★★
② 도안성 Design ★★★★★
③ 희귀성 Rarity ★★★☆☆

☞ 우표 구성 : 4종 중 1종
  Stamp Composition : 1 of 4 stamps

소형쉬이트 2종   2 Souvenir Sheets

우표로 보는 태권도 발자취 The Evolution of Taekwondo as Seen Through Postage Stamps

XI-11. 요르단 태권도 우표
A Taekwondo Stamp from Jordan

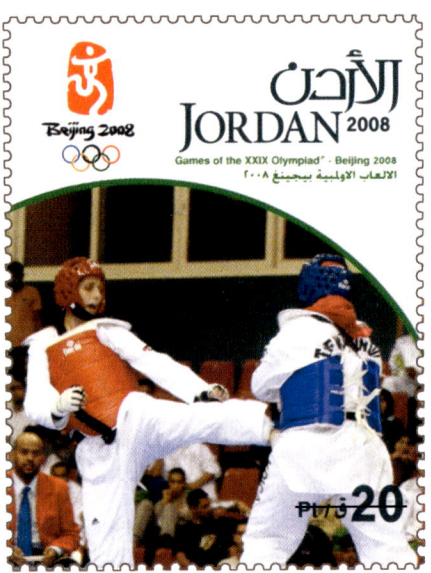

요르단이 베이징올림픽 기념으로 두 번째 태권도 우표를 선사했다. 태권도 경기에서 두 선수가 겨루는 장면과 함께 부심과 관중이 포함된 흥미로운 사진이 그대로 도안되었다. 베이징올림픽에서 요르단 선수가 입상을 하지 못했지만 훌륭한 선수가 여러 명 있다. 2006년 도하 아시안게임에서 금메달을 수상한 알 바퀴트(남자부.-54kg급), 은메달리스트 쿠트쿳(여자부.-72kg급), 자밀 알 쿠파쉬 선수(남자부.-67kg급)가 잘 알려져 있다. 요르단에는 70개의 태권도장이 있고, 그 중 40여 개가 수도 암만에 있다. 예의(禮義), 인내 등 태권도의 기본 정신이 전통적 가치관을 중시하는 중동의 정서와 잘 맞아 태권도가 발전하는 요인으로 보인다.

The Hashemite Kingdom of Jordan issued its second Taekwondo stamp to commemorate the Beijing Summer Olympics. This stamp depicts an interesting photograph of two competitors sparring that also includes a corner judge and some spectators. At the Beijing Summer Olympics, Jordanian competitors did not earn any medals. However, they are a good group of well-known competitors. At the 2006 Doha Asian Games, Al Bakhit earned a gold medal in the 54kg male division, Kutkut a silver medal in the 72kg female division, and Al Khuffash a silver medal in the 67kg male division. There are 70 active Taekwondo schools in Jordan, and 40 of them are located in Amman, the capital. It appears that the development of Taekwondo depends on the fact that the basic tenets of Taekwondo, such as courtesy and perseverance, match values in Middle Eastern cultures which emphasize traditional values.

☞ 국가명 : 요르단 II. 2008
　 Nation : Jordan II

☞ 자료 평가 Evaluation :
① 태권도가치성 Taekwondo Value ★★★★★
② 도안성 Design ★★★★★
③ 희귀성 Rarity ★★★☆☆

☞ 우표 구성 : 4종 중 1종
　 Stamp Composition : 1 of 4 stamps

기념 초일봉투
First Day Cover

XI-12. 온두라스 태권도 우표
A Taekwondo Stamp from Honduras

중미 카리브해 연안 국가의 온두라스가 베이징올림픽 기념으로 두 번째 태권도 우표를 발행했다. 우표에는 도복을 입고 두 사람이 겨루는 그림이 도안되었는데 태권도인지 가라테인지 구별하기가 쉽지 않다. 가라테는 현재 올림픽 종목이 아니므로 베이징 올림픽 기념으로 태권도 종목이 우표에 선택된 것으로 판단된다. 온두라스는 베이징올림픽 태권도 경기에서 입상하지 못했지만 중미 대회에서 활약하고 있다. 태권도 유단자인 포르피리오 로보 소사 온두라스 대통령은 "한국인 송봉경 사범으로부터 받은 가르침 중 정치인으로 냉정하며 침착하게 삶을 살 수 있도록 교훈을 준 점이 기억에 남는다. 한국 문화 전반에 대해 큰 경외심을 갖고 있다. "고 2010년 열린 한국 · 온두라스 정상회담에서 언급했다.

Honduras, by the Caribbean Sea, issued its second Taekwondo stamp to commemorate the Beijing Summer Olympics. The stamp depicts a couple of competitors sparring in uniforms, but it is hard to discern whether they are wearing Taekwondo or Karate uniforms. Since Karate is not an official Olympic discipline, they are understood as Taekwondo uniforms in commemoration of the Beijing Summer Olympics. Honduras did not earn any medals in the Olympics, but it is active in Taekwondo competitions held in Central America. The President of the country, Mr. Porfirio Lobo Sosa is a black belt, which was mentioned at the summit meeting between the Republic of Korea and Honduras held in 2010. As a politician, he remembers the lessons on how to be calm and poised among many other teachings by Korean Master Bong Gyung Song. Mr. Sosa has great respect for Korean culture in general.

Taekwondo Stamp No. 131

☞ 국가명 : 온두라스 II. 2008
　Nation : Honduras II

☞ 자료 평가 Evaluation :
① 태권도가치성 Taekwondo Value ★★★★★
② 도안성 Design ★★★★☆
③ 희귀성 Rarity ★★★★☆

☞ 우표 구성 : 4종 중 1종
　Stamp Composition : 1 of 4 stamps

기념 초일봉투
First Day Cover

우표로 보는 태권도 발자취 The Evolution of Taekwondo as Seen Through Postage Stamps

XI-13. 러시아 태권도 우표
A Taekwondo Stamp from Russia

Taekwondo Stamp No. 132

☞ 국가명 : 러시아. 2008
　　Nation : Russia

☞ 자료 평가 Evaluation :
① 태권도가치성 Taekwondo Value ★★★★☆
② 도안성 Design ★★★★★
③ 희귀성 Rarity ★★★☆☆

☞ 우표 구성 : 3종 중 1종
　　Stamp Composition : 1 of 3 stamps

베이징올림픽을 기념한 러시아 우표에 태권도가 담겨있다. 1988년 서울올림픽 이후에 문호가 개방된 러시아가 태권도 문을 열었다. 1989년 러시아 체육장관이 재미 외교관 시절 태권도 스승인 미국의 이준구 사범을 러시아에 초청하여 태권도를 심었다. 이후 이정기, 이상진, 김종길 사범이 진출하여 활약했다. 그 동안 러시아태권도협회는 유럽태권도선수권대회를 2회 개최하고 1996년 세계대학선수권대회를 유치했다. 최근 2010년에는 러시아 태권도 시범단이 국기원(원장 강원식)을 방문하여 합동 시범을 준비했다. 양국 시범단은 러시아 모스크바에서 열리는 '제2회 주러 한국대사배 태권도대회'에 합동 시범공연을 보인다. 에브제니 클리치니코프 씨가 러시아태권도협회 회장을 맡고 있다.

Taekwondo is featured on a stamp issued by the Russian Taekwondo Federation to commemorate the Beijing Summer Olympics. Russia opened its door to Taekwondo after the Seoul Summer Olympics in 1988 as part of its open-door policy. While the Russian minister of Athletics was in the US in 1989, he invited his Taekwondo Master, Grandmaster Jhoon Rhee, to introduce Taekwondo to Russia. After that, Jung Ki Lee, Sang Jin Lee, and Jong Gil Kim went there to promote Taekwondo. Since its inception, the Russian Taekwondo Federation has organized the European Taekwondo Championship twice, and hosted the World University Taekwondo Championship in 1996. Recently, in 2010, the Russian Taekwondo Demonstration Team visited the Kukkiwon (whose current is President Won Sik Kang) and prepared a joint demonstration with the Korean National Taekwondo Demonstration Team. Both national demonstration teams will perform a joint demonstration at the 2nd Korean Ambassador's Cup Taekwondo Championships to be held in Moscow, Russia. The Russian Taekwondo Federation is led by its current President, Mr. Evgeny Klyuchnikov.

소형쉬이트　A Souvenir Sheet

XI-14. 튀니지 태권도 우표
Two Taekwondo Stamps from Tunisia

북아프리카 지중해 연안 국가인 튀니지가 베이징올림픽 기념으로 두 종의 우표를 선사했다. 우표에는 올림픽 오륜기과 베이징 올림픽 엠블렘을 중심으로 여러 종목들이 배치되고 그 중에 태권도 발차기 그림이 포함되어 있다. 두 종의 우표에는 색깔을 다르게 처리한 조그만 크기의 태권도 픽토그램이 실렸다. 튀니지는 베이징 올림픽 태권도 경기에서 메달을 따지 못했다. 하지만 이번 대회 여자부에서 최연소로 참가했던 벤 함자 카올라 선수가 튀니지 사상 첫 올림픽 메달 가능성을 열었다. 그녀는 주니어 세계선수권대회와 프레올림픽에서 우승했기에 차기 올림픽에서 기대되는 튀지니의 희망이다.

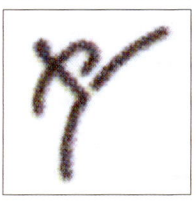

The Tunisian Republic, a Mediterranean country in North Africa, issued two Taekwondo stamps to commemorate the Beijing Summer Olympics. In the center of the stamps, you can see the Olympic emblem and the Beijing Olympics' emblem. Around the center are stylized stick figures representing diverse sport disciplines, including a Taekwondo kicking scene. On both stamps are small Taekwondo pictograms in various colors. Tunisia did not earn any medals in the Taekwondo championships at the Beijing Summer Olympics. However, the youngest female competitor, Khaoula Ben Hamza, opened the door to the possibility of earning an Olympic medals for the first time in the history of Tunisia. She has earned medals at the World Junior Taekwondo Championship and Pre-Olympics, and is considered Tunisia's Olympic hopeful.

Taekwondo Stamp No. 133-134

☞ 국가명 : 튀니지 Ⅰ. 2008
　Nation : Tunisia Ⅰ

☞ 자료 평가 Evaluation :
① 태권도가치성
　Taekwondo Value ★★★★☆
② 도안성 Design ★★★★☆
③ 희귀성 Rarity ★★★☆☆

☞ 우표 구성 : 2종 중 1종
　Stamp Composition : 2 stamps

우표로 보는 태권도 발자취 The Evolution of Taekwondo as Seen Through Postage Stamps

XI-15. 리비아 태권도 우표
A Taekwondo Stamp from Libya

☞ 국가명 : 리비아, 2008
  Nation : Libya

☞ 자료 평가 Evaluation :
  ① 태권도가치성
    Taekwondo Value ★★★★☆
  ② 도안성 Design ★★★★★
  ③ 희귀성 Rarity ★★★☆☆

☞ 우표 구성 : 기념우표 1종
  Stamp Composition : Single stamp

아프리카 북부 지중해 해안을 접한 리비아에서 펴낸 베이징올림픽 기념 우표에 태권도 그림이 나왔다. 우표에는 다른 네 종목과 함께 중앙 윗부분에 품새 태극 7장에 나오는 외산틀 막기가 그려져 있다. 올림픽에서 태권도 경기는 겨루기만 거행되는 만큼 겨루기 관련 이미지가 도안되었으면 하는 아쉬움이 있다. 리비아는 2007년에 베이징 올림픽 아프리카 지역 예선을 개최했는데 이 대회는 리비아가 사상 처음으로 개최하는 아프리카 대륙 규모의 국제 대회였다. 28개국 88명의 선수가 참가한 이 대회에 한국의 삼성전자가 20여명의 "삼성 희망의 시범단"을 파견하여 태권도 시범과 교육 활동을 공식 후원했다. 리비아 대통령 경호관까지 역임했던 김용광 사범이 리비아에 태권도를 전파하는데 공을 세웠다. 70년대 중반 강문현 사범도 가세했다. 리비아 태권도협회는 1979년에 등록되었고 모하메드 반닥씨가 회장이다.

A Taekwondo figure appears on the stamp to commemorate the Beijing Summer Olympics issued by Libya, a Mediterranean country in North Africa. On the stamp, you can see the Oe-san-teul makki of Taegeuk Chiljang Poomsae on the upper middle area of the stamp. Four other disciplines are represented on the stamp. I wish that a Taekwondo sparring image were depicted, since only the sparring aspect of Taekwondo is performed in the Olympics. Libya hosted the African Regional Selection Tournament for the Beijing Summer Olympics in 2007. This was the first international African tournament that Libya had ever hosted. 88 competitors from 22 countries participated in the championship. Samsung Electronics sponsored a Taekwondo demonstration team and educational activities by dispatching the "Samsung Demonstration Team of Hope," consisting of 20 members, to Libya. Master Yong Kwang Kim, who was a body guard of the Libyan president, contributed to the dissemination of Taekwondo in Libya. The Libyan Taekwondo Federation was registered in 1979, and is led by its current President, Mr. Mohamed Moh. Khalifa Ali Bandak.

XI-16. 소말리아 태권도 우표 2종
Two Taekwondo Stamps from Somalia

아프리카 대륙 동부 인도양 연안의 해안국 소말리아가 베이징올림픽 기념으로 첫 태권도 우표를 발행했다. 우표에는 역대 올림픽 태권도 경기에서 중국에 금메달을 선사한 두 명의 유명한 여자 선수가 실렸다. 위 선수는 시드니에 이어 아테네올림픽에서도 여자부 +67kg급 금메달을 수상한 첸종 선수이다. 첸종 선수는 베이징올림픽 8강전에서 영국의 사라 스티븐슨에게 아깝게 패해 메달권 진입에 실패했다. 아래 선수는 베이징올림픽 여자부 49kg급에서 우승을 차지한 우 징위 선수이다. 우 선수는 태권도 경기 종목에서 주최국 중국에게 유일한 금메달을 제공했다. 중국은 남자 80kg급에서 주귀 선수가 동메달을 추가했다. 소말리아태권도협회는 1997년에 등록되었고 아웨이 아바티씨가 회장이다.

The Republic of Somalia, located on the east coast of Africa and by the Indian Ocean, issued its first Taekwondo stamps to commemorate the Beijing Summer Olympics. On the stamps, two famous female competitors, who had earned gold medals in the Olympics, are featured. The competitor on the top is Chen Zhong, who earned the gold medal in the 67kg female division at the Athens Summer Olympics as well as at the Sydney Summer Olympics. Chen Zhong lost in the quarter final match against Sarah Stevenson of Great Britain at the Beijing Summer Olympics. The competitor on the bottom is Wu Jingyu, who earned the gold medal in the 49kg female division at the Beijing Summer Olympics. Ms. Wu earned the only gold medal for the host country, China, in the Taekwondo event. Zhu Guo added a bronze medal in the 80kg male division for China. The Somali Taekwondo Federation was registered in 1997 and is led by its current President, Mr. Aweys Mohamed Abati.

- 국가명 : 소말리아. 2008
  Nation : Somalia
- 자료 평가 Evaluation :
  ① 태권도가치성 Taekwondo Value ★★★★★
  ② 도안성 Design ★★★★★
  ③ 희귀성 Rarity ★★★★☆
- 우표 구성 : 4종 중 2종
  Stamp Composition : 2 of 4 stamps

XI-17. 상투메프린시페 태권도 우표 6종
Six Taekwondo Stamps from São Tomé and Principe

Taekwondo Stamp No. 138-143

- 국가명 : 상투메프린시페 II- 1~6. 2009
  Nation : São. Tomé and Principe II- 1~6
- 자료 평가 Evaluation :
  ① 태권도가치성 Taekwondo Value ★★★★★
  ② 도안성 Design ★★★★★
  ③ 희귀성 Rarity ★★★☆☆
- 우표 구성 : 6종 중 6종
  Stamp Composition : 6 of 6 stamps

아프리카 상투메 프린시페가 한번에 6종의 태권도 우표를 파격적으로 선사했다. 베이징올림픽 태권도 종목 금메달리스트 6명을 각 우표에 담아 올림픽의 영광을 되새겼다. 이 우표들은 2009년 한국이 개최한 '필라코리아 제24회 아시아 국제우표전시회'를 기념하기 위해 특별히 제작되었다. 한국은 1984년, 1994년, 2002년 등 세계우표전시회를 3회나 개최하기도 했다.

The Democratic Republic of Sao Tome and Principe, in Africa, issued 6 special Taekwondo stamps. They put a Taekwondo gold medalist on each of the stamps to highlight the glory of the Olympics. These stamps were specially designed to commemorate the PHILAKOREA 2009 24th Asian International Philately Exhibition held in Seoul in 2009. South Korea has organized a world stamp exhibition 3 times; in 1984, 1994 and 2002.

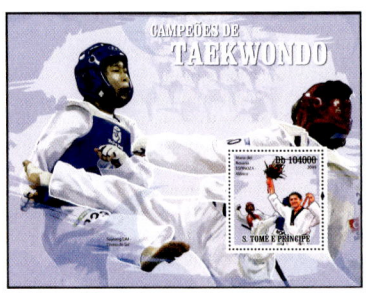

상투메 프린시페가 두 번째로 발행한 태권도 우표 6장에는 여자부 4명과 남자부 2명의 선수들의 금메달 수상 장면과 경기 모습이 실렸다. 여자부 +67kg급 멕시코의 마리아 에스피노사 선수가 금메달을 목에 걸고 축하꽃다발을 높이 들었다. 여자부 57kg 한국의 임수정 선수가 금메달을 손에 쥐고 환한 웃음을 띠고 있다. 여자부 67kg급 한국의 황경선 선수도 우승의 기쁨을 누리고 있다. 임수정과 황경선은 한국 태권도 선수로서 사상 처음으로 우표에 나왔다. 여자부 49kg급 중국의 우징위 선수도 즐거운 표정으로 금메달을 목에 걸고 있다. 남자부 80kg급 이란 태권도의 영웅 하디 사에이가 금메달이 입에 물고서 짜릿한 금 맛을 보고 있다. 남자부 58kg급 멕시코의 기예르모 페레스 선수가 금빛 대열에 합류했다. 베이징올림픽 태권도 경기에는 남녀 각각 4명씩 총 8명의 우승자가 배출되었는데 아쉽게도 남자부 한국의 손태진(68kg급)과 차동민 선수(+80kg급)가 이 우표에서는 제외되었다.

On the six stamps issued by Sao Tome and Principe, you can see the medal award ceremonies and competition scenes of 4 female and 2 male gold medalists. On one stamp, Maria del Rosario Espinoza , the 67kg female division winner from Mexico, is wearing the gold medal around her neck and raising a celebration bouquet. On another, Su Jung Lim from South Korea, winner of the 57kg female division, is holding the gold medal in her hand and smiling cheerfully. Kyung Sun Hwang, the South Korean winner in the 67kg female division, is enjoying her victory. Su Jung Lim and Kyung Sun Hwang are the first South Korean Taekwondo athletes to appear on stamps. Wu Jing Wei, from China and winner in the 49kg female division, is wearing her gold medal happily. Hadi Saei is biting his medal to taste the gold. Mexico's Guillermo Perez, winner in the 58kg male division, is wearing his gold medal and waving to the crowd. There were 8 gold medalists in the Beijing Summer Olympics, 4 in the female division and 4 in the male division, unfortunately however, South Korea's Tae Jin Sohn, winner in the 68kg male division, and Dong Min Cha, winner in the 80kg male division, were excluded from this set.

우표로 보는 태권도 발자취   The Evolution of Taekwondo as Seen Through Postage Stamps

XI-18. 기니비사우 태권도 우표
A Taekwondo Stamp from Guinea-Bissau

Taekwondo Stamp No. 144

아프리카의 기니비사우가 베이징올림픽 기념으로 세 번째 태권도 우표를 선사했다. 우표에는 여자부 49kg급 우승자 중국의 우 징위 선수의 금메달 수상 모습과 경기 장면이 도안되었다. 중국의 우 선수는 소말리아, 상투메프린시페에 이어 기니비사우까지 3개국의 공식 우표에 등장하는 유명 인물이 되었다. 베이징 하계 올림픽에 참가한 나라 수는 기니비사우를 포함해 205개국에 이른다. 베이징 과학기술대학교 체육관에서 거행된 태권도 경기에서 남녀 64명씩 총 128명의 선수들이 참가하여 열전을 벌였다. 베이징올림픽에 참여한 심판진으로 29개국에서 29명이 선발되었다. 세계태권도연맹은 올림픽 거행 직전 선임된 심판들을 대상으로 다가오는 베이징올림픽 태권도 경기에서 공정한 심판을 다짐하는 '올림픽 심판보수교육'을 개최했다.

☞ 국가명 : 기니비사우 III. 2008
　Nation : Guinea-Bissau III

☞ 자료 평가 Evaluation :
① 태권도가치성 Taekwondo Value ★★★★★
② 도안성 Design ★★★★★
③ 희귀성 Rarity ★★★☆☆

☞ 우표 구성 : 4종 중 1종
　Stamp Composition : 1 of 4 stamps

소형쉬트
A Souvenir Sheet

The African nation of the Republic of Guinea Bissau issued its third Taekwondo stamp to commemorate the Beijing Summer Olympics. The stamp depicts Chinese athlete Wu Jingyu, winner of the 49kg female division, holding her gold medal with a competition scene as the background. Chinese competitor Wu became quite the celebrity, being featured on three different stamps issued by Somalia, Sao Tome and Principe and Guinea Bissau. The number of participating countries in the Beijing Summer Olympics reached 205, including Guinea Bissau. At the Olympic Taekwondo championships held at the Beijing Science and Technology University Gymnasium, 128 competitors, 64 male and 64 female, engaged in heated contests. 29 referees from 29 countries were recruited to judge the matches, and the World Taekwondo Federation organized an "Olympic Referee Refresher Seminar" for these appointed referees in order to ensure fair judging.

XI-19. 베이징올림픽 주최국 중국의 태권도 소재 우편 자료
Several Taekwondo-Themed Postal Items from China, The Host Country of the Beijing Olympics

중국은 시드니올림픽부터 베이징올림픽까지 금메달을 모두 4개나 따낸 태권도 강국이지만 베이징올림픽을 기념한 공식 태권도 우표를 발행하지 않았다. 대신 우편엽서, 나만의 우표, 봉투 등 여러 우편 자료들이 중국 올림픽위원회에서 제작되어 발매되었다.

Even though the People's Republic of China emerged as a Taekwondo power by earning 4 gold medals from the Sydney Summer Olympics to the Beijing Summer Olympics, it did not issue a Taekwondo stamp to commemorate the Beijing Summer Olympics. Instead, a variety of items ranging from post cards to customized stamps and envelopes were designed and issued by the Beijing Organizing Committee for the Olympic Games.

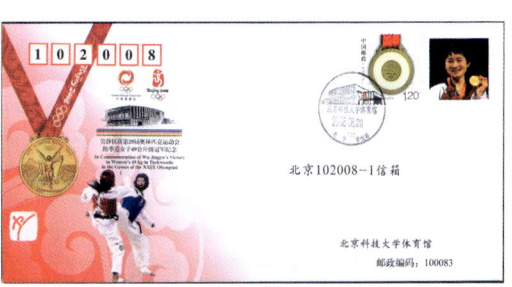

우표로 보는 태권도 발자취　The Evolution of Taekwondo as Seen Through Postage Stamps

쉼터 · Break Time

한국 '태권도의 날' 기념 나만의 우표
A Customized Cover & Stamp from South Korea for Taekwondo Day

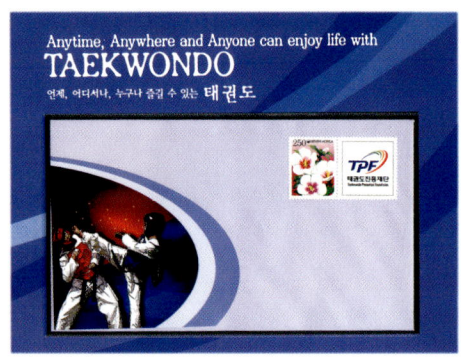

베이징올림픽이 끝난 직후인 2008년 9월 4일 한국은 '태권도의 날'을 기념하는 기념 우편자료를 제작했다. 1994년 9월 4일 파리에서 개최된 제103차 IOC 총회에서 태권도가 올림픽 정식종목으로 채택된 날을 기념하기 위해 '태권도의 날'이 지정되었다. 태권도진흥재단(이사장 이대순)은 나만의 우표와 봉투 등 우취 수집용 자료를 담은 6쪽짜리 우표첩을 발행했다

South Korea issued a customized cover and stamp to commemorate Taekwondo Day, September 4th, 2008, right after the Beijing Summer Olympics. Taekwondo Day was designated to celebrate the adoption of Taekwondo as an official event at the 103rd IOC General Assembly Session held on September 4th, 1994. The Taekwondo Promotion Foundation (Chairman Dai Soon Lee) issued a six page booklet including customized stamps and envelope.

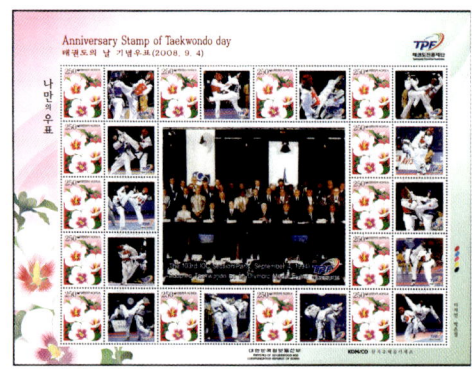

 # 2012년 제30회 런던 하계올림픽 정식종목 거행 예정

Taekwondo Will Be an Official Sport at The 30th Olympiad
– The 2012 London Summer Olympic Games –

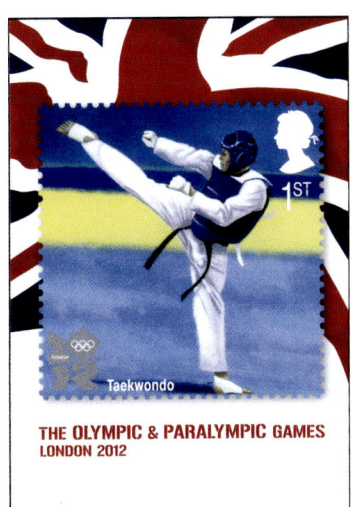

태권도는 2005년 싱가포르 IOC총회에서 과반수가 넘는 지지를 얻어 2012년 런던하계올림픽에서도 정식종목으로 유지하기로 했다. 아울러 2009년 베를린 IOC집행위원회는 2016년 하계올림픽에서 기존 26개 종목에 태권도를 그대로 존속시키기로 결정했다. 이로서 태권도는 2012년 런던올림픽에 이어 2016년 브라질 리우자네이로 하계올림픽에서도 올림픽 종목으로 무난히 개최된다. 태권도는 2000년 시드니 하계올림픽 정식종목으로 첫 선을 보인 후, 5회 연속 올림픽 종목 자리를 지켜내어 국제 스포츠로서 확고한 위상을 보여주고 있다.

At the 2005 IOC General Assembly meeting, a majority of the members voted for Taekwondo to be approved as an official event for the 2012 London Summer Olympics. And, in Berlin in 2009, the Executive Board of the IOC Executive Committee decided to keep Taekwondo as one of its existing 26 official events. Thanks to these decisions, Taekwondo will remain as an official event for both the 2012 London Summer Olympics and the 2016 Brazil Summer Olympics in Rio de Janeiro. With its adoption as an official event in the 2000 Sydney Summer Olympics, Taekwondo has maintained its position for 5 consecutive Olympics, thus demonstrating its widespread popularity as an international sport.

2012년 런던 하계 올림픽을 기념하여 주최국 영국이 발행한 태권도 기념 엽서
Postcards issued by the United Kingdom, the host country of the 2012 London Summer Olympic Games.

우표로 보는 태권도 발자취 The Evolution of Taekwondo as Seen Through Postage Stamps

XII-1. 런던올림픽 주최국 영국에서 발행된 태권도 우표 1종

Taekwondo Stamp No. 145

2012년 런던 하계올림픽 기념 첫 태권도 우표가 영국에서 발행되었다. 이번 태권도 우표는 영국 하계올림픽 주최국 기념우표일 뿐 아니라 우표의 종주국 영국에서 나온 우표라는 점에서 더욱 가치 있고 돋보인다. 우표에서는 태권도 경기에서 한 선수가 펼치는 발차기 공격 장면이 도안되었다

The United Kingdom of Great Britain issued its first Taekwondo-themed stamp in 2010, to commemorate the 2012 London Summer Olympics. The value of this stamp continues to increase not only for it being the first London Summer Olympics commemorative stamp, but also because it was issued by the country where stamps first originated. The stamp depicts a scene of a taekwondoist attacking with a kick in a Taekwondo match.

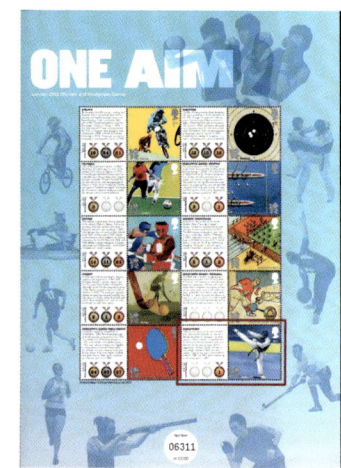

런던올림픽 기념 소형시트
a Commemorative Souvenir Sheet

☞ 국가명 : 영국. 2010
　Nation : Great Britain

☞ 자료 평가 Evaluation :
① 태권도가치성 Taekwondo Value ★★★★★
② 도안성 Design ★★★★★
③ 희귀성 Rarity ★★★☆☆

☞ 우표 구성 : 10종 중 1종
　Stamp Composition : 1 of 10 stamps

함께 나온 우표세트
Accompanied Stamp Set

A Taekwondo Stamp from Great Britain, the Host Country For the 2012 London Summer Olympic Games

지난 2009년 발행된 10종의 올림픽 종목 우표 발행에 이어 런던 올림픽 개최 2년을 앞둔 기념으로 태권도를 포함한 10종의 올림픽 및 장애자올림픽 종목이 2010년 발행되었다. 지난 베이징올림픽 태권도 경기에서 동메달을 따낸 영국 선수의 이름을 새긴 특이한 소형시트가 함께 발행되었다. 영국에는 오래 전부터 박수남, 하승수, 신운섭 사범들의 활약으로 태권도가 널리 퍼져 나갔다. 박수남씨는 세계태권도연맹 부회장을 맡아 왕성한 행정 활동을 펴고 있다. 영국 태권도협회는 1977년에 등록되었고 에드리안 트랜터씨가 회장이다.

After the issuing of the 10 Olympic stamps in 2009, 10 more Olympic and Paralympic Games discipline stamps were issued in 2010, two years before the London Summer Olympics. In addition, a souvenir sheet was issued which included a special inscription about the British competitor who had earned a bronze medal in the Taekwondo championships at the Beijing Summer Olympics. Taekwondo has grown considerably in the UK, thanks to the activities of Masters Soo Nam Park, Seung Soo Ha, and Woon Sup Shin, among others. Master Soo Nam Park is currently serving as a vice president of the WTF, and is an active administrator. The British Taekwondo Control Board was registered in 1977 and is led by its current President, Mr. Adrian Tranter.

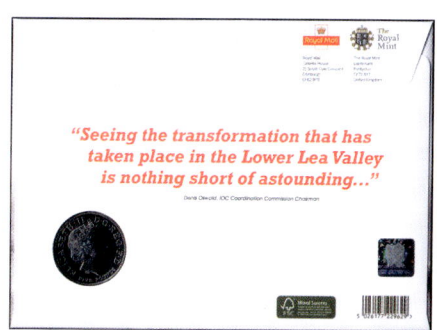

5파운드짜리 런던올림픽 기념 주화가 포함된 초일 봉투
The First Day Cover with Five pound Commemoration Coin issued by the United Kingdom

5파운드짜리 런던올림픽 기념 주화가 포함된 초일 봉투
The First Day Cover with Five pound Commemoration Coin issued by the United Kingdom

우표로 보는 태권도 발자취 The Evolution of Taekwondo as Seen Through Postage Stamps

영국 우정성은 2012년 런던 하계 올림픽을 기념하기 위해 우표의 종주국답게 여러 가지 다채로운 우취용 상품을 제작하여 큰 인기를 끌고 있다. 우표, 증정용 우표팩, 초일봉투, 코인 초일봉투, 기념우표가 동봉된 우편엽서세트, 소량 우표첩, 소형시트 등 갖가지 상품들이 런던올림픽 기념품으로 발매되고 있다.

Mint Stamps, a Presentation Pack, First Day Covers, Coin Covers, Set of Ten Stamp Cards, a Retail booklet, Commemorative Sheet, and Postcards all issued by the United Kingdom, the Host Country for the 2012 London Summer Olympic Games.

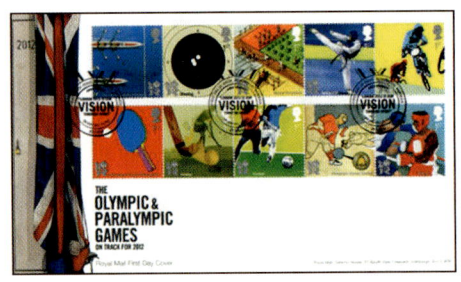

초일봉투
First Day Cover

설명카드가 동봉된 증정용 우표 세트
A Presentation Pack with an Information Card

우표를 함께 담은 우편엽서 세트
A Postcard Set with Stamps

쉼터 · Break Time

2016년 제31회 리오데자네이로 하계올림픽 정식 종목거행
Taekwondo will be An Official Sport at The 31st Olympiad
- The 2016 Rio de Janeiro Summer Olympic Games

태권도 종목은 2016년 리오데자네이로 하계 올림픽에서도 정식종목으로 거행될 예정이다. 앞으로도 각 나라가 태권도 우표들을 계속해서 발행하게 되고 장차 언젠가는 지구상의 모든 나라들이 태권도 우표를 펴내는 날이 올 것이다. 태권도는 이미 한국의 것이 아닌 세계인의 것이 되었다. 무엇보다도 중요한 것은 태권도를 하는 모든 사람들이 각 개인의 행복과 세계평화를 위해 올바른 태권도 정신과 가치를 누리고 확장해가길 기원한다

Taekwondo competition will be held as an official sport at the Rio de Janeiro Summer Olympics in 2016. Taekwondo stamps will continue to be issued in more countries, and the day will soon come when all the countries of the world will have issued their own Taekwondo stamps, for Taekwondo has risen from the national level, to being recognized as a global sport. Above all, I wish that the Taekwondo spirit and value become deeply rooted, so that all Taekwondoists can practice the sport for their personal enjoyment and world peace.

2016년 리오데자네이로 올림픽 가상 우표
A Possible Taekwondo Stamp for the Rio 2016 Olympics

예의와 존경, 인내와 집중, 자신감과 호연지기 등 태권도 정신을 표현한 나만의 우표
A Customized stamp expressing the Taekwondo spirit:
Manner and Respect, Endurance and Focus, and a Fair, Confident and Dignified Spirit

우표로 보는 태권도 발자취 The Evolution of Taekwondo as Seen Through Postage Stamps

해설 I. 놀랄만큼 다채로운 '태권도 테마 우표'
Appendix I. The Amazing Variety of Taekwondo – Themed Stamps

☞ '태권도 테마 우표'의 가치

원래 우표란 우편 업무에 쓰이는 지폐와 같은 증권(금권)으로서 정부의 홍보 매체로도 사용된다. 그 나라의 역사, 문화, 풍물, 위인 등을 소개한 대중 문화이자 고상한 취미 분야로 간주된다. 세계 각국에는 수많은 우취 인구가 활동하며 해마다 국제 규모의 우표작품 경쟁대회가 여러 나라에서 열린다.

우취 분야는 올림픽 문화와도 깊은 관련을 맺는다. 국제올림픽위원회 규정을 보면 올림피즘은 체육 경기 이상의 것이며 문화·우표·학술·조각·음악 등 종합 프로그램의 일환으로 국제스포츠우표 전시 행사를 열도록 되어 있다. 태권도와 같은 특정한 분야의 우표는 그 분야가 정부 차원에서 인정하고 권장하는 스포츠이자 문화 종목으로 승격되었음을 의미한다. 태권도 입장에서 이들 우표들은 대단히 유용한 가치를 갖는다. 태권도의 위상을 인식시키는 홍보와 문화 전시 자료가 될 뿐 아니라 교육적 소재로도 활용될 수 있다

☞ The Value of a 'Taekwondo-Themed Stamp'

Originally, a stamp was considered to be like a share of stock, or a bank note, used for postal services as well as a medium of publicity for government. They are also considered a form of mass public culture which can introduce the history, culture, institutions, customs, and historical figures of a country. There is a large and growing philatelic population throughout the world and international stamp competitions are held each year in many countries.

Philately has a long and storied relationship with Olympic culture. According to the codes of the International Olympic Committee, Olympism transcends the realm of simple athletic events. It is expanded to include international sports stamp exhibitions, which are held as a type of supporting program conducted to share culture, stamps, sculptures and music. The issuing of specific stamps, such as Taekwondo-themed stamps, is a sign that the sport is approved and promoted by the government and has been elevated to the level of cultural product. From the perspective of the Taekwondo society, these stamps possess extremely useful value. They are not only resources and modes of publicity and cultural exhibition to help people recognize the prestige of Taekwondo, but also a great educational tool.

태권도가 한국의 국기(國技)임을 강조한 세인트피에르 앤미켈론(캐나다 동부 섬나라) 우표.
This stamp, from Saint-Pierre & Miquelon,(An island country in the Eastern sea of Canada) shows Taekwondo as a Korean national sport.

서울올림픽 문화행사인 국제우표전시회 기념 한국 우표. 태권도 그림도 포함되어 있다.
A Korean stamp which includes a Taekwondo pictogram that was displayed in the international stamp exhibition held at the Seoul Olympic culture event.

☞ '태권도 테마 우표'란?

태권도를 소재로 발행된 공식 기념우표를 뜻한다. 태권도 종목을 소개하기 위해 태권도 경기 장면이나 발차기, 기술 동작이 도안되어 발매된 우표이다. 정부 소속의 우정국이 발행한 공식 우표에 한하며 개인이나 단체의 주문형 우표인 '나만의 우표'는 제외된다. 기념할 만한 스포츠 대회나 올림픽 우표 속에 태권도 이미지나 글자가 담겨있으면 태권도 우표가 된다. 태권도 우취 자료로는 소형시트, 관제엽서, 일부인(날짜가 표시된 소인)이 찍힌 실체봉투, 초일봉투, 맥시멈카드, 미터스탬프 등이 포함된다.

☞ What is a 'Taekwondo-Themed Stamp'

They are the commemorative stamps officially issued using Taekwondo as a theme. They depict competition scenes, kicks, or other technical movements to introduce and promote the discipline of Taekwondo. They include official stamps issued by the Post Office Department of a government, and exclude "individually-issued stamps" made by an individual or an organization. If Taekwondo images or inscriptions are included on the stamp to commemorate a sport or Olympic event, it becomes an official Taekwondo commemorative stamp. Taekwondo philatelic resources include small sheets, post cards, stamps, envelopes with postal markings, first day issue envelops, maxim cards, and postage meterstamps.

☞ 태권도 테마 우표 발행 상황

1970년대에 태권도는 동양무예의 한 종목으로 한국 내 뿐 아니라 해외에 널리 보급되면서 우표의 소재로 등장하기 시작했다. 당시 태권도 우표에는 다른 무술과 태권도를 혼동한 도안이 종종 나온다. 태권도가 유수한 국제 경기 종목으로 채택되면서 태권도 수련이나 경기 장면을 담은 제대로 된 태권도 이미지가 담긴 우표들이 나오기 시작했다.

☞ The Issuing of Taekwondo-Themed Stamps

Taekwondo started to appear as a stamp theme in the 1970s thanks to its dissemination, both within Korea and internationally, as one of the East Asian martial arts disciplines. Among the stamps issued during that time, it is common to find designs confusing Taekwondo with other martial arts. With the adoption of Taekwondo as an international competition event, proper Taekwondo stamps began to appear which depict Taekwondo practice or competition scenes.

그림엽서에 관련 우표를 붙이고 기념일부인을 찍은 맥시멈카드. 이란 태권도 영웅 하디 선수가 도안되었다.
This maximum card, where a Taekwondo stamp and seal are displayed on a Taekwondo postcard, was designed by Iranian Taekwondo hero, Hardy.

1988년 서울하계올림픽 기념 잠비아 소형쉬이트. 태권도 도안이 어색해 보인다.
An oddly designed souvenir sheet issued by Zambia commemorating the 1988 Seoul Summer Olympics.

우표로 보는 태권도 발자취 The Evolution of Taekwondo as Seen Through Postage Stamps

☞ **태권도 테마 우표가 발행되는 명목(사유)**

태권도 우표는 스포츠 또는 올림픽 대회를 기념하는 우표 세트에 태권도 종목이 포함되어 발행되는 경우가 많다. 태권도가 올림픽 정식종목이 되면서 대중적 인지도가 높아지면서 각종 스포츠나 올림픽 대회를 기념하는 태권도 우표가 선보이기 시작했다. 총 124건의 태권도 우표를 발행 명목별로 구분하여 살펴보면 아래와 같다.

1) 아테네, 베이징 등 올림픽 대회 기념우표 : 총 65건.
2) 아시안게임, 시게임, 판암게임, 유니버시아드게임 등 국제 스포츠 대회 기념 : 26건
3) 세계태권도대회, 아시아태권도대회, 유럽태권도대회 등 태권도 대회 기념 : 8건
4) 전국체육대회 등 각국 국내 스포츠 대회 기념 : 8건
5) 국가별 문화 상징물, 스포츠 활동 권장 등 계몽 및 기념 : 13건
6) 아동, 청소년 교육 상징으로 동양무술 및 태권도 기념 : 3건
  국내 및 국제 스포츠 대회와 올림픽 종목으로서 태권도 경기 관련 우표가 107건으로 87%를 점유했다. 이는 태권도 경기가 올림픽을 비롯한 세계 스포츠 대회에 채택되어 보급이 활성화된 성과로 볼 수 있다.

벨기에가 발행한 태권도 초일봉투. 미국, 프랑스, 독일 등 선진국에서 태권도 우표가 나오길 기대해 본다.
A first Day Cover issued by Belgium. I hope USA, France, Germany, and other developed countries will issue their own Taekwondo – Themed stamps in the future.

☞ **The Reasons for the Issuance of Taekwondo-Themed Stamps**

Taekwondo stamps are often issued to commemorate certain sports events or Olympic Games. The general public's heightened awareness of Taekwondo, due to its adoption as an official Olympic event, has resulted in the more frequent appearance of Taekwondo-themed commemorative stamps for various sports events, including the Olympic Games.

Here is a list of the main reasons for the issuance of the 124 cases of Taekwondo-themed stamps featured in this book:

1) Stamps to commemorate the Summer Olympic Games such as those in Seoul, Sydney, Athens and Beijing : a total of 65
2) Stamps to commemorate international sports events such as the Asian Games, City-sponsored Games, Pan-Am Games, and Universiade : a total of 26
3) Stamps to commemorate Taekwondo championships such as the World Taekwondo Championships, Asian Taekwondo Championships, European Taekwondo Championships, etc. : a total of 8
4) Stamps to commemorate national sports games such as the "National Athletics Championships" : a total of 8
5) Stamps to commemorate cultural symbols or to promote sports activities or education campaigns : a total of 13
6) Stamps to symbolically promote Taekwondo or East Asian martial arts for the education of children and young adults : a total of 3

Taekwondo stamps related to Taekwondo tournaments including national and international sports games and the Olympic Games consist of 107 cases comprising 87% of the Taekwondo stamps included in this book. This shows the wide spread popularity of Taekwondo tournaments at international sports games and the Olympics.

☞ 동양무예의 교육적 의미를 담은 우표

태권도는 인종과 국가, 종교를 넘어서서 예의, 인내, 충효 등 생활 신조와 철학적 실천을 추구하는 동양무예의 한 종목이다. 여러 동양무예 중 특히 태권도는 아동과 청소년 교육을 위한 건전한 여가 활용을 위한 것으로서 어느나라에서든지 사회적 호응도가 높다. 동양무예의 교육적 기능에 주목하여 어린이와 청소년을 올바르게 선도하는 계몽적 성격을 띤 우표도 선보였다. 태권도 우표 발행은 현재 진행형이다. 앞으로도 태권도가 올림픽 종목으로 존속되는 한, 해마다 세계 각국의 새로운 태권도 우표들이 등장할 것이다.

☞ Stamps Featuring the Educational Significance of Asian Martial Arts

Taekwondo is an East Asian martial art through which people can pursue the philosophical practice of life skills such as courtesy, perseverance, loyalty, etc., regardless of ethnicity, nationality, or religion. Among the many East Asian martial arts, Taekwondo in particular has achieved immense social popularity in many countries as a sound leisure activity for the education of children and young adults. In fact there are even stamps emphasizing the building of character, in order to guide children and young adults in the right direction by focusing on the educational benefits of East Asian martial arts. The issuing of Taekwondo stamps continues to grow. As long as Taekwondo remains an official Olympic event in the future, countries throughout the world will issue more new Taekwondo-themed stamps every year.

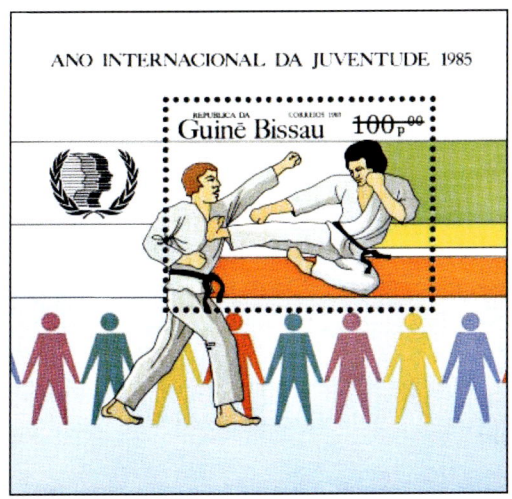

태권도 발차기와 함께 '예의와 존경'의 동양 무예 정신을 표현한 온두라스 우표(1985) 2종. 동양무예의 정신적 가치가 묘사된 보기 드문 우표이다.
Two Honduran stamps, one showing the manners and respect that are expressed through Martial Art disciplines, the other with Taekwondo kicks. It is rare to find a stamp depicting the spiritual value of East Asian Martial Arts.

'국제 청소년의 해' 기념 기니비사우 우표(1985). 청소년들의 건전한 여가활동으로서 태권도 등 동양무예의 역할을 인정하여 우표로 발행된 좋은 예이다.
A Guinea-Bissau souvenir sheet commemorating the year of the International Youth in 1985. A fine example of Taekwondo and other East Asian Martial Arts being approved as a means of sound education for youth.

우표로 보는 태권도 발자취 The Evolution of Taekwondo as Seen Through Postage Stamps

해설 II. 이것이 최고의 '태권도 우표' – 지상우표갤러리
Appendix II. The Best Taekwondo Stamps – The Stamp Gallery

세계 최초의 태권도 우표는 1969년 전국체육대회 기념으로 한국에서 발행되었다.
The First Taekwondo Stamp in the World was issued in Korea in 1969 for the National Athletic Games.

태권도 우표를 가장 많이 발행한 나라는 태권도 종주국답게 한국이 총 9건 9종의 공식 우표를 발행했다.
Korea published the largest quantity of Taekwondo Stamps. 9 kinds of 9 cases of official stamps were released.

싱가폴이 한국 이외의 나라중 1985년 최초의 태권도 우표를 발행했다.
Singapore was the First Country to issue a Taekwondo stamp outside of Korea in 1985.

한국 이외의 국가중 태권도 우표를 가장 많이 발행한 나라는 베트남으로서 무려 6회 6종의 태권도 우표를 발행했다.
Vietnam released 6 kinds of 6 cases of Taekwondo Stamps, the largest quantity of Stamps outside of Korea.

한국 이외의 최초의 태권도 테마 공식 기념우표는 1988년 바레인에서 발행된 서울올림픽 기념우표이다.
Bahrain was the First Country to issue a stamp specifically commemorating Taekwondo outside of Korea in 1988 for the Seoul Olympics.

최초의 태권도 인물 우표로 영광을 차지한 호주의 로렌 번즈 선수
Lauren Burns of Australia is the first case of a Taekwondo stamp commemorating a Taekwondoist.

희귀한 태권도 우표 자료⟨1⟩은 발행 매수가 적어 구하기
어려운 시드니올림픽기념 쿠웨이트 소형쉬트.
This, the rarest Taekwondo Stamp ⟨1⟩, was released as
a souvenir sheet by Kuwait for the Sydney Olympics.

희귀한 태권도 우표 자료⟨2⟩는 바르셀로나올림픽 기념
나이지리아 천공 에러우표.
This Nigerian stamp is a very rare item which includes an
error in perforation.

최초의 올림픽 주최국 태권도 기념우표는
2004년 아테네올림픽 기념으로
그리스에서 나왔다.
The first official Taekwondo stamp of
the Olympic host country was issued
by Greece in 2004.

가장 특이한 모양의 태권도 우표는 베이징올림픽 기념
베트남 우표로서 평행사변형의 모양이다.
The most uniquely shaped Taekwondo Stamp was issued by
Vietnam in the shape of a parallelogram.

가장 아름다운 태권도 우표는 시드니의 명물
오페라하우스와 함께 도안된 라오스 소형쉬트.
The most beautiful Taekwondo Stamp released
by Laos containing the famous Sydney Opera House.

해설 Ⅲ. 국가별 태권도 우표 발행 현황
Appendix Ⅲ. Taekwondo Stamps Issued by Country

2010년 12월 현재 전세계 68개국, 124건 145종의 태권도 소재 우표가 발행되었다.
124 cases and 145 kinds of Taekwondo stamps have been published from 68 countries as of December, 2010

아시아 총 24개국 54건 62종
24 Countries, 54 Cases and 62 Kinds from Asia

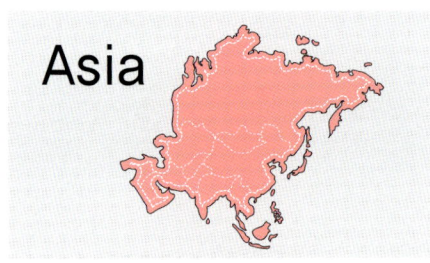

No.	국가명(Country)	건수(Case)	종류(Kind)
1	한국 SOUTH KOREA	9	9
2	베트남 VIETNAM	6	6
3	북한 NORTH KOREA	4	9
4	대만 CHINESE TAIPEI	4	6
5	필리핀 PHILIPPINES	3	3
6	바레인 BAHRAIN	2	2
7	이란 IRAN	2	2
8	이스라엘 ISRAEL	2	2
9	요르단 JORDAN	2	2
10	네팔 NEPAL	2	2
11	싱가폴 SINGAPORE	2	2
12	타지키스탄 TADZHIKISTAN	2	2
13	중국 CHINA	1	1
	마카오(포르투갈령) PORTUGESE MACAO	1	1
	마카오(중국령) CHINESE MACAO	1	1
14	쿠웨이트 KUWAIT	1	2
15	브루나이 BRUNEI	1	1
16	부탄 BUTAN	1	1
17	홍콩 중국 HONG KONG CHINA	1	1
18	인도네시아 INDONESIA	1	1
19	일본 JAPAN	1	1
20	카자흐스탄 KAZAKHSTAN	1	1
21	라오스 LAOS	1	1
22	말레이시아 MALAYSIA	1	1
23	카타르 QATAR	1	1
24	예멘 YEMEN	1	1
	총계 Total	54	62

9종 · 9 kinds

6종 · 6 kinds

3종 · 3 kinds

2종 · 2 kinds

 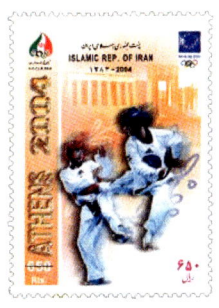  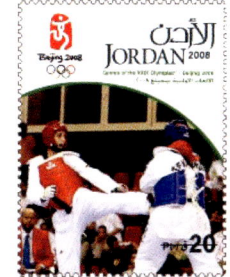

1종 · 1 kind

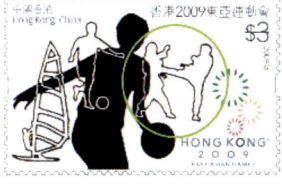   

우표로 보는 태권도 발자취   The Evolution of Taekwondo as Seen Through Postage Stamps

아메리카 총 15개국 25건 27종
15 Countries, 25 Cases and 27 Kinds from Americas

No.	국가명(Country)	건수(Case)	종류(Kind)
1	에콰도르 ECUADOR	4	4
2	엘살바도르 SALVADOR	3	4
3	도미니카공화국 DOMINICAN REPUBLIC	3	3
4	코스타리카 COSTA RICA	2	2
5	온두라스 HONDURAS	2	2
6	도미니카 DOMINICA	1	2
7	아르헨티나 ARGENTINA	1	1
8	브라질 BRAZIL	1	1
9	쿠바 CUBA	1	1
10	그레나다 GRENADA	1	1
11	과테말라 GUATEMALA	1	1
12	멕시코 MEXICO	1	1
13	니카라과 NICARAGUA	1	1
14	세인트피에르앤미켈론 SAINT, PIERRE & MIQUELON	1	1
15	세인트키츠앤네비스 SAINT, KITTS & NEVIS	1	1
16	트리니다드앤토바고 TRINIDAD & TOBAGO	1	1
	총계 Total	25	27

4종 · 4 kinds

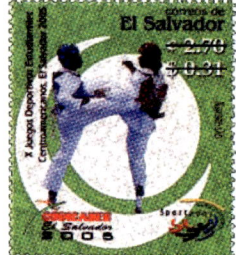

3종 · 3 kinds

2종 · 2 kinds

1종 · 1 kind

Europe

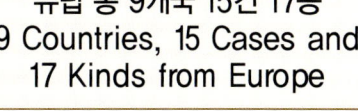

유럽 총 9개국 15건 17종
9 Countries, 15 Cases and 17 Kinds from Europe

No.	국가명(Country)	건수(Case)	종류(Kind)
1	터키 TURKEY	2	3
	터키계 사이프러스 TURKISH CYPRUS	3	4
2	그리스 GREECE	2	3
3	러시아 RUSSIA	1	1
	러시아령 타타르스탄 RUSSIAN TATARSTAN	1	1
4	벨기에 BELGIUM	1	1
5	보스니아헤르체고비나 BOSNIA & HERZEGOVINA	1	1
6	불가리아 BULGARIA	1	1
7	영국 GREAT BRITAIN	1	1
8	루마니아 ROMANIA	1	1
9	세르비아 SERBIA	1	1
	총계 Total	15	17

6종 · 6 kinds

3종 · 3 kinds

2종 · 2 kinds

1종 · 1 kind

1종 · 1 kind

 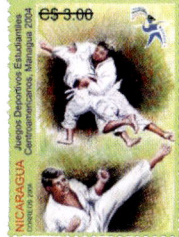   

우표로 보는 태권도 발자취 The Evolution of Taekwondo as Seen Through Postage Stamps

아프리카 총 17개국 27건 38종
17 Countries, 27 Cases and 38 Kinds from Africa

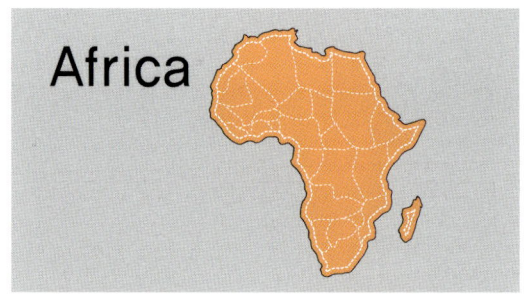

No.	국가명(Country)	건수(Case)	종류(Kind)
1	베냉 BENIN	3	6
2	이집트 EGYPT	3	3
3	기니비사우 GUINEA - BISSAU	3	3
4	상투메프린시페 S.TOME.E.PRINCIPE	2	7
5	튀니지 TUNISIA	2	3
6	카보베르데 CAPE VERDE	2	2
7	나이지리아 NIGERIA	2	2
8	기니 GUINEA	1	2
9	소말리아 SOMALIA	1	2
10	콩고 CONGO	1	1
11	리비아 LIBYA	1	1
12	모로코 MOROCCO	1	1
13	니제르 NIGER	1	1
14	세네갈 SENEGAL	1	1
15	스와질랜드 SWAZILAND	1	1
16	잠비아 ZAMBIA	1	1
17	짐바브웨 ZIMBABWE	1	1
	총계 Total	27	38

7종·7 kinds

6종·6 kinds

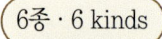

3종·3 kinds

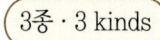

2종·2 kinds

오세아니아 3개국 3건 3종
3 Countries, 3 Cases and 3 Kinds from Oceania

No.	국가명(Country)	건수(Case)	종류(Kind)
1	호주 AUSTRALIA	1	1
2	키리바시 KIRIBATI	1	1
3	뉴칼레도니아 NEW CALEDONIA	1	1
	총계 Total	3	3

1종 · 1 kind

1종 · 1 kind

  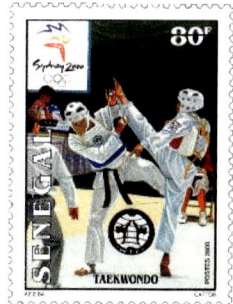 

우표로 보는 태권도 발자취 The Evolution of Taekwondo as Seen Through Postage Stamps

저자 우취 활동상 I – 신문 기사 및 기고문
Author's Philatelic Activities I
– Articles in Newspapers & Magazines

저자 우취 활동상 II – 태권도 우표작품
Author's Philatelic Activities II
– Philatelic Works of Taekwondo

저자 우취 활동상 III - 〈태권도 작품액자〉 전시회
Author's Philatelic Activities III
– Exhibition of Taekwondo Philatelic Work

태권도 우표 작품 액자 Philatelic Work

2006 코리아 오픈 태권도대회
2006 Korea Open Taekwondo Championships

2005 진천 화랑 문화축제
2005 Jinchon Hwarang Taekwondo Festival

우표를 활용한 태권도 역사 강의
A Lecture on Taekwondo History using Taekwondo stamps

저자 우취 활동상 IV – 우표작품 증정 및 기타
Author's Philatelic Activities IV – Presentations and Etc.

국군 테마작품'을 연세대 학군단에 기증하는 모습. 연세대학교 여러 곳에 필자의 우표작품 액자가 걸려 있다.
The author presented the philatelic work on 'Korean Military'. There are several philatelic works in Yonsei University

월드컵 우표 액자
The World Cup Stamp Frame

'독도 사랑 행사'의 일환으로 필자는 '독도테마작품'을 독도박물관에 기증했다(2010년 10월).
The author donated the philatelic work 'Dokdo, The Far Eastern Korean Island' to the Dokdo Museum for the event of the Taekwondo peoples' social benefit.(October 2010)

태권도 우표 정보에 대해 영국 우취가이자 태권도 유단자인 마이크 히스 씨로부터 큰 도움을 받았다.
Mr. Mike Heath, a British philatelist & Taekwondo black belt, provided a lot of detailed information of the Taekwondo stamps.

해외에서 태권도 우표를 발송한 우편봉투
Envelopes that had Taekwondo Stamps mailed from Overseas

참고 문헌 및 자료
- References -

◎ 문헌 자료

- 강기석, 『태권도 반세기, 인물과 역사. 이야기 한국체육사』. 국민체육진흥공단. 2001
- 강원식, 이경명, 『우리 태권도의 역사』. 상아기획. 2002
- 국기원, 『태권도 교본』. 오성출판사, 2006
- 김석년, 『서울, 1988 – 제24회 올림픽 공식화보집』. (주)오리콤. 1988
- 김승제, 『외국우표로 본 한국의 모습』. 으뜸출판사. 2009
- 김영선, 『태권도 역사론』. 연세대 태권도최고지도자과정 교재. 1997
- 김운용, 『위대한 올림픽』. 두산동아. 1990
- 대한태권도협회 홍보실, 『(계간) 태권도 1-7호』. 대한태권도협회, 1971-1972
- 박상운, 『테마틱 우취 ; 이론과 실제』. 우취문화사, 2007
- 서성원, 『태권도 현대사와 길동무하다』. 상아기획. 2007
- 설성경, 『실존인물 홍길동』. 중앙 M&B. 1998
- 세계태권도연맹, 『Handbook Taekwondo』. W.T.F. 1996
- 세계태권도연맹, 『Taekwondo & The Olympic』. W.T.F. 2009
- 이경명, 『태권도의 어제와 오늘』. 어문각. 2002
- 이경명, 『한국 전통무예의 철학, 태권도』. 형설출판사. 2000
- 이규석, 『태권도의 탐구 논리』. 이규석교수회갑기념 논총간행위원회, 2001
- 이진수, 『신라화랑의 체육사상 연구』. 보경문화사, 1990
- 태권도진흥재단, 국기원, 『지구촌 끝까지 I & II』. (재)태권도진흥재단. 2006

◎ 인터넷사이트
- 국기원 http://www.kukkiwon.or.kr
- 대한태권도협회 http://www.koreataekwondo.co.kr
- 두산네이버백과사전(EnCyber) http://100.naver.com
- 마이크 히스 태권도우표 http://www.flickr.com/photos/mikeheath
- 무카스 http://www.mookas.com
- 세계태권도연맹 http://www.wtf.org
- 아시아태권도연맹 http://www.asiantaekwondounion.org
- 연합뉴스 http://www.yonhapnews.co.kr
- 엘비스기념관(경기도 파주) http://www.elvishall.com
- 월드태권도신문 http://www.w-taekwondo.com
- 위키피디아백과사전 http://en.wikipedia.org
- 태권도신문 http://www.tkdnews.com
- 태권도진흥재단 http://www.tpf.kr

◎ Bibliography

- Kang, Ki-seok, *A Half Century of Taekwondo, People & History*. the Korea Sports Promotion Foundation. 2001.
- Kang, Won-sik & Lee, Kyong-myong, *Our Taekwondo History*. Sang-A Publishing Co., 2001.
- Kim, Seok-nyun. *SEOUL '88*. Oricom Co., 1988.
- Kim, Seung-jae, *The Features of Korea as through Foreign Postage Stamps*. Ueddeum Publishing, 2009
- Kim, Young-sun, *Theory on Taekwondo History*. Textbook of Yonsei Taekwondo Masters' Course. 1997.
- Kim, Un-yong. *The Greatest Olympics*. Doosan Dong-A Co., 1990.
- Kukkiwon, *Taekwondo Textbook*, O-Sung Publishing Co., 2006.
- Lee, Jin-soo, *Research on the Physical Ideology of Hwarang, Silla*. Bojyung Publishing Co., 2002.
- Lee, Kyong-myong, *Yesterday and Today of Taekwondo*. Eomoongak Publishing Co., 2002.
- Lee, Kyong-myong, *Taekwondo ; Korean Traditional Martial Arts*. Hyung Seol Publishing Co., 2000.
- Lee, Kyu-suk, *The Searching Logics on Taekwondo*. Prof. Kyu-suk Lee's Sixtieth Birthday Commemoration Article Collection Committee, 2001.
- Park, Sang-un, *Thematic Philately ; Theory and Practice*. Philatelic Culture Co., 2001.
- Press Department of K.T.A., *Taekwondo (Quarterly Magazine)*. Korea Taekwondo Association., 2001.
- Seol, Sung-kyung, *The Real Man, Hong Gildong*. Jung-Ang M&B Publishing Co., 1998
- Seo, Sung-won, *Traveling with Modern Taekwondo History*. Sang-A Publishing Co., 2007.
- The World Taekwondo Federation. *Handbook Taekwondo*. W.T.F. 1996.
- T.P.F & Kukkiwon, *Until the End of the Global Village*. the Taekwondo Promotion Foundation. 2006.
- W.T.F., *Taekwondo & The Olympics*. The World Taekwondo Federation. 2009.

◎ Internet Site

- Asian Taekwondo Federation – http://www.asiantaekwondounion.org
- Elvis Hall(Paju, Kyungki-do, Korea) – http://www.elvishall.com
- Korea Taekwondo Association – http://www.koreataekwondo.co.kr
- Kukkiwon – http://www.kukkiwon.or.kr
- Mike Heath's Taekwondo Stamp – http://www.flickr.com/photos/mikeheath
- Mookas Korea – http://www.mookas.com/index.asp
- Naver Doosan EnCyber – http://100.naver.com
- Taekwondo News – http://www.tkdnews.com
- Taekwondo Promotion Founfation – http://www.tpf.kr
- Wikipedia – http://en.wikipedia.org
- World Taekwondo Federation – http://www.wtf.org
- World Taekwondo Newspaper – http://www.w-taekwondo.com
- Yonhap News – http://www.yonhapnews.co.kr

국가별 찾아보기
Country Index

Argentina 168
Australia 128
Bahrain 104 115
Belgium 130
Benin 92 93 162 163
Bhutan 118
Bosnia & Herzegovina 121
Brazil 132
Brunei 54
Bulgaria 123
Cape Verde 134 158
China 41
Chinese Taipei 49 56 60 159
Congo 150
Costa Rica 136 156
Cuba 68
Dominica 103
Dominican Republic 71 87 167
Ecuador 73 75 108 124
Egypt 70 85 116
El Salvador 77 82 83
Great Britain 184
Greece 146
Grenada 78
Guatemala 67
Guinea 157
Guinea-Bissau 66 79 180
Honduras 72 173

Hong Kong, China 61
Indonesia 53
Iran 50 151
Israel 69 88
Japan 55
Jordan 119 172
Kazakhstan 133
Kiribati 152
Kuwait 138
Laos 140
Libya 176
Macao, China* 57
Macao, Portugal* 102
Malaysia 48
Mexico 84
Morocco 86
Nepal 59 170
New Caledonia 169
Nicaragua 81
Niger 64
Nigeria 80 117
North Korea 110 111
Philippines 135 155 165
Qatar 58 138
Romania 122
Russia 174
Russian Tatarstan* 143
Saint Kitts & Nevis 89

Saint Pierre & Miquelon* 44
Sao Tome and Principe 171 178 179
Senegal 142
Serbia 90
Singapore 46 47
Somalia 177
South Korea 28 30 32 33 35 36 38 40 42
Swaziland 105
Tadzhikistan 94 139
Trinidad and Tobago 154
Tunisia 125 175
Turkey 106 166
Turkish Northern Cyprus* 65 76 114
Vietnam 51 52 120 137 153 164
Yemen 141
Zambia 107
Zimbabwe 74

* 표시는 국가 승인이 안된 자치정부를 뜻한다.
* Autonomous region not recognized as an independent country

우표로 보는 태권도 발자취
The Evolution of Taekwondo as Seen Through Postage Stamps

- 지 은 이 : 김영선 / Author : Young Sun Kim
- 발 행 인 : 문상필 / Publisher : Sang-Phil, Moon
- 편집디자인 : 명성진 / Designer : Sung-Jin, Myung

- 초판발행 : 2011년 1월 6일
- 발 행 처 : 도서출판 상아기획 / Sang-A Publishing Company
- 주   소 : 서울시 영등포구 문래동1가 39번지 센터플러스 715호
  Address : Room 715, Centerplus Bldg, #39, Mullae-dong 1-ga, Youngdeungpo-gu, Seoul, Korea.
  Tel : 82-2-2164-2700 / Fax : 82-2-2164-2999
- E-mail : 0221642700@hanmail.net
- www.tkdsanga.com

- 인   쇄 : 명진씨엔피 Tel : 02-2164-3000
  Printing Office : Myung Jin Creative & Printing. Co., Ltd

- 저작권은 작가에게 있습니다.
- 잘못 만들어진 책은 구입처나 본사에서 교환해 드립니다.
- 본 은 국민체육진흥공단의 기금 및 태권도진흥재단 협찬으로 기획됨.
  This book is published with the support from the Korea Sports Promotion Foundation and the Taekwondo Promotion Foundation.

ISBN 978-89-91237-67-4
책값 29,000원 USD 40.$